8J

DARK HEARTS

Dark Hearts

THE UNCONSCIOUS FORCES
THAT SHAPE MEN'S LIVES

Loren E. Pedersen

SHAMBHALA
BOSTON & LONDON
1991

Shambhala Publications, Inc.
Horticultural Hall
300 Massachusetts Avenue
Boston, Massachusetts 02115

Shambhala Publications, Inc.
Random Century House
20 Vauxhall Bridge Road
London SW1V 2SA

9 8 7 6 5 4 3

Printed in the United States of America
on acid-free paper
⊗

Distributed in the United States by Random House, Inc.,
in Canada by Random House of Canada Ltd., and
in the United Kingdom by the Random Century Group.

Library of Congress Cataloging-in-Publication Data

Pedersen, Loren E., 1941–
    Dark hearts: the unconscious forces that shape men's
lives / Loren E. Pedersen.
        p. cm.
    ISBN 0-87773-491-7
    1. Masculinity (Psychology) 2. Anima
(Psychoanalysis) 3. Men—Psychology. 4. Jung, C. G.
(Carl Gustav), 1875–1961. I. Title.
    BF175.4.M3P43   1990   89-43323
    155.3'32—dc20   CIP

To the memory of my brothers,
Michael and Dennis

Dark Hearts in need
Of a Song to sing
And a Safe Place
From which to be Reborn.

I am not a mechanism, an assembly of various sections.
And it is not because the mechanism is working
    wrongly, that I am ill.
I am ill because of wounds to the soul, to the deep
    emotional self
and the wounds to the soul take a long, long time, only
    time can help
and patience, and a certain difficult repentance
long difficult repentance, realisation of life's mistake,
    and the freeing oneself
from the endless repetition of the mistake
which mankind at large has chosen to sanctify.

—D. H. LAWRENCE

Contents

Acknowledgments

IT HAS ALWAYS SEEMED TO ME that the purpose of writing a book ought to be the education of the author as well as of the reader. In my case I had the good fortune of having the support, encouragement, and direct assistance of a number of individuals, all of whom in different ways enriched and educated me throughout the long process of creating *Dark Hearts*. The men I have worked with in group therapy and analysis contributed the "heart" of this book by sharing generously their dreams, fantasies, and journal notes. I thank them for much of what I have learned over the past seven years about the psychology of men and for the profound experiences we all went through together. I am indebted to my agent, Rosalie Siegal, for her kind support and her success in finding the publisher best suited to produce this book. I am also indebted to my editor, Emily Hilburn Sell, whose incisive thinking and good humor made our work together a pleasure. Her meticulous editorial skills have taught me much about writing. My thanks also go to my colleague and good friend, Frank R. Wilson, M.D., whose support, encouragement, and lunches at the "author's corner" of Speidini's kept the spirit of writing alive; to John Beebe, M.D., Jean Bolen, M.D., Joseph Henderson, M.D., Wayne Detloff, M.D., Eric Greenleaf, Ph.D., and Alexander J. Nemeth, Ph.D., for reading drafts of the manuscript and being available for consultation; to Anne Francis, whose summary of many books was an immense help in my research; to Ruth Pierce, for her support and the many relevant readings she provided over the last two years; to Gerald P. Macdaid, of the Center for the Applications of Psychological Type, for his kindness in answering many research questions about psychological type and the Myers-Briggs Type Inventory; and finally, most of all, to Karen Diane, to whom I owe an immeasurable debt of gratitude for her seemingly endless hours of research, criticism, and tolerance over the last two years.

Dark Hearts

Introduction

Toward a Male Psychology

MUCH OF WHAT IS CURRENTLY UNDERSTOOD of male psychology and men's behavior is reported through a growing literature concerned primarily with women's experience of men. In the seventies and eighties this literature was contained within a tremendous outpouring of information concerning the psychological, social, and economic dimensions of women's lives. In any library or bookstore we find whole sections devoted to women's psychology and women's issues. In colleges and universities around the country we also find numerous newly created programs in women's studies. Feminism seems to have come of age; in the meantime there remains a corresponding paucity of information of any depth about men.

Over twenty years ago I read Simone de Beauvoir's *The Second Sex*. Up until that time I had not thought in terms of women's liberation or feminism, and certainly not specifically in terms of masculine psychology. I recall being impressed by the depth of feeling expressed in de Beauvoir's account of women's secondary place in contemporary Europe. In the United States, Betty Friedan's *The Feminine Mystique* further elucidated the social and psychological restrictions of women's roles in the modern world. There have since been increasingly impassioned and eloquent

accounts of the social, political, economic, and even moral ine-
qualities between men and women.

As a result of feminism we are now seeing a new, more positive
valuation of women and the feminine through a resurgence of
popular literature—ranging from women's self-help books to the
mythology of the Goddess. However, one of the unfortunate
consequences of this literary abundance is a popular view that
the majority of men are rather brutish, shallow, self-seeking,
overintellectualized, and unemotional creatures. Or, as Warren
Farrell notes in his recent book, if women's questions about men
could be summed up into one, it would be, "Why are men such
jerks?"[1] It seems to me that much of the current literature about
men focuses on the *symptomatology* of men's behavior rather
than on an understanding of the deeper roots of the issues that
men are struggling with.

Of what is known about men little seems to have come from
men themselves, either as laymen or as psychologists and psychoanalysts (and this in spite of the fact that men are represented
in these latter professions far more frequently than women). Is
this because women make more interesting subjects of study for
male authors? Or is it because men are prone to look outside of
themselves? Is there a general reluctance among men to look
more deeply at themselves? Traditionally, much of what has been
represented in literature as "psychology" has been assumed to
apply equally to both sexes; however, since men have typically
found it more difficult to allow themselves to seek psychological
treatment they are decidedly underrepresented as actual subjects
of study or as patients. This has created a bias due to both the
preponderance of female patients, clients, and subjects as well as
the confusing overuse of the pronoun *he/him* in psychological
literature. Perhaps the most telling evidence for the imbalance of
information about men is the fact that the great body of literature
devoted to developmental psychology is extensively referenced
and researched largely with respect to the role of the mother in
the emotional and psychological life of the child. This emphasis
reflects the lack of involvement with children that fathers them-

selves have traditionally demonstrated, as well as a lack of professional interest in the importance of the role of the father in family life. It is an alarming fact that the overwhelming attention currently being focused on fathers instead has to do with them as perpetrators of incest. As we shall see, there is a disturbing amount of objective support for this attention.

Masculinity has left its imprint, if not footprint, on science and philosophy in its attempt to study everything but itself. Scientific methodology itself has recently come into question, with its masculine bias being viewed as a determinant of some of its "objective" outcomes. My approach to studying masculinity is neither philosophical nor scientific per se. I am not writing to *prove* anything, but to plant a psychological garden with "seeds"—ideas, facts, theories, experiences of working with men in analysis, and some of my own personal psychological and life experiences. Rather than promising a particular outcome, I invite the reader to sow his or her own seeds as part of a mutual exploratory process. What I want most clearly is for men to grow, and I believe that growth now must come from the inside.

Psychology itself has always been the errant child of science, forever trying to justify its existence by reference to "scientific" rigors and laws. There are, however, no laws of psychology, at least none that I know of. Psychiatry similarly grew up as an unwanted child of medicine and neurology, and it has yet to achieve a healthy separation from its parents. Try as it may, psychology has not yet, and perhaps never will, achieve the status of a purely scientific discipline. Even the nature of science itself, according to new concepts of field theory and quantum physics, has become much more relative than had ever been thought under the old notions of traditional Newtonian physics. We know, for example, that a personal bias is not only inevitable but can find its way into our "scientific" results. In its pursuit of a scientific status some of the gains of psychology have been dubious and reductive; some of the quintessential values of human experience have been lost as proper subject matter. This so often happens when discrete pieces of human behavior are separated from their

natural history, context, and environment and put under a mag-
nifying lens, as in the case of behaviorism. The "scientific" study
of dreams, for example, has resulted in the conclusion in some
quarters that they are merely "random neuronal firings of the
cortex" with no significant meaning in and of themselves—
certainly an example of *reductio ad absurdum*. Years of study of
discrete bits of human behavior have resulted in a contemporary
insult to the nature of human consciousness by the most influential behaviorist of American psychology, B. F. Skinner: "A scientific
analysis of behavior must, I believe, assume that a person's
behavior is controlled by his genetic and environmental history
rather than by the person himself as an initiating creative agent."[2]

Science and religion are strange bedfellows, forever trying to
stay out of each other's way, but both wanting to lay claim to the
ultimate "truth." As truth seekers they always wind up in a similar
bed, but, unfortunately, when points of view don't jive, the
Procrustean bed is invoked. I don't think we can all be stretched
or shortened forever, so all disciplines may have to learn to share
a bigger bed.

The "Energy" of Consciousness

If consciousness can be said to be "composed" of anything, it
might be thought of as being composed of energy. Further, since
energy seems to express itself in polarities, we might think in
terms of masculine and feminine *energies,* rather than masculine
and feminine qualities belonging to, or being carried by, a
specific sex. In this sense, masculinity and femininity are polarities within consciousness itself, much as positive and negative
valences co-exist in varying proportions in nature.

In the prehistorical, matrilineal period consciousness seems to
have been expressed as primarily feminine, with the archetypal
symbolism of the mother—that is, having to do with the cycles of
nature, farming, reproduction, and birth—being dominant.

As we moved out of the matrilineal period and into the patriarchy, consciousness became more masculine—that is, more goal-oriented, product-oriented, linear, and scientific. The scientific revolution was a high period of masculine dominance in all spheres; at that time the feminine principle or energy became comparatively dormant. The exteriorized products of masculine dominance have both increased the quality of life through technological, scientific, and medical advances; at the same time they have sown the seeds of a technology and science potentially capable of annihilating all life.

Historically and psychologically men and women increasingly became identified with the particular qualities of masculinity and femininity, as though these qualities belonged exclusively to the domain of their sex. The concepts of *masculine* and *feminine* became so fraught with cultural stereotypes and sex role biases that issues of inherent sexual orientation and gender identification have generated inflammatory arguments about the validity of so much as even labeling an attribute or a person one way or the other. In current psychology and sociology the patriarchy and masculine attitudes have now become the "dark side" of consciousness, particularly in the feminists' view.

We are becoming more aware of this dark side in terms of damage to the environment, the nuclear problem, the centuries of war that have been waged by men, and the harmful effects of domineering attitudes toward women. Men, as "carriers" of that tradition, are inextricably associated with this dark side of consciousness. The destructive effects of patriarchal attitudes have also resulted in a form of masculine masochism that men unconsciously perpetuate and perpetrate against themselves and each other.

As the environment and the planet itself begin to regain their rightful place in human values, and as women vie for equality in all spheres of life, the feminine pole of consciousness seems to be on the rise again. Feminine consciousness appears to be reemerging in the form of an affirmation of life, in contrast to the negation that has resulted from the overdeveloped, one-sided pole of masculinity. Women are not allowing themselves to be dominated by the patriarchal attitude as it is manifested in men.

At the same time, men are faced with the necessity of retreating from their overly exogenous orientation and coming to terms with the dormant feminine component of their own personalities. The present challenge is to integrate and balance the masculine and feminine energies of consciousness *within* both men and women.

My initial interest in men's psychology began with a curiosity about myself as a man, particularly in the context of my relationships to women and to other men, and because of a need to understand the spontaneous products of my unconscious—my dreams. These interests deepened when I entered Jungian analysis while I was in graduate school. I began to wonder whether there even was a psychology of men as distinct from women, and I further speculated that, just as women have been socially and economically disadvantaged, men may have become emotionally and spiritually disadvantaged in their own right.

As a very young man I read Freud fairly extensively, developing a great respect for him as a pioneer in the exploration of the unconscious, particularly as expounded in his *Interpretation of Dreams*. At the same time I found little that made sense to me by way of understanding the psychological differences between men and women. In fact, in this respect I found Freud's work confusing and perhaps a reflection of his own personal and cultural biases.

It is noteworthy that Freud based a great deal of his psychology of women on the concept of penis envy, and he also implicitly based a great deal of his psychology of men (though he didn't put it in those terms) on the Oedipus complex. Even though it is nearly a hundred years since the foundation of psychoanalysis, we have been left with a historical and theoretical legacy from which we have not quite psychologically recovered. The use of these concepts has not only been unfair to women but a great injustice to the psychology of men as well. Freud's theories need to be reevaluated in the light of his own personal bias as well as the external factors that shaped his thinking about both men and women.

The incest taboo and the Oedipus myth have been of particular interest to me; the function of the symbolic aspects of incest as well as its literal enactment, including psychological incest, is an area of grave psychological and social concern. In this book I attempt to rethink some of the significant aspects of the Oedipus complex as it applies specifically to the father-son relationship, and its consequences in incest.

In reading the works of C. G. Jung, and in my personal Jungian analysis, I began to feel that there was a more viable psychological context for understanding myself as a man, and I also discovered a potential theoretical basis for beginning to understand masculinity. Jung's concept of the archetypes of the collective unconscious, when added to my understanding of the personal unconscious, seemed to offer a fertile ground from which to explore the deeper aspects of men's behavior.

When I was seven years old I had the following dream.

> I am in my childhood home, a three-story red-brick walk-up flat on the near north side of Chicago. I am walking down the hallway from the second-floor apartment. As I reach the stairway I notice that tree roots are beginning to break through holes in the plaster walls, growing rapidly out from one side of the hall into and seemingly through the other side. As I move downward, more and more of them break out, so that in a short while there are so many that I am almost completely ensnared. I struggle, climbing downward, trying with greater and greater difficulty to find my way through the roots. They become so thick that finally it seems like it is going to be impossible to get to the outside. I feel increasingly fearful with the certainty that I would not be able to find my way through them. I wake in a panic.

This apparently simple dream mystified me for many years. It was not until I entered analysis almost twenty-five years later that

I could begin to understand its profound significance for my entire psychological, emotional, and spiritual life. Its tremendous impact signaled the first indication of an internal process that I could not ignore. This dream helped me to embark on what I later came to understand as the *individuation process.*

According to Jung, it is through individuation—the human being's "progressive realization of wholeness" in life—that the psyche demonstrates a propensity for growth and a natural movement toward the integration of the personality.[3] There is an inborn and natural tendency of the psyche to strive to attain "wholeness." But this process requires the participation of the individual, who must become aware of the archetypal processes that attempt to reflect themselves through the unconscious by way of images and the powerful emotions that accompany them.

My childhood dream, as well as a number of subsequent experiences, led me to develop a somewhat uncanny and irrational sense of knowing that my life was not entirely my own doing. That is, it seemed as if there was a process unfolding within me that I did not entirely control and about which I needed desperately to become aware, since I also felt emotionally stuck and was often subject to bouts of severe depression that I couldn't understand. I "confessed" this seemingly odd premonition about my life to my analyst early on, fearing that he might think me even more ill than I was. I was relieved when he acknowledged not only that this feeling was not as bizarre as I thought, but also that it was deeply important for me to cultivate it.

It was through my analysis that I discovered the individuation process as personally meaningful. The symbols of death, dismemberment, and rebirth, as well as the images of mothers and female figures I encountered in my dreams and fantasies, fascinated me, because I had had little knowledge of them when I entered analysis. I had always thought of my ego as being the center, if not the totality, of my psyche. On the other hand, my unconscious had often seemed to have a life of its own, which both puzzled and intrigued me. To understand these symbols and their importance to my life I began to study them in greater depth; this process, as we shall see, began my encounter with my *anima,* my own inner feminine. It was through this process that I began to find the meaning of my life.

For myself, and for men in general, such an exploration often leads back to the most primordial images and symbols of the mother, as she is encountered as far back as the beginnings of life itself. It is as if we must return to these images to discover the metaphors and the roots of our psyche's beginnings. Because a man's mother is the first and most important woman in his life, she is also the forerunner of his inner image of the feminine.

The rich and complex concept of the anima can be a tool for deepening our understanding of significant aspects of a man's behavior. The anima is a man's contrasexual or contrapsychological side, about which he is most often unconscious. Becoming more aware of this inner woman helps him to see that "she" is a prominent factor in some of the most important dimensions of his behavior, including his relationships. For the purpose of discussing certain aspects of male psychology and male behavior I have purposefully restricted my discussion of the role of the anima to some specifically pragmatic functions, hopefully without diminishing its overall meaning in other contexts. Some may say that using the term *anima* in this way has the effect of reducing some of its breadth and depth and that it should not even be used apart from its female counterpart, the *animus.* To those readers I offer my apology. I have more to say about the anima even in this restricted framework, but the constraints of time and space have prevented me from doing so. It may be for women to expound on the *animus* further, as I don't believe that the men who have written about this aspect have done the concept great justice in the past.

Why men (as distinct from women) behave in particular ways is, of course, relative and complex. Human behavior in general is conditioned by many factors, including the historical, cultural, and social context, as well as the levels of collective consciousness current in any historical period. Obviously, not all men behave alike. In this sense, then, I am attempting to approach the concept of *anima* as one factor among many in male behavior.

When I became a psychologist, and particularly when I later became a Jungian analyst, I was struck by the fact that there are so few men in analysis. I began to cultivate an interest in working with male patients and then began to observe—in their behavior, images, dreams, and fantasies—what I felt were distinct differences in how the unconscious male, as compared to female, psyche describes itself. In particular, the archetype of the anima seems to be a man's *dark heart*—a frequently unknown, often unexplored, and mysterious substrate of his personality that offers itself as a *prima materia* from which much psychological and spiritual understanding might come.

In 1982 I finally had enough male patients in my private practice to begin a men's group comprising six men, all of whom were also in personal analysis for the duration of the group. That group met virtually every week for six years. During that time we also met once or twice a year for two-day intensive sessions. At the end of those six years there were three men left: one had dropped out, one had died of a heart attack, and another had committed suicide.

My personal experience, as well as my experiences with other men in analysis, comprises much of the clinical basis of this book. Some of the men I have worked with have generously contributed parts of their own material in the form of dreams, fantasies, journal notes, and personal experiences. These clinical experiences have provided and continue to provide a rich source of material to enhance our understanding of the male psyche.

I hope that my observations and experience will encourage men in their efforts to continue or begin a psychospiritual journey into the deeper recesses of their unconscious. I also hope that women's understanding of men will be enhanced and that this will enrich their appreciation of the value and power of the feminine as they see it portrayed in the psychological and spiritual experiences of men.

This book is not an attempt to exhaustively define masculinity or male psychology, but to begin a deeper exploration of the male psyche by casting some light on the dark hearts of men.

□ 1 □

Anima: Men and Their Inner Women

For there is a boundary to looking.
And the world that is looked at so deeply
wants to flourish in love.

Work of the eyes is done, now
go and do heart-work
on all the images
imprisoned within you; for you
overpowered them: but even now you don't know them.
Learn, inner man, to look on your inner woman,
the one attained from a thousand
natures, the merely attained but
not yet beloved form.

—RAINER MARIA RILKE

Collective Images

ONE OF C. G. JUNG'S greatest contributions to the study of the psyche was his recognition of the collective unconscious—the fascinating world of archetypal images he discovered through investigating the dreams and fantasies of his patients. In contrast to the personal (subjective) unconscious, which consists of the once conscious but then repressed or forgotten elements of an individual's life experiences, the collective unconscious consists of elements that are primal psychic structures, or forms. In the early years of his analytical work, Jung recognized that these collective images were common to many of his patients' material. He tried to understand these images by tracing their origins, finding parallels in history, religion, early myths, fairy tales, and in the symbolic aspects of alchemical writings. He discovered that the forms of these images (rather than the images themselves) are seemingly "genetic," in that they are part and parcel of the human psyche. They generally remain unconscious, however, except when activated during times of stress, emotional crisis, psychosis, or during important developmental periods of life.

Archetypes are the catalysts of consciousness; they are primordial forms which manifest in the clothing of a particular culture while retaining a common underlying form. Archetypes may act almost like transducers, converting energy contained in the unconscious to a more conscious differentiated form. In biology the instincts are precursors to the archetypes insofar as they facilitate adaptation of the organism to its environment and promote survival-specific behaviors. As far as we know human beings have outgrown most of the "pure" instincts and instinctually mediated behavior; the archetypes may be the closest equivalents to instinctually mediated behavior.

We can gain a deeper understanding of a man's behavior in relationships if we include an appreciation of the archetype of the anima, an unconscious factor that shapes the way men feel and act. In the most general way, the anima refers to a man's *unconscious personality*, which Jung considered to be feminine. *Anima* is a Latin word meaning "soul" or "breath." This concept is peculiar to Jungian psychoanalysis, as opposed to Freudian and other psychoanalytic theories. Because Jungian analysts have in the past written for each other and not for the general public, the concept of the anima is unfamiliar to most people; however it is as familiar to Jungian analysts as the Oedipus complex is to their Freudian counterparts.

Conversely, the construct which refers to woman's unconscious masculine personality is called the *animus*, the Latin word for "mind." The animus personifies the Logos principle, acting as a bridge between a woman's ego and her own creative resources in the unconscious. These definitions are the traditional ones; in recent years they have been rethought by some Jungians so that the anima/animus constructs are now considered to be within the psyches of both men and women.[1]

Jung recognized early in his own life the importance of a man's internal feminine images and the dynamic role they could play in his psychological and emotional development. He recounts in his autobiography that, following his break with Freud, he became disoriented and emotionally disturbed. He began to pay close attention to his dreams in order to try to understand what was happening to him. In some of these dreams he encountered important feminine images—in one a young girl of about eight, and in another the figure of the blind Salome who accompanied Elijah. He also encountered a feminine voice that broke into his awareness from time to time and came to him in his directed fantasy, and with which he developed a dialogue. Of these figures he said:

> The essential thing is to differentiate oneself from these unconscious contents by personifying them, and at the same time to bring them into relationship to consciousness. That is the technique of stripping them of their power. It is not too difficult to personify them, as they always possess a certain degree of autonomy, a separate identity of their own. Their autonomy is a most uncomfortable thing to reconcile oneself to, and yet the very fact that the unconscious presents itself in that way gives us the best means of handling it. . . . It is she who communicates the images of the unconscious to the conscious mind, and that is what I chiefly valued her for. For decades I always turned to the anima when I felt that my emotional behavior was disturbed and that something had been constellated in the unconscious. I would then ask the anima: "Now what are you up to? What do you see? I should like to know."[2]

Redefining Masculinity and Femininity

When Jung refers to inner feminine and masculine qualities, we must be careful to realize that he was not speaking about *gender*, per se. Nor was he referring to the social and cultural stereotypes of these qualities and the often erroneous ideas of what it means to be a "real" man or woman.[3]

In American society, the conventional masculine ego is still often represented as tough, strong, virile, independent, realistic, thinking, unfeeling, and so forth. The feminine ego, on the other hand, is thought of as soft, tender, weak, passive, dependent, emotional, and nurturing. In spite of individual variations on these qualities, the collective stereotypes continue to be so strong that we reflect them in much of our literature, advertising, music, art, and movies.

Such "qualities" need to be viewed with caution and some reservation, however, or notions of masculinity and femininity are likely to devolve into cultural stereotypes, and the depth and breadth of the concept of the anima/animus will become increasingly narrowed. We also need to avoid an implicit (or explicit) psychological sexism through the reductive use of such socially current clichés as "men can't express their feelings" and "women can't think."

A current Jungian view of the concept of the anima includes the notion that both men and women have an anima, just as both have an animus. The anima is seen to interpenetrate the animus as a larger dimension of human experience, making a *syzygy*, or pair, each helping to clarify the other.[4] We must keep in mind that we are speaking here about relative psychological qualities and not fixed or unalterable attributes based on biological or sexual determinants. Any particular man, then, may be seen as behaving and responding from a combination of: specific life experiences, culturally fostered sex role expectations, as well as innate archetypal patterns. If sex is defined in the metaphorical, rather than strictly biological, sense, men and women each have access to the psychological worlds of both masculinity and femininity. For men, anima can then be seen as a developmental potentiality of the *otherness* missing in one-sided notions of masculinity.

Current social roles define masculinity and femininity as opposites that are gender specific. This tends to result in value judgments. When a man is described as "acting effeminate," for example, he is actually being described in two ways rather than one. *Webster's* dictionary defines *effeminate* as "having the qualities generally attributed to women, such as weakness, timidity, delicacy, etc.; unmanly; not virile."[5] The synonym given is *female.* In American culture femininity is a trait conventionally ascribed to women, so to be *effeminate* means behaving "not like a man"; or, it means behaving "like a woman." The effeminate man is removed from the class *male* and placed in the class *female,* with the effect that the effeminate man is no longer a "real" man.

Our collective consciousness and psychological defenses are apparently still so strong that we cannot tolerate the presence of much otherness within the same sex. Herein lies a major dilemma for contemporary man: femininity, as otherness, has to be relegated to the psychosexual garbage heap or one is not a "real man." Men unfortunately choose to follow the path that is expected of them, and perpetuate this choice for themselves and their sons. And, as we will see in chapter 7, the contribution of this choice to homophobia is significant.

The Bipolar Anima

There is another aspect of the anima that makes our understanding of it difficult—namely, its bipolar quality. The anima is usually split into two aspects: the positive (often more conscious) pole, and the negative (often more unconscious) aspect. Although both aspects are projected onto outer women, the initial projection is usually the positive one, in the sense that it is "seen" from a more conscious perspective. The positive pole is the infatuating or idealizing pole; the ego initially perceives its projection as being the whole person. The negative pole of the image is frequently imbedded in or occluded by the positive pole; they are not experienced consciously at the same time. The more painful experiences a man has of the feminine, the more suppression of the negative pole; the ego is then unaware of the negative aspects of the anima image. The effect of this process is to create an inner image of a *wounded woman*. The negative pole may only emerge after a period of time, which will vary according to the individual's level of self-reflection and vulnerability.

With the suppression of the negative pole of the feminine image there is a corresponding *impoverishment of consciousness*. Suppression carries with it a loss of some of the fullness or richness of human experience, no matter how successfully repressed the painful experiences are. This impoverishment of consciousness is also an impoverishment of life, since the unconscious saps the energy of consciousness and causes unnamed fears, anxieties, and seemingly unexplainable depression. We shall see later how this happened to Harry Haller, the protagonist in Hermann Hesse's novel *Steppenwolf*.

A fascinating quality of the psyche is that it seems to autonomously desire a reintegration of the split-off parts of itself; it demands an integration of the opposites contained within it. For a man, this is a major function of the anima, which functions as a bridge between the ego and the unconscious. Because of this innate capacity, a man is able to gain access to the deeper parts of his personality, where lie the unresolved developmental tasks that his ego has tried to leave behind, but from which his anima won't let him escape. The anima specifically allows him access to his capacities for interpersonal relatedness, differentiated feeling, creativity, spirituality, and further development of his consciousness. If ego perpetually ignores the demand of the anima for reintegration, this ignorance may lead to far-reaching and sometimes tragic consequences.

The Persona

Before we can go more deeply into the concept of the anima we need to first consider the concept of the *persona*. *Persona,* or "mask," is a word borrowed from early drama, where it designated the role that one played. Psychologically, the persona refers to the outermost layer of personality, which is largely socially defined. Each of us has a persona, which is natural and actually helps facilitate social interaction. Sometimes one's job, profession, or economic status itself defines the persona. One function of the persona is to facilitate a certain degree of social identity and sensitivity, without which one would be experienced as socially inept or naive. However, the persona also hides. When a man becomes overidentified with the persona, he is left with a constricted and shallow view of himself. Paradoxically, he develops an overinflated view of his conscious sense of ego, since so much value is placed on his outer personality; on the other hand, he suffers a loss of a sense of inner self and a connection to the unconscious.

Insofar as the anima is a personification of parts of his unconscious, it can be seen as the antithesis of the persona. Since it is the function of the anima to create a more viable connection to the unconscious. overreliance on the persona may in some cases block access to the unconscious altogether.

Sam, one of the men in my group, had a dream that dramatically illustrates this:

> I am getting ready to make the Academy Award presentation for the best actress. On a practice sheet I have Joan Crawford's name. I am nervous and concerned that when I am given the envelope I will fumble the papers. I ask myself, "How do I know Joan Crawford will win the award? What movie was she in?" Then I remember that it will all be printed on the envelope they give me. I remember that since I am on the radio and cannot see the audience I should pace my voice and time my humor. As the time grows near I ask myself, "Why am I giving the award, since it is always given by the best male actor of the last year?" Then I remember that I was in a film with several other men. At that I become totally calm and relaxed. I gather my strength and take control.

My opening line of humor is, "Who is Sam? Why, he is so unknown that I hardly know who he is!"

This dream is a particularly delightful example of the persona problem; it even includes metaphors from acting. It is a creative attempt of the unconscious to make Sam aware that he is in fact "acting" and that the questions he asks himself in the dream are indeed questions he needs to be asking. His various attempts to reassure himself ultimately fail when, at the end, he asks himself the most critical question of all: "Who is Sam?" The grandiosity of being identified as the apparent best actor of the year is offset by his lack of knowledge about who he really is. That is, the greater his identification with the persona, the greater the likelihood that he doesn't know himself in any depth. The values and even the feelings expressed by a man caught in the persona are likely to be those he thinks he is supposed to have—those that are socially conventional—which may in fact be neither his own, nor based on values that have much depth for him.[6]

In Arthur Miller's play *Death of a Salesman,* we see in the character Willy Loman a particularly poignant and tragic example of persona identification. At the end of the play Willy has committed suicide. His wife and sons try to make sense of his death:

LINDA [*Willy's wife*]:   He was so wonderful with his hands.

BIFF: He had the wrong dreams. All, all wrong.

HAPPY (*almost ready to fight Biff*):   Don't say that!

BIFF: He never knew who he was.

CHARLEY (*to Biff*):   Nobody dast blame this man. You don't understand. Willy was a salesman. And for a salesman there is no rock bottom to the life. He don't put a bolt to a nut, he don't tell you the law or give you medicine. He's a man way out there in the blue, riding on a smile and a shoeshine. And when they start not smiling back—that's an earthquake. And then you get yourself a couple of spots on your hat, and

you're finished. Nobody dast blame this man. A salesman is got to dream, boy. It comes with the territory.

BIFF:　Charley, the man didn't know who he was.[7]

No man can read or see this play without feeling an uncomfortable coldness inside. Willy's suicide was an act of resolution of a
self not known; when his persona finally failed, so did his life.
Since he never knew himself with any depth he knew no one
else, not even his wife or his sons. At the end only his son Biff
seemed to begin to understand the real problem: Willy just didn't
know who he was.

A man is naturally less familiar with his unconscious personality
than he is with his persona. If it is the persona with which he is
most closely identified then for him that is the whole of who he
is. Unless a man is unusually introspective or has undergone
psychological analysis he may regard the persona as the sole basis
of his personality. In this sense the persona can be an obstacle to
self-awareness, preventing access to the deeper parts of the self,
particularly the anima.

One of the functions of the anima is to help a man become
more connected to a deeper sense of self. A wonderfully clear
example of this function can be seen in Hermann Hesse's novel
Steppenwolf, in the relationship between Harry Haller and a
mysterious woman, Hermine. At the outset, Harry is a cultured
and overly intellectual man trying to live out his persona. He is
depressed and suicidal, and then he meets Hermine, who foretells
that he will fall in love with her, and also that he will carry out
her last order, which she won't tell him until the right moment.
She introduces him to his forgotten instinctual side, to his shadow
side, personified by Pablo, the coke-snorting jazz musician whom
he at first resents and despises for being so open and crude.
Hermine introduces him to a woman with whom he has a hot
affair, and she produces in him dreams of his repressed instinctual nature. She teaches him to dance, to make passionate love, to

laugh at his overly somber nature, and to accept his split-off aggressiveness. All of this is carried out in the Magic Theatre, within which he finally comes to accept himself more fully, for who he really is. Hermine's last order is that he must kill her when he finds her lying naked with Pablo. This scene throws him into a jealous rage, and he murders Hermine; that is, he finally "kills off" his anima since she has by then served her final purpose by bringing him into contact with the darkest part of his psyche.

In trying to understand some of the deeper aspects of a man's relationship to women we need to understand that his conscious ideas of women represent only one facet of what he experiences with actual women. The anima, or *inner woman,* as a conditioner of his personal relationships, is derived from both personal and archetypal images of female figures. The quality and types of a man's experiences of his personal mother, mother surrogates, sisters, as well as the other women he encountered in early life, all contribute to the inner feminine in his psyche. These inner images are also influenced by social and cultural descriptions of femininity.

To a man, the outer woman represents a large part of his life's mysterious, unresolved otherness. Whether or not a man is conscious of it, the inner struggle with the masculine/feminine polarity is one of his life's greatest issues. Among other things, behind every man *is* a woman, whether he is successful or not. The deeper truth, however, is that the most influential woman in his life is not the outer woman but the personal and archetypal internal representation of the feminine image—his anima. The outer woman, or women, often correspond in many ways to this unconscious anima image, since it is upon her, or them, that this image is projected.

In order to make a connection to this inner woman, a man first needs to "find" her. Men—particularly those in analysis—have the opportunity to find the inner woman in their dreams and to establish a relationship with her.

Fusion of the Anima with the Shadow

The inner woman eventually helps a man to clarify his relationship with the outer woman. But the connection to the anima also involves confronting his *shadow,* the male personification of those parts of himself that he has disowned because they interfere with his persona image. (I will elaborate on the shadow in chapter 6.) If a man is overly reliant on his persona orientation the effect may be that his anima and shadow exist in a state of *fusion,* or contamination. An excellent example of this is seen in Sam's dream about a girl named Misty:

> I am working for a police department, and we are looking for a missing girl. The police department has hired a consultant and he is helping me. We are driving in a hilly area, and along the way we see a road where all the rock formations are exposed. There is a thin cap of rock that is harder than the rock below, and I remember that a caprock can sometimes come sliding down, slipping on the surface of the softer underlying rock, resulting in a landslide.
>
> The two of us drive to a ridge overlooking a valley below. I say to the consultant that no one has seen the girl in this valley, but if they only looked from above, they could easily miss her because not all the valley is visible from here. As we climb down into the valley the trail is very steep, and many rocks are dislodged beneath our feet and tumble down below us. The consultant comments that this is more difficult than he thought it would be. I tell how consultants can charge twice as much and that he is to stay with me.
>
> In the valley are two sets of buildings; we explore the one to the left. There is one two-story building and a separate two-room, one-story building. I remark to the consultant that when women sleep in the two-room building police patrol the area, ostensibly to protect them but really to stop them from pandering. The missing girl is not here.
>
> We go to the other set of buildings to the right, which

is a duplicate of those to the left, except that they are dark, vine-covered, and have wrought iron grills over the windows. I climb up to the second story with the consultant, and we work our way along the outside, holding onto the grills. I am able to get inside. I discover that one of the grills is loose and find a false front to the lower part of the window. We do not locate the missing girl. We are now concerned that there is a killer at large who may have killed the girl.

There is a carving in the rock with some symbols. I know the missing girl is named Misty. There is a paved area leading from the road to the base of this rock-carved symbol. I tell the consultant that the girl's name is Misty and that she is in the set of buildings to the right. I know by the symbol carved in the rock.

We go back to the office to be fitted with guns, bullet-proof vests, etcetera, and to get more help in searching out the killer. I know about the loose grill and the false-front window, and I think that I can trap the killer there. As I am putting on the bullet-proof vest J. [his ex-wife] comes to me, and we embrace tenderly and passionately. I am crying and wrought with emotion. I know that I must take off my wedding ring to search for the missing girl and the killer. I ask myself, "Why do they allow policemen to cry and become so emotionally wrought-up before they go out to kill someone?" By being so emotionally wrought-up a policeman could easily lose his mental alertness and his will to kill.

This is a wonderful portrayal of Sam's search for his anima. Following are his associations and my interpretations: he is working for the police, a stereotypical image of the "good guys," who represent to Sam authority, power, and exaggerated masculinity. I am the "consultant" in the dream, whom he needs to help him find the girl. This is a dangerous undertaking since there could be a "landslide"; that is, the whole venture could collapse on him. He senses that his inner work is going to be difficult when the consultant says that the search is "more difficult than he thought it would be." But Sam is willing to "pay twice as much" since he so badly needs this help. This aspect is particularly important, since Sam had a poor relationship with his actual father and was emotionally abandoned by him. His real father could never have helped him in this important task, so he needs a "consultant." One set of buildings is "vine-covered"—here is a place where no one has been in a long time. It is "covered over," and the place he goes to look has a "false front," an allusion to the persona. It is here that he discovers that there may be a "killer at large." Now the task is to locate the shadow and kill him before rescuing the anima. This is important because it indicates that the anima is contaminated by, and fused to, the shadow; they need to be separated so that the shadow can be seen as part of the ego.

It is at this point that Sam knows the name of the woman— Misty—which means blurred, dimmed, indistinct, obscure, or vague. This aptly describes the image of the anima to his ego. With his new knowledge we know that we have to first find the shadow. He reinforces the stereotypical masculine defensive position by getting even more help, putting on bulletproof vests, and being fitted with guns. When he says that he must "take off his wedding ring" to search for the missing girl and the killer, he acknowledges that his outer relationship must be put on hold until he deals with the shadow and finds the missing inner woman. At the same time his ex-wife is there, and they tenderly embrace. In spite of his attempts to control his emotions, he is overwhelmed with feelings that he cannot prevent from intruding into the job that needs to be done. In order to get to the anima he must first find the shadow, of whom she is a captive. Here he asks a critical question: "Why do they allow policemen to cry and become so emotionally wrought-up before they go out to kill someone?" This indicates the conflict he feels between "being a man" in the social-conventional sense of being in control, especially of his feelings, and being deeply connected to the more emotionally vulnerable part of himself, the anima. Being "in control" and the simultaneous presence of strong feelings is contradictory to him. Losing his "will to kill" could have devastating consequences for his need to be empowered in the world as a man.

Sam's dream powerfully describes the excitement of a man in search of the inner woman, as well as his anxiety about needing to come to terms with his shadow and possibly giving up his usual more defended masculine orientation to the world.

Jung elaborates on the importance of the anima as a personification of the unconscious and the relationship of the anima to the disowned parts of the ego:

> If the anima figure (the personified unconscious) is separated from ego-consciousness and therefore unconscious, it means that that there is an isolating layer of personal unconscious embedded between the ego and the anima. The existence of a personal unconscious proves that contents of a personal nature which could really be made conscious are being kept unconscious for no good reason. There is thus an inadequate or even non-existent consciousness of the shadow. The shadow corresponds to a negative ego-personality and includes all those qualities we find painful or regrettable. Shadow and anima, being unconscious, are then contaminated with each, a state that is represented in dreams by "marriage" or the like. But if the existence of the anima (or the shadow) is accepted and understood, a separation of these figures ensues. The shadow is thus recognized as belonging, to the ego.[8]

Projection

Realizing the anima is a critical factor in the development of masculine consciousness, not only because much of the success or failure of men's relationships hinges upon the integration of this otherness, but also because the anima is responsible for a man's connection to his unconscious. If a man cannot gain access to the unconscious, he may remain stuck at the persona level and never move beyond a superficial orientation to life.

For a man to become aware of the anima, he must identify the anima's images in his dreams, fantasies, or projections onto actual women in the outer world. Having identified these images, he must then struggle with and reclaim them as projections in order to access the potentialities the anima represents for himself.

In psychoanalytic theory, *projection* was originally defined as a defense mechanism against thoughts, feelings, or impulses that were unacceptable to the ego—as a way of protecting the self-image of the ego. Freud saw defenses as neurotic mechanisms that protected the ego from painful feelings it did not want to acknowledge. From a more contemporary and especially Jungian perspective, however, while projection may be at times a neurotic defense, its function is also seen as positive.[9] Projection is one of the ways by which we may eventually become aware of the unconscious parts of ourselves that are in need of deeper understanding and integration, such as the anima. The complete absence of projection, on the other hand, could result in a narcissistic preoccupation with oneself; all of a man's emotional energy would be self-contained, resulting in a rather withdrawn and schizoid orientation to women and to the world.

One form of projection, *projective identification,* occurs when the content of the projection is so identified with the other person that there is little chance of the projection being seen through or withdrawn. The projection and the carrier of the projection become inseparably fused in the mind of the projector. The projector, of course, is unaware of either his projection or the other person. To an extent, all projections are projective identifications because there is always some identification (however unconscious) with the content that is being projected. This is true even in negative identifications, such as shadow projections in which the projector maintains that the other is "not-like-me" or "not-me."[10]

This might sound like a conscious process, but it is really not that at all: like all archetypal entities, the anima is itself a "projection-making" factor. Anima projections always involve an identification, but it is precisely the ignorance that one is projecting something of oneself that makes the behavior of the one carrying the projection so mysterious to the projector. We are surprised when we find that the "other" is not who we thought they were. When a relationship seemingly "doesn't work" anymore, what is more likely happening is that our projections aren't holding when we still want them to. If we don't understand this and simply withdraw what was being projected, we will inevitably find another person on whom to project.

A great story of projective identification is Somerset Maugham's semi-autobiographical novel, *Of Human Bondage.* The protagonist, Philip, has an obsessive "love" for Mildred, a woman who is quite unfit for him and who is in fact bent on exploiting and humiliating him. His apparently masochistic preoccupation with her causes his medical studies to suffer, but he can muster no reason to unshackle himself from her. He even humiliates himself by mentioning his club foot as an appeal to her sympathy, but there is none forthcoming. In a final gesture, he finally begs her to marry him, but Mildred tells him she is going to marry someone else. After an interlude without her, Philip meets a new woman, Norah, who is the opposite of Mildred. But, instead of falling in love with her as she does with him, he once again returns to Mildred, who is now pregnant by the man she was supposed to marry. Philip agrees to look after her and the baby; however, this reunion is short-lived. When Philip introduces Mildred to a friend, she runs off with him to have an affair, which Philip, out of desperation, agrees to finance if Mildred promises she will later return to Paris with him. She does not keep her promise, resurfacing as a prostitute after she has been abandoned by Philip's friend. Philip once again takes her in and supports her, on the condition that she give up prostitution. At this point she makes overtures to him, which he rejects; in a fit of rage she destroys his apartment and his belongings. She disappears again until she discovers that she is in need of his help. She looks him up, and he finds that she has syphilis. He prescribes some medicine for her and tells her of the seriousness of the condition and again implores her to give up prostitution. She apparently neither takes the medicine nor gives up prostitution; that finally ends the relationship.

On the surface, Maugham seems to be telling us that in love there can only be unhappiness and misery: "He did not know what it was that passed from a man to a woman, from a woman to a man and made one of them a slave: it was convenient to call it sexual instinct; but if it was no more than that, he did not understand why it should occasion *so vehement an attraction to one person rather than another* [italics added]."[11]

On a deeper level, Philip's obsession might make sense if we look at it as a form of projective identification of his anima and assume that he was trying to become conscious of some split-off, unconscious aspect of his emotional life and his relationship to his abandoning mother. Herein lies some clue to his "vehement attraction"—his seemingly paradoxical fascination with Mildred. From the standpoint of rational consciousness the attraction not only doesn't make sense, it seems to be a futile and self-defeating undertaking. Looked at as an unresolved developmental task, as something unconscious, the attraction makes much more sense: it is an identification with some split-off part of himself. The compulsion to unite with Mildred can in this way be seen as a prospective function of Philip's psyche to resolve his early emotional woundedness.

Young Philip's father has died six months before the opening scene of the novel. Philip goes to pay his last visit to his mother, who is dying in a hospital after having given birth to a stillborn child. Now orphaned, Philip, who is only nine years old, is sent to live with his godmother and uncle, who don't look forward to having responsibility for him. His godmother loves him but is unable to express her affection directly. His uncle is cold, selfish, disinterested, and filled with meaningless platitudes.

The main theme of the story actually begins when Philip, now a young man, decides to give up his attempt to become an artist and decides instead to go to medical school, following in his father's footsteps. Shortly thereafter, he meets Mildred in an encounter marked by her snubbing him. The beginning of their relationship follows directly upon the death of his aunt, the embodiment of his last strong emotional childhood attachment to a woman.

Unconsciously, Philip is now desperately in need of reconnecting with the anima, which is still fused with his early experience of the feminine: the anima is sick, emotionally unavailable, and abandoning. Mildred is an apt character in that she herself is also deeply wounded, she is unable to relate to him emotionally, she will continually abandon him, and she will eventually die in spite of his attempts to save her. (She also continually wants to abandon her own child, whom Philip keeps trying to save, and who also dies.)

Philip's saving grace, psychologically, is that he develops some capacity for self-reflection, arriving at the realization that with respect to Mildred there is nothing more he can do. He eventually sees his obsession as a form of disease that he must overcome, and although one can surmise that she never completely leaves his mind, the fascination with Mildred is finally resolved with his realization that there is nothing he can do to make her love him. Perhaps it is her death that frees him. The anima projection is finally withdrawn; Philip can become aware of the futility of trying to recapture the love he lost when his mother and godmother abandoned him through death. Although he never becomes consciously aware of the identification of his relationship with his mother and with Mildred, one gets the feeling that the attachment issue is finally resolved existentially.

Perhaps Maugham's novel was an attempt at some resolution in his own life. Many years after Maugham wrote this novel, at the age of ninety, he says: "Perhaps the most vivid memory left to me is the one which has tortured me for more than eighty years—that of the death of my mother. I was eight when she died and even today the pain of her passing is as keen as when it happened in our home in Paris."[12]

Unconscious Choices

Most of us think that we are aware of much, if not all, of what we perceive. However, unconscious perception is a phenomenon familiar to psychologists, especially in the area of motivation and choice. Psychologists know that outer perceptions can be influenced and even distorted by inner needs and drives.

In psychological experiments it is consistently found that individuals will distort the spelling and meaning of words based on their inner needs. For example, the word *moat* will frequently be misperceived as *meat* by hungry subjects, but will be perceived correctly by nonhungry subjects. *Canker sore* will be perceived as *cancer sore* by patients who have a morbid fear of cancer.[13] Other interesting examples come from ethological studies demonstrating that animals are capable of responding to extremely small verbal and nonverbal cues given by humans. The human informant does not have to be aware that he or she is signaling this information.[14]

Even more compelling evidence of unconscious perception comes from experiments in hypnosis, in which subjects are given suggestions for what are called *positive* and *negative hallucinations*. A positive hallucination involves "seeing" objects that are not actually present in the environment; a negative hallucination involves not seeing objects that *are* present. Subjects not only go along with the suggested misperceptions, but they also attempt to rationalize them when confronted with contradictory information. For example, if it is suggested to a person that a glass of water that is supporting a book be perceived as absent, the subject will not only not perceive the glass, he or she will attempt to explain why the book appears to be suspended in the air. Even more dramatic are the cases of hysterical deafness or blindness in which the person is fully "conscious" and yet temporarily loses the ability to see or hear.

The point is that the perception of information is quite an elaborate, complex, and highly selective process involving unconscious communication. Even though we are not fully conscious of doing so, we are constantly evaluating our perceptions and filtering those that we wish to exclude from consciousness. In this way, information that has been excluded from consciousness does not simply go away, it is stored in the unconscious; some of its more emotionally charged contents then become the basis for what we later unconsciously perceive in others. Self-perceptions that are alien to the persona are also excluded by the ego and become part of our perception of others. In this sense unconscious perceptions can become the primary means by which partners "choose" each other.

In clinical work with couples, the therapist is often amazed at how closely the partners "fit," in the sense that they play out respective poles of a particular complex. Not all women can carry the unconscious potential of a particular man's anima projections, and so there is undoubtedly method to the madness of a man who falls in love with only certain women—even if those women are not "good" for him, as in the case of Philip's "vehement attraction." Similarly, individuals with multiple marriages find themselves continually reconstellating the same unresolved issues or problems.

Another illustration of this dynamic is seen in families where there is physical or sexual abuse of children. Why do at least eight out of ten women who were molested as children marry men who molest their children? It is certainly not that they consciously want their children to experience the same grief and suffering they experienced themselves. A more likely explanation is that these women unconsciously perceive and marry men who have anima wounds very much like the anima wounds of their own fathers.

In a much publicized case that was popularized by the NBC television special "Burning Bed," a woman who suffered twelve years of physical abuse finally poured gasoline on her sleeping husband and burned him to death, to the "approval" of millions of Americans. She was acquitted of the murder, and "justice" was apparently done. Few people know that a short time later this same woman married another abusive man who also molested her daughter. That she was abused for so many years is indeed a human tragedy; that she murdered her husband is a tragedy of equal measure. But the unconscious acting-out of their mutual violence did not bring understanding. The cycle began anew soon after the old cycle ended. This is a tragic example of the mutual unconsciousness of two people locked into fixated projections.

When men blame "women" or women fault "men," there is a danger of turning away from each other as if they were not coconspirators; each then further projects the *bad object*, whether it be onto individuals or as a collective projection onto a particular group. *Splitting* is the label given to this dynamic of projection. The polarization between men and women is increased and the consciousness of both is decreased by one-sidedly projecting blame. Splitting leaves the developmental tasks of both parties unresolved.

In a prospective way, however, the unconscious component of the initial attraction may serve to bring each side of the relationship face to face with the developmental task of the anima that is still in need of conscious understanding and integration.

The Anima as Conditioner of Relationships

In counseling couples, I have often observed that beneath the persona level there is a particular dynamic that formed early in the relationship. This dynamic involves an unconscious agreement, as if there was a conspiracy of the anima and animus at work—a *conspirato*, a "breathing together." In other words, men don't just "do things" to women, and women don't just "do things" to men; they do them together in order to learn about themselves by becoming aware of the particular way the unconscious anima/animus dynamic influences their relationship. Particular anima/animus problems are often the residuals of defective and unsatisfactory early parent-child relationships, which have left both adults imbedded in childhood identifications. Recurring emotionally poor relationships are created and recreated out of an internal world of bad objects who dwell in the unconscious as secret persecutors—at first exciting desire and then denying satisfaction.[15]

One example is the dynamic of Sally and John, who struggled for years with John's alcoholism. Sally was always after John to get involved in some treatment program. The harder she tried to influence him to get the help he needed, the more entrenched his resistance became. His actual need for treatment retreated into the background as the struggle with Sally waged on, creating greater and greater discord between them.

They claimed to love each other; he felt that their relationship would be fine if only she would stop trying to determine whether or not he needed treatment. She felt the relationship would be fine if he would just go and get the treatment he needed. Sally's father was also an alcoholic, and her resultant father-complex caused her to unconsciously treat her partner like a weak father. Since she could never trust her father she was never able to trust another man. For her, men were fathers who acted like sons who couldn't take care of themselves. Trust, in her eyes, became the central focus in the relationship: if there could be no trust there could be no relationship. The proving ground of trust became whether John would get treatment. John, on the other hand, felt that Sally needed to trust him to get the treatment he chose for himself.

Why would Sally choose as her partner someone with a demonstrated history of untrustworthiness and stay with him for ten years? Why wouldn't John simply get the treatment he needed and let it go at that? The answer, in part, is that on the one hand he unconsciously needed to play out the role of the rebellious son until he could become aware that his wife was fused with his anima-as-mother. John's mother was secretive, rigid, domineering, and opinionated. She was a suffocating mother who could not let her son really live his own life because she could never live her own. Since she lived through him, his life could not be his own. As a further consequence, she was unable to have any genuine empathy for her son's life apart from her own. When he began drinking and was unable to function, his mother was always there to take care of him, at the same time reinstituting her control and reinforcing the idea that he was incapable of managing his own life. The tremendous ambivalence this brought up in John caused him to oppose his mother—and mother substitutes—in order to protect his own sense of integrity. Unfortunately, rather than being truly liberating, his oppositional behavior had the effect of perpetuating his dependency on his wife as well as his mother.

It was no accident that John chose Sally, who was so much in need of a man to take care of, as a way of saving her father. He experienced Sally as another form of the mother who was trying to control him and live her life through him. But of course it was not Sally who controlled his life but his anima, with which Sally was unconsciously fused. John's internal representation of the anima was of an angry, resentful woman who wanted to dominate his life by telling him what to do. And, at the same time, she was also someone more than willing to take care of him. He tended to be passive and to hide any angry feelings of which he was afraid. His anger was only expressed indirectly through his rebelliousness.

Sally, for her part, unconsciously perceived her father's emotional distance as a weakness that could only be bridged by "mothering," a lesson she learned from her mother. She felt she needed to "save" her father in order to get her own inner child's needs taken care of. Her veiled wish to be taken care of could not be met no matter how hard she tried. John's mother-complex fits well with a woman who feels emotionally weakened by a father unable to meet her needs. But John responded to her need to "mother" him as if she were the powerful mother trying to control his life.

And so, each partner was confronted in their relationship with projections that "fit" one another and functioned to perpetuate their own childhood dramas. The conflict between them, then, represented a developmental block for each of them—one that needed to be fully understood before they could outgrow their respective parent-child dynamics. They had to become aware of the unconscious projections and expectations they were putting on one another, begin to withdraw them, and try to understand the developmental significance of the problem they had been living out. Sally needed to become conscious of her unresolved problem with her father so she could grow up as a woman in her own right. John needed to become conscious of his mother-complex and separate his anima image from Sally so that he would begin to take care of himself.

"Stages" of the Anima

Predifferentiation is a normal quality of infancy and some aspects of childhood. In adult life differentiation takes on greater significance because of the need not only to achieve a greater diversity of behavior but also to reincorporate what was split off in early life, in order to arrive at a sense of wholeness of one's personality. This growth in adult life involves gradually enlarging the sphere of consciousness to include more and more parts of the self that were fused to parental images, abandoned in early life, or simply never experienced consciously.

The knowledge that unconscious perception plays such an important part in our choice of romantic partners introduces another dimension into the way we perceive the experience of "falling in love." Why don't we say "rising in love"? *Falling* may be the more apt figure of speech in that the experience often involves a descent into unconsciousness. We are drawn by the unconscious power of a resonant otherness into a realm in which reason, logic, and practicality are submerged beneath a magical fantasy caused by the confluence of a man's anima and a woman's animus. Often when a man emerges from that experience he wonders how anything that began as something so seemingly sweet could turn so bitter in the end.

The anima has a multifarious role in the growth of a man's

personality; her predominant images determine to a large extent his outer relationships with actual women, and she also reflects his inner relationship to the unconscious. The anima's projected image appears to be at a developmental level that corresponds to an inner development of feminine qualities. For this reason, a man is going to be unconsciously attracted to women with a developmental level similar to his own.

The unconscious attraction or fascination a man feels for a particular woman can act almost like a spell, causing him to feel lured to her in what sometimes amounts to a compulsion. The intensity of those feelings is related to his perception of "something" in her which beckons him in a sometimes uncanny way, signaling the activation of an anima image.

The particular images of the anima, which are present at any given period of a man's life, span the spectrum of all female personifications. These images include, among others: the female child, the adolescent, the young woman, the mother, the witch, the seductress, the old wise woman, and the spiritual guide. Each image represents a particular developmental achievement in a man's early identifications with the feminine and also points to his potential for further growth.

While it is not fair to speak of exact stages of the anima, there do seem to be some developmental levels of the image that correspond to different levels of psychological development in men. The earliest of these is the anima as young girl or child. Men for whom the anima is consistently portrayed as a child are often emotionally immature and tend to be rather narcissistic in their relationships, sometimes alternating between symbiotic attachments and emotional coldness. They are extremely demanding, have a low frustration tolerance, and are subject to bouts of rage or prolonged depressions when their needs are thwarted or threatened. They also have a poor sense of interpersonal boundaries and a tendency to impulsively act out their wishes as well as their frustrations. In spite of occasional appearances to the contrary, they relate to their partners as mothers, that is, as women who are, by and large, there to meet their needs. As children they may have been emotionally neglected, abandoned, or abused.

When the anima most frequently occurs as an adolescent we find men who tend to be flighty, unstable, and unpredictable in their relationships. These are the classical Don Juan–type of men, who continually move from one relationship to another. They are often superficially charming and have a lofty romanticism that can be flattering and seductive. They are frequently infatuated, but their enamored attachments are short-lived. Rather than being neglected by their mothers, they more frequently have been overindulged and consequently have an inflated sense of self-worth. Because of this, their pride is easily injured, and they feel unrecognized and undervalued. If this type of anima-possessed men ever do settle down they can also become *warriors*—compulsive achievers with type A personalities and little sense of realistic limits in the outer world. Such men rarely know how much is "good enough" or when it's time to stop. Since they have such difficulty setting limits for themselves, their children often have a difficult time measuring up to their standards and may even become their competitors. Relationships with partners often revolve around attempts to mold them into the women they want them to be, rather than allowing them to be who they are.

Unfortunately, we have the least amount of clinical information about men who are developmentally "normal." The reason for this is that few have sufficiently disturbed relations in adult life to warrant treatment. Therefore, it is difficult to know much about the anima images of a mature man, except through studying the transformation of anima imagery as it occurs in the course of analysis. Those men who have undergone successful analysis seem to develop anima images that are more consistently of adult women as well as images of the feminine that have a more spiritual aspect to them. At that point it may be no longer worthwhile to label personifications of the feminine as the anima. Jung referred to this when he said that such personifications are converted into bridges to the unconscious when the contents of the unconscious became assimilated.

The more spiritual aspect of the feminine is often portrayed as an old wise woman. This image may occur throughout a man's life as a precursor and potentiality for a spiritual relationship to the feminine, in spite of his current developmental struggles.

The Wounded Anima

The image of the *wounded anima* is a frequent occurrence in the dreams of men who are overidentified with their personas. These men may discover that the women they marry or their daughters have characteristics that correspond to these anima images.

Charles, a man of forty-three, came for treatment after having been arrested for having a sexual relationship with his daughter. The relationship had started when his daughter was only nine years old; Charles had become fascinated by her emerging sexuality and had developed a compulsion of wanting to be physically closer to her. His compulsion led to inappropriate touching and years later to a full-blown sexual relationship. His wife was aware of his inappropriate contacts with their daughter, but tried to ignore them. As it turned out, she had also been molested by her father at the age of ten.

Charles's case is an example of anima identification that remains at the level of the young child. In such instances a man may project much of his emotional and sexual energy onto an actual female (or even male) child—often his own child, or a relative. When the anima development is at this level there is a strong tendency toward incest and pedophilia. The man may suffer from impairment of his adult sexuality, resulting in impotence or other sexual problems with adult women. He may also be an exhibitionist or a voyeur. This man often suffers from guilt and shame resulting from these preoccupations. While he usually knows his behavior is wrong, he nevertheless has a strong compulsion to act out his fantasies.

A man with an anima of this young age often had a mother who was emotionally cold or even absent, who was critical and demanding, or who punished by withholding affection and approval. His relationship with his father was probably characterized by emotional abandonment, resulting in a cool and distant association with him. His mother may also have been emotionally withdrawn from her husband, so there was little modeling of anything approaching mature love or acceptance. As a man, it is difficult for him to be nurturing with others, since he received so little himself. He is also extremely vulnerable to rejection or even slight criticism. He may be demanding of others to accept him without qualification and demanding of himself as a compensating defense against being found lacking in any way. He can also be demanding and critical of his children, while at the same time harboring the expectation they will approve of him. He often tends to be distant and uninvolved in the ongoing lives of his children; for such a man his most intense emotional involvement usually occurs around his sexual compulsiveness.[16]

Another example of the wounded anima can be seen in the case of Jack. For many years Jack was able to skillfully sport an outwardly jovial and capable persona. He was successful in his business and apparently quite happy—except for the fact that he was married to a woman who was chronically depressed for many years. He never understood how or why she could be so depressed since he seemed to have provided her and the family with "everything they needed." On the other hand, he often had recurring dreams of a mysterious and unknown woman—his anima—who was a pale, quiet, depressed, and withdrawn woman. The dreams were simple vignettes of seeing her walking down the street, seated in the park, or sometimes just standing in the hazy distance. She was always alone and she always engendered a tremendous fascination in him; she never spoke and seemed to disappear almost as quickly as she appeared.

Here we can see the anima compensating for Jack's disconnected feeling. When a man is overidentified with his persona he likely has little development of differentiated feeling, causing him to relate to others in a superficial way. Because he has little emotional depth we say that his anima is *wounded*. His outer woman may in fact also be deeply wounded, particulary by her father, and he may try to save her from her suffering. However, in this case, because it was Jack's wounded "outer" woman who carried his anima, when she received treatment, discovered the source of her own difficulties, and began to work them out, he began to emotionally *decompensate*—that is, he began to lose his facile emotional superficiality and became plagued with depressive feelings and uneasiness about his own life. In effect what happened was that as she improved, she no longer needed to unconsciously carry his wounded anima for him. He was then left to face his problems, without even understanding where they were coming from.

After his wife's treatment Jack decided to come in himself. He began, with my encouragement, to have a dialogue with his mysterious inner woman. At first she wanted nothing to do with him. She said, "You've never had anything to say to me, why should I talk to you?" and walked away. Finally he was able to get her to speak at greater length. This time she said, "I'll talk to you, but I don't think you'll like what I have to say." I encouraged him to tell her that it was important that she speak to him, and I said that he might have to promise to listen to her. As she spoke, she transformed into a furious, enraged, almost animallike creature who ranted at him, cursed him, and told him how she despised him for his aloofness and feigned superiority. She told him what a fake human being he was. She went on for the better part of twenty minutes and then collapsed in a heap on the floor. He was stunned, frightened, and shocked at all of what she had said. When he opened his eyes, he started to cry and simply said, "She's right." At subsequent sessions we went back to her again. In time she was entirely transformed: she was composed, peaceful, and beautiful. She also seemed wise, compassionate, and open. He asked her what he could do to repay her for "opening his heart." She said, "Don't forget me. Take me on walks—in the park, by the ocean—take me to church, and at night before you sleep, keep me in your open heart."

In the course of my own analysis, at a critical point I had the following dream:

> I am walking down a deserted street in the late afternoon. I come upon a house where I see a young pretty girl of about fourteen or fifteen with blonde hair sitting in the window. She is looking outside and seems quite sad, as if she is very depressed. Moved by her sadness, I go to the door of the house and knock. The girl's mother comes to the door, and when she opens it I notice that there is a man's suit hanging on the inner closet door. I somehow know that this girl's father has died. I then ask the mother if perhaps I can take the girl for a walk as though to help her. The mother agrees and goes to get the young girl, who comes to the door. Being somewhat inside the house I turn to open the door to go out again, and as I reach for the door handle a hand comes from behind me and grasps the handle of the door and opens it ahead of me. I notice that his hand is of a very old woman but seems to be coming from the young girl. As I turn around after stepping outside, I notice that the young girl has turned into a very old but wise and kindly woman with silvery grey hair. As we step outside she takes my arm in hers and asks very warmly, "Now tell me, how are you?"

This dream is not unlike a fairy tale or myth that portrays a relationship between the hero and a maiden in distress. The dream begins with a lack of harmony that must somehow be overcome: the young girl is forlorn, the mother is emotionally unavailable, and the father is absent. The means of working with this is to help the young girl overcome her grief by bringing her "outside" the house of mourning, away from the depressed mother. The father also needs to be found.

The anima image is fourteen or fifteen years old; she is sad and depressed, as is the mother. With respect to her own animus development, she may be stuck in adolescence. She is abandoned by her father—whether emotionally, psychologically, or physically—with the result that her own animus growth is developmentally arrested. She also needs a man to play out the *good father* for her. As the hero, I am moved by her sadness to go and help her. The goal is to change the prevailing conditions by becoming the good father. The anima is presented in three developmental aspects: the young girl, the depressed mother, and at the end of the dream, the old wise woman, who is a more mature and spiritually oriented aspect of the feminine. So "accessing" the young girl leads to the transformation of the feminine into a more mature archetype.

This dream, particularly the shift from my initial concern for the young girl to the old woman's concern for me, moved me profoundly. The girl is the young, wounded, feminine part of my psyche, which was stuck in adolescence. Her defenses corresponded to my own: I was experiencing a sense of melancholy and mourning for the "death" of my own father. This dramatically pointed out some significant aspects of my "anima problem."

The developmental aspect of this anima imaged dated back at least to when I was three years old and witnessed my own father leaving my mother. I never saw him again. My defenses were already so developed that I didn't perceive my father as leaving me; I only perceived him as leaving my mother. I felt as though I was left with the responsibility of taking care of her. Assuming this responsibility left me in a position of seeing my mother, and by extension unconsciously perceiving all women, as being deeply wounded, abandoned, and in need of being cared for.

The dream characterized one of my unconscious attitudes toward women at that time: I saw them as unable to take care of themselves and myself as their self-appointed caretaker. In outer life I unconsciously found women who were looking for a "good father" to save them from their suffering. As it turned out, their fathers had not been emotionally available to them. My father was "dead" in my psyche, and my attempts to heal myself in outer life were characteristically aimed at dealing indirectly with my own depression by taking care of wounded women. In the dream, the act of beginning to care for the young girl introduced the possibility of transformation, of having the door opened for me by the archetypal old wise woman.

The need to separate from the depressed mother corresponds to the masculine need to separate from the actual mother, and particularly to free the anima from her influence, which is usually the most dominant influence. If a man is unable to separate his inner feminine from his mother he will always be unconsciously responding to the outer woman as though she were part mother, and this can cause problems in relationships.

Men who are stuck at this level often find adolescent girls (young maidens) a focus of fascination and intrigue, since they themselves may not have had the opportunity to experience the emotional fullness, blooming sexuality, freedom, and ambiguity of their own adolescence. Men who had to "grow up" too soon, or who had unusual responsibilities during these years, may "return" to adolescence later on by becoming irresponsible and flighty, or by rejecting the more traditional adult values in other ways.

The Inner Woman in Analysis

A man's first confrontation with the inner feminine may occur in analysis. One of the greatest problems a man faces in analysis is that this confrontation may mobilize extremely strong, possibly overwhelming, emotions for which he feels unprepared. In the initial stages, the relationship with the analyst may feel like a regression to the original parent-child relationship. As a result, a man may become very defensive and may even precipitously quit analysis before the deeper work can be accomplished. On the other hand, when he is successful in withstanding this regression and its consequent mobilization of the unconscious, true transformation of his personality may take place.

Paradoxically, the more in touch with his inner feminine a man is, the more comfortable he is likely to be with the process of his inner self-exploration. As we have seen, the anima, as a man's potential connection to his unconscious, may appear personified in his dreams and fantasies. Sometimes a man will report that long before analysis began he had many dreams involving a mysterious, intriguing, or seductive female figure. He may have fallen in love with her and always felt disappointed about losing her when he awoke. It is as if this inner woman was trying to teach him. She may also be frightening, because initially she may be contaminated by negative experiences of the mother during childhood.

Sometimes the anima appears in the early dreams of analysis. For example, one man had the following dream soon after he began treatment (prior to this he had never remembered a dream):

> I am on a business flight to New York with E. I get up to go to the bathroom. As I open the bathroom door I notice a pair of headphones dropping into my hands. When I get to the toilet it is almost totally red inside. I think to myself that some woman must have had her period and didn't flush the toilet. I flush it. We arrive at the airport, and I see my sister and her husband and a large group of children. We are all walking along looking for a ride when we meet B. and his wife and son (B. was my high-school principal). The first sentence from them is Mrs. B. asking if I bought my mother a present. She knows that we have just come from staying three days with my mother. I feel very guilty when I tell her no—I hadn't even thought about it. We say goodbye. A little later my sister arrives with a car and asks me to hop in. She starts off into the suburbs, and I then realize that I had been headed to the hotel to be with my business partner, but I decide to continue on with them. We go into the house they have rented, and as I start to explore I find it is very strange. First of all it has many rooms. I find myself exploring room after room. At first the rooms seem to be empty, but as I proceed they start to be filled. I notice many bedrooms and beds. I then flash that this house must have belonged to an older

couple and they have made it over so that all of the children and their children's children, etcetera could stay there when visiting. As I go downstairs, it is apparent he has even used every inch of what would normally have been a low basement, for bedrooms. I open one interesting door, and there is a marvelous children's room containing a kitchen and everything needed. The ceiling is the height for children. It is such a wonderful children's playroom I want to call J. who is in the house to come see it. Another low room has two double beds in it and two yellow lights over the far bed. There are two switches near me—one for each light—that I turn on and off to check them out. The yellow light from them is very interesting somehow. I am amazed at the number of people the house can sleep and start to count the beds. After counting the double beds or their equivalent I stop counting. I now remember that a little earlier a small boy arrived at the house, and when I opened the door he asked where his grandparents were. I said I didn't know—we were just renting the house. He started to look frantic and went running through the house yelling for his grandparents. I then end up upstairs where I find many marvelous objects in the room. I am wondering where they all came from—room after room. There is furniture and objects of great worth. As I come to the end of the house there is a railing and stairs leading down to a store below, and I see many people standing in line to do some trading. I then realize that this entire building belongs or belonged to Grandfather, and the marvelous objects in all of the rooms came from the store below, which no longer seems to belong to him. At any rate, a stern woman walks up the stairs with a sign that says the room below is closed. I say that is all right because I have no desire to go down there anyway. I remark that I haven't been aware they were there, because I didn't want to intrude. She responds in a displeasing voice saying that the people upstairs over the store must not know either, because they and their children were making a lot of noise. I then turn to the right and leave her and enter a series of rooms that hold exhibit or display cases. The cases hold marvelous displays of intricate oriental models, and there are other displays beyond that which I can't see well.

Immediately following this dream he has this powerful fantasy:

> I am playing in the hot tub being in love with the moon. I glance over the side and can see the women having their full moon summer solstice ritual. I continue to play, occasionally sneaking a peek over the side at the women I can see standing in a circle on the other side of the fence, nude. All of a sudden I have a flash that if I look once again I could lose my soul—not only could I, but I have the terrifying feeling that I *would* lose my soul if I even accidentally peeked. I dash out of the tub with my eyes covered with my hand and grab my towel and use it to shield my eyes as I put the cover on the hot tub. I quickly dress, and as I am doing so E. comes running out of the house. I want to warn him of the danger of looking at the women, but before I can decide to do this, he is gone—taking a safe path. I put on my robe with my hood on and walk quickly with my head covered to the safety of my room. Later I sense that I recently received an enormous flash of feminine energy and that my male psyche was scared to death of being killed.

His first dream introduces him to the feminine in his psyche, portrayed by the powerful archetypal image of menstrual blood in the bathroom. This rather involved dream is staged as an interruption in a business trip (a movement away from his outer life), which leads him in a regressive way back to the inner world of childhood. He is delighted to find this world and to discover that it all belongs to his grandfather. But the way is blocked by a stern woman who announces that this area is closed. The dream depicts his need to return to childhood, to rediscover the archetypal father (in his grandfather's house) which contains so many parts of himself that he has never seen before. However, the way is blocked by a woman who represents the part of his mother that blocked his development in childhood. It is clear that before he will be able to discover the unknown parts of himself—the "mysterious things"—he will have to confront the feminine.

In his fantasy following the dream, the archetypal feminine returns again, as nude women celebrating the summer solstice. He initially wants to avoid the images of the feminine in both the dream and the fantasy: in one case by flushing away the menstrual blood, and in the other by hiding his eyes to prevent the loss of his soul. The "loss of soul" idea is a serious omen for a man about to explore his unconscious, for he takes the chance of losing his usual orientation to consciousness, which has not previously allowed any access to the unconscious. In this case, the sudden confrontation with the nude women in their ritual, an archaic symbol of the anima, is overwhelming; it causes him to panic and to temporarily lose his ego orientation.

These two eruptions from the unconscious initiated this man into a process of remembering and recording his dreams—a fruitful source of unconscious material that allowed him to further explore his inner women.

The Spiritual Quest and the Anima

A man's creativity and spiritual needs are reflected by his experience of the anima in his outer as well as inner life. As guide to the unconscious the anima personifies the connection between outer and inner, and between the psychological and spiritual dimensions of life.

An example of this can be seen in the life of the Trappist monk Thomas Merton. Merton was a writer, poet, social activist, and a man who struggled literally all of his life with the need to find spiritual and psychological fulfillment. When he was six years old his mother died prematurely. Following her death he only sporadically lived with his father; then, when he was sixteen, his father died of a brain tumor. Merton's many writings, dreams, and personal journals, as well as writings about him, vividly describe his ongoing struggle to reconcile his inner spiritual quest with his need to relate to the outer world. His struggle embraced the polarities of self-determination versus external authority, action versus contemplation, solitude versus social involvement, and masculine versus feminine—all aspects he needed to come to terms with in his effort to feel a sense of inner spiritual peace.

These opposites seemed to make up much of the paradoxical nature of Merton's attempt to discover himself throughout the course of his life. He had an immense craving for solitude and at the same time was driven by a desire to have an impact on the outer world. Toward the end of his life he seemed to accept this polarity as "God's mercy:"

> I have also had to accept the fact that my life is almost totally paradoxical. I have also had to learn gradually to get along without apologizing for the fact, even to myself. . . . It is in the paradox itself, the paradox which was and still is a source of insecurity, that I have come to find the greatest security. I have become convinced that the very contradictions in my life are in some ways signs of God's mercy to me; if only because someone so complicated and so prone to confusion and self-defeat could hardly survive for long without special mercy.[17]

Two of his dreams of the anima seem to illustrate his struggle:

> One night I dreamt I was sitting with a very young Jewish girl of 14 or 15, and that she suddenly manifested a very deep and pure affection for me and embraced me so that I was moved to the depths of my soul. I learned that her name was "Proverb," which I thought very simple and beautiful. And also I thought "She is of the race of St. Anne." I spoke to her of her name, and she did not seem to be proud of it, because it seemed that other young girls mocked her for it. But I told her

that it was a very beautiful name, and there the dream ended.

A few days later when I happened to be in a nearby city, which is very rare for us, I was walking alone in the crowded street and suddenly saw that everyone was Proverb and that in all of them shone her extraordinary beauty and purity and shyness even though they did not know who they were and were perhaps ashamed of their names—because they were mocked on account of them. And they did not know their real identity as the Child so dear to God, who from the beginning was playing in His sight all days, playing in the world.

Thus you are initiated into the scandalous secret of a monk who is in love with a girl, and a Jew at that! One cannot expect much from monks these days. The heroic asceticism is no more.[18]

And then:

He dreamed that a distinguished woman Latinist came to talk to the novices about St. Bernard, only instead of talking to them she sang in Latin. The novices giggled and were restless and Merton was distressed at their reaction. In the middle of all this, the late Abbot, Dom Frederic, entered, the singing stopped and everyone stood up. Merton suddenly realized the *he had violated the cloister by bringing in a woman* and apologized in an undertone. The Abbot asked where she came from, and Merton replied, 'Harvard,' in a loud whisper that he knew she overheard. At this point the scene changed, and the novices were all in an elevator going down from the top of the building. Merton escorted the Latinist down by the stairs instead, but by now her clothes were torn and dirty, she was puzzled and sad and silent, and her Latin seemed to have deserted her.[19]

Evocation of the Anima

It is sometimes quite helpful to have men use an imagery exercise called *active imagination* to help establish a dialogue with the anima images that come up in dreams or fantasies. This "dialoguing with the unconscious" is a powerful technique that creates a means of approaching unconscious material. It is particularly designed to help a man to establish contact with the image when he hasn't had any previous experience of the anima. Initially it is usually carried out with the therapist's help; later, when the patient is comfortable with this procedure, he is able to do it on his own. The patient is guided through this exercise with the following instructions: "Don't try to 'make' anything happen. It may not work if you get too involved in *trying* to make it happen, so just try to allow things to develop on their own and let the primary purpose be to establish a dialogue with your inner woman. You will be treating the image as if she were a 'real' person for whom you feel respect regardless of her appearance, values, age, or attitude toward you. Your purpose is to establish a bargaining dialogue with her in order to become more informed about anything she has to say about you, especially as she reveals feelings that she may have and feelings that may be evoked in you. You need to resist the temptation to reach out to her physically, even in the event that she appears seductive and enticing to you. Especially in the beginning, sexuality may be a cover for deeper feelings in each of you. There should be minimal physical *action* between you in the dialogue; rather, the emphasis needs to be on the experience of being with her to learn what she may have to say to you as well as to discover the *emotional* content of the interaction.

"To begin with, allow yourself a minimum of a half hour for this exercise; be prepared to spend an hour if necessary. Find a place where you will be undisturbed. The place should also be physically comfortable, quiet, and conducive to relaxation. Sitting or lying in a recliner chair, couch, or comfortable upright chair would be best. For a few minutes, turn your attention away from the external environment and focus on the rate and rhythm of your breathing. It is best if you can allow yourself to breath abdominally and slowly, inhaling through your nose and exhaling through your mouth. Let your eyes close as if you were going to take a nap. Most likely you will at first 'see' nothing in your mind's eye except the darkness. Enjoy this darkness and quiet for a minute or two and allow yourself to appreciate the time you are taking to relax and to learn something about your inner woman. When you feel comfortable, begin to *allow* the image to slowly form in your mind's eye of a woman you have never met before. She may be of any age, from any period of history, or even of a race that is different from yours. If visual images are difficult for you, try other representations. For example, try to hear some sound that alerts you to her presence; or feel with your senses some presence of her in your vicinity; or become aware of any emotions that begin to arise for you as you begin to try to experience her presence. Be patient and allow *whatever* representation that feels comfortable for you to begin to form. Whatever it is, let it begin to fill out in greater detail until it seems that her presence becomes 'real' to you, even though you are fully aware that you are producing this imagery yourself.

"As you see her, or begin to sense her presence, remember that you are going to treat her as a person for whom you feel respect, whatever form or appearance she may have. Try not to make judgments about any aspect of her even though there may be parts of her you may not find immediately acceptable. Begin your dialogue by thanking her for appearing to you and telling her you want to learn something about yourself from her. Tell her that you are open to what she has to say, even if you don't understand at first what that may be. You don't have to agree to *do* anything except to simply listen and respond to what she has to say. Remember that this is a 'bargaining' dialogue; you don't have to agree or disagree with anything she says or do anything that she may request of you. If she asks you to do something, simply ask how doing that will help you understand yourself better. Listen to her, and when it feels like you have heard (for the time being) what she has to say, then ask her what she needs from you. Again, you don't have to agree to do anything for her, just listen and remember what she says she needs from you. After she does that, ask her how your providing this will help you understand yourself better. Listen carefully to what she says and note what feelings this dialogue gives rise to. Most dialogues will seem to come to a natural conclusion, ending with the agreement to meet again on another occasion. After you finish the dialogue, write down in a journal what was said and how you felt about what was said. Ask questions in your journal about what possible significance this dialogue had for you; ask yourself if it brought up positive and/or negative feelings that you need to understand better. Make detailed notes about the appearance of the inner woman, and particularly note whether there was some transformation of the image of her as the dialogue proceeded. Each time you 'visit' with her, record your dialogue and notice any changes that occurred in your feelings, as well as any changes that occurred in your inner woman's appearance, attitude, or feeling toward you."

Summary

The anima is not only derived from a man's personal experiences with women he has known in his life, but also an archetypal figure with whom he must reckon if he is to grow psychologically and spiritually. The anima manifests as an inner image or series of images that occur in his dreams and fantasies, as well as in his projections onto the outer women he meets. As the personification of his unconscious, the anima is an important means of accessing his deeper self. To use this means fully, however, a man must be willing to examine the images of the anima when he experiences them. One of the primary ways a man can gain access to these images is through struggling to withdraw and understand his projections onto outer women.

A conscious acknowledgment of the anima allows a man access to the deeper parts of his personality, generally to his unconscious. It allows him the potential, particularly through his relationships with women, to reintegrate otherness and to resolve his developmental blocks. In that way he is able to access his capacity for greater interpersonal relatedness, differentiated feeling, and creativity; he is able to gain an increased awareness of himself.

An Anima Poem

"For Whom have I Sought if not for You?"

In pursuing her, was it not you I sought?
When longing and loneliness multiplied my desires,
    and 'she' became a plenitude of 'hers,'
wasn't it you who were the only one?

And in changing dress, food, habits, friends
    in renouncing certain things and affirming
others
    in saying 'no' and saying 'yes,'
was it not you I sought?

Making my path crooked and narrow
    as if its difficulty alone
    would lead me to you
I became my own enchantment,
mistaking my search
for the finding of you.

So eager I was to lose that which I held dear
    I ran from you when often you were too close,
for fear I might find you
before my delusions of 'that which is'
    had time to abandon me.

Yet, you never left me.
In spite of my searching,
you pursued me—
    as close as my heart beat
    as near as the sound of my breathing.[20]

—Bob Shelby

□ 2 □

The Emergence of the Great Mother

> The importance of consciousness is so great that one cannot
> help suspecting the element of *meaning* to be concealed some-
> where within all the monstrous, apparently senseless biological
> turmoil, and that the road to its manifestation was ultimately
> found on the level of warm-blooded vertebrates possessed of a
> differentiated brain—found as if by chance, unintended and
> unforeseen, and yet somehow sensed, felt and groped for out of
> some dark urge.   —C. G. JUNG

Evolution

THE MATERIAL EVOLUTIONISTS would have us believe that the
consequences of the evolutionary process have been random in
their value—based, perhaps, on "happy accidents" or on survival
of the fittest, but not necessarily representing a process of progressive improvement.[1] Why life should have arisen in the first
place may remain one of the unsolved mysteries of humanity; but
observing that it has arisen, and witnessing the magnitude of the
transformations within it, I am in awe of what seems to be the
operation of an inexplicable wisdom in nature, which in my mind
speaks to more than random effects. One sees the development
of increasingly complex forms of life with greater and greater
capacities for differentiation, culmination in *Homo sapiens
sapiens.*

Evolution is characterized by progressively higher levels of specialization of function, as well as by increasingly subtle and diverse possibilities of behavior, all in the face of often phenomenal adversity and opposition to change. In fact, adversity has often had the consequence of enhancing specialization and adaptation. Can we find a parallel to this in the evolution of collective consciousness? It strikes me that the individuation process provides such a parallel, as we shall see.

In order to continue our discussion of the psyche of contemporary man, we need to first make a digression to the origins of life and the beginnings of sexual differentiation. In particular, looking far into the past will disclose some of the significant evolutionary landmarks that have given rise to our images of *mother,* not only as a biological creature but as an archetypal form. Obviously, the biological mother as we know her today didn't always exist; it was only through a series of maturational biological innovations that she came into being in the first place. We will be better able to understand and appreciate the significance of the archetypal mother by tracing her ancestral origins as far back as the primordial sea out of which life itself arose.

Beginnings: Mother as Nature

As far as we can determine, life on this planet has existed for over three billion years. Prior to eight hundred million years ago life consisted primarily of single-celled organisms which were contained in the watery mass of the earth.[2] Gradually multicellular organisms arose, creating change within the very environment that produced them. Because they were capable of sexual reproduction, they had available the primary raw material for evolutional diversity; this was the beginning of the differentiation of organisms.

It was only four hundred million years ago that life finally moved toward the land. This emergence of the first forms of life out of the water was a prototypal event that was to be duplicated in varying forms throughout the history of higher forms of life.

Water, the seas, and oceans were the *primordial mother* even before sexual differentiation.

Then, approximately three hundred million years ago, through a remarkable evolutionary event, amphibians were freed from their dependence upon water. This was the origin of the amniote egg and its shell, which allowed evolution to continue on land, first in the form of reptiles.[3] This amniote egg, produced and carried by a female, heralded a rudimentary but distinct form of the mother, since by this time there was not only clear sexual reproduction but functional differentiation: only one sex gave birth. We can say that here the mother occurred as a biological creature for the first time in history.

Emergence of Human Consciousness

Our ancestral family, *Hominidae,* goes back five to ten million years. About two million years ago important developments in human evolution and consciousness began to take place: of biological significance, an evolutionary diversion away from the apes and the emergence of *Homo habilis;* and, of psychological significance, the onset of the substrate from which the distinct attributes of human consciousness would eventually emerge, as signaled by an astounding increase in brain size.[4]

This dramatic change in cortical capacity allowed for increasing levels of sophistication in manual dexterity, the emergence of language, and the development of higher mental functions, including an ability to conceptually abstract, to form symbolic representations, and—the capacity which finally separated humans from all other species—to self-reflect. This unique potential for self-reflection was the substrate for the emergence of consciousness.

Accompanying encephalization was an equally dramatic change in sexual capacity, which reshaped the nature of human reproduction and behavior. Previously the female typically mated only when in heat.[5] And when she became pregnant, mating ceased.

Only after weaning did the estrus cycle and mating behavior return. Gradually females became capable of greater and greater periods of heat; that is, they became capable of intercourse for longer periods of time, and they began having intercourse sooner after parturition. Eventually females could have intercourse virtually all of the time, and more children in shorter periods of time. This naturally created increasing demands on the mother's time.

Also, as a result of beginning to walk on two feet instead of four, the female pelvic structure shifted and the birth canal narrowed. This, along with the increase in cranial size, necessitated shorter gestation periods and earlier births, thus creating a situation in which human newborns were technically premature as compared to other species.[6] The human infant came to require an even more extensive period of nursing, contact, nurturance, and learning, which was largely provided by the mother.

As human infants required longer periods of care from the mother, patterns of bonding and attachment must be presumed to have gained greater importance for both infant and mother. Mothers must have become more "motherly" as their parenting responsibilities and attachments increased. The infant was more dependent because it was less physically capable and its own identity took longer to form. In fact, the earlier the infant is born, the greater the mother-infant fusion. We now know only too well the tremendous physical and emotional vulnerability of the human infant and how disruptions in the mother-child bond have severe consequences for the further psychological development of the child.[7]

Division of Labor and Social Organization

Longer periods of dependency seemed to increase the division of labor between the sexes, because the mother was required to spend more time with the infant and less time food gathering and hunting. It seems that, from this point on, males spent increasing amounts of time away from the home camp, while females spent a corresponding amount of time nursing and caring for their dependent infants and plant gathering at the home camp.[8]

As the role of mothering demanded increasing contact and time with the infant, the role of the father in family life remained relatively unimportant. It is likely that as the demands of motherhood increased, the mother's capacity to hunt and gather diminished, creating an even greater responsibility for the males to be away from the family group. Males remained largely on the periphery, as the polygynous "impregnators" and hunters.[9] It was not even known, of course, whether a particular male was the father of a specific child, so this naturally reduced the potential for a father-child relationship. In fact, at this time there was not even the acknowledgment that impregnation was related to conception.

The increase in the sexual capacity and fertility of females naturally led to a greater need and capacity for emotional bonds within monogamous relationships. As a result of the mother's need to spend more time caring for her children she became more dependent upon the male, or males, for assistance and support in food gathering. This further change in the division of labor gave rise to increasingly complex forms of social interaction, leading to patterns of kinship and "family ties." Even the first hominids some four million years ago had begun to establish patterns of social interdependency with rudimentary rules of kinship. This movement toward more monogamous relationships was probably superseded by the formation of exogamous bonds, to ensure access to other groups and as a reaction against endogamous tendencies, specifically incest.

Endogeny and Exogeny

Evolution can be viewed as the dynamic interplay and gradual integration of the most basic set of opposites I describe as *endogenous* and *exogenous:* behavior or development that occurs largely from within, and that which occurs largely from without. Thus we could say that life began at the extreme pole of endogenous development. The "primordial soup" of single-celled organisms was a very lengthy, largely endogenous process of constant self-reproduction that spanned a period of two billion years or so. At the same time there was a lesser exogenous tendency, without which there could not have been differentiation at all. The first specific signs of exogeny came with the development of multicellular organisms and sexual reproduction—the beginning of true differentiation.

The concepts of exogeny and endogeny also apply to the development of kinship systems—specifically as the cultural customs of *exogamy* and *endogamy*. Exogamy describes a movement of individuals away from the tribe or clan by out-marrying, while endogamy describes the tendency to remain within, and hence the incest tendency.[10] While there are social and economic reasons for exogamy,[11] there are also powerful psychological factors that require the balancing of inner-directed and outer-directed behavior. It is interesting that concomitant with the formation of the matrilineal family structure and closer family ties, there was a corresponding development of the practice of exogamy. It would seem that, while the newly evolved structure was a positive social, economic, and emotional development, it also contained endogenous tendencies that presented dangers to the individuals within it, such as a tendency to remain too long within the group, and a regressive tendency toward a more undifferentiated state of consciousness.

By excluding the grown sons of the group, exogamy emphasized a solidarity of the females, thus forming one of the bases of the matrilineal system: lineage could only be traced through the mother. It also tended to both isolate the men and force them to form an identification outside of their home group. In this way the practice of exogamy not only functioned endogenously in forming primitive group marriage systems; it also functioned exogenously by creating a disassociation of men from their family and the feminine and further reinforcing their exogenic identity as food gatherers, hunters, and providers.

Both endogenous and exogenous tendencies can have either positive or negative effects on the individuals within the group. For example, if a group is overly endogenous, in response to a need to be tightly cohesive, its members may not have opportunities for self-exploration and growth and may tend toward incestuous relationships. Conversely, if a group is exogenous to the point of prematurely excluding its members, individuals may suffer from a sense of rejection and low self-esteem. Kinship systems and individuals therefore require a blending of endogenous and exogenous tendencies to ensure the stability and cohesion of the group on the one hand, and to protect the integrity of the individual members on the other. In this way, throughout human history, consciousness at both the collective and individual levels has evolved from the dynamic interplay of these two basic tendencies.

The Family

The family structure is a dynamic microcosm of both endogenous and exogenous tendencies, beginning as a highly dependent endogenous framework. As life proceeds, the individual gradually becomes liberated from the family matrix as well as from the collective values of his or her society. By balancing growth in both endogenous and exogenous directions, the psychological life of the individual progresses along lines of greater differentiation, personal responsibility, and emotional freedom.

Alongside the rise of the family as the basic social structure was the development of the incest taboo, which prohibited the natural endogenous tendencies within the family from being carried too far. The positive pole of the endogenous tendency for the family is that parents create children who are "part of them," and this confers on the child an identity as an important member of the family group. Overt incest within the original family is endogenous behavior in the extreme—family members are not only creating from within, but *staying* within. This tendency is counterbalanced by the incest taboo, which keeps extreme endogenous behavior from stifling growth and development within the family matrix.

It seems natural that extreme endogenous tendencies are most often represented by the archetypal feminine, specifically as the mother. Both the archetypal and personal mother represent the epitome of creation from within. This is why symbols of the ocean (such as the "primordial soup") may still refer back both to the unconscious in general and to the mother in particular.[12]

In the case of men and their mothers, we see endogenous behaviors in the wish to maintain the security and attachment of the early mother-child bond. Positive endogenous behaviors include those of nurturance and containment within the family group, while also respecting the integrity and independence of the individual. Negative endogenous behaviors are those of smothering, restraining, and restricting, which function to keep the individual only within the original group, leading in some instances to endogamy and incestuous family ties.

Positive exogenous behaviors represent natural moves away from the family, as in the initiation rites of pubertal boys. Negative exogenous behaviors are those in which there is an extreme or premature movement away from the group, causing either isolation of the individual or an exaggerated degree of separation from the original family, such as when a child is rejected or abandoned by one or both parents. We also see specific exogenous behaviors designed to extricate children from the matriarchal matrix in which they have become imbedded. I discuss this in relation to boys' initiation rites and to the hero's journey, in chapter 3.

A major problem for modern men is that counterphobic defenses against feelings of dependency on their mothers are later projected onto their partners. This causes them to move even further away from the family as a source of support and identity. Expressed in terms that I have been describing, this amounts to a form of negative exogenous behavior, in which men live in a state of anxiety of being overcontained and unable to maintain a healthy sense of either attachment or separation with their partners and their children. At the same time, the negative endogenous tendency of incest in the form of sexual molestation of children by their fathers is manifest today at an almost epidemic level.

The question needs to be asked: "Why has this tendency taken such an extreme form?" The answers need to be sought among several critical issues of men's early development. Modern men seem to be caught between the extreme poles of the incest archetype: on the one hand they are largely disassociated from the family and the feminine, primarily investing themselves in exogenous pursuits; and on the other they are plagued by unconscious regressive endogenous tendencies with the potential for incest. This dilemma can be made more clear by looking at the first and most critical developmental task of men—the separation from the mother. To do this we need to look more closely at the rise of the matriarchal system.

Mother

A man's personal mother, as well as the archetypal images of the mother in his psyche, exerts a dominant influence on his experience of the inner feminine, and consequently on his manner of relating to outer women. As we have been born from the mother psychically as well as physically, it behooves us to understand how deeply ingrained our relationship to the mother archetype is. This relationship, because of its inherently unconscious nature, can be communicated to consciousness only through the language of the symbol. In this sense, individuation cannot proceed without symbolization.[13] An appreciation of this is essential to understanding male psychology in particular, since for men the differentiation of themselves is a critical developmental task—and essential for individuation.

After my childhood dream of being impeded and ensnared by tree roots, as recounted in the Introduction, the power and emotional impact of the mystifying symbol of the roots captivated me for many years. There was nothing in my conscious experience to which I could relate this symbolization; I had to look elsewhere. This search for meaning initiated the conscious individuation process. I see now that this dream not only symbolized a tremendous conflict in my unconscious but also portrayed an entanglement in the archetypal mother, an expression of the unconscious in a very primal form. In order to comprehend these images I had to not only understand the nature of my experiences with my own mother; I also had to discover a source that was beyond my personal mother.

This source was the realm of the collective unconscious and its archetypal images. These archetypal forms amplify the personal dimension of our experience by supplying a transpersonal context that extends backward to the earliest symbols created by the psyche. It is helpful to briefly review some of the origins of these archetypal symbols as they were represented in the earliest art of prehistory.

The Last Ice Age and the Beginnings of Art

Prehistoric art, such as the cave paintings at Lascaux in France and Altimira in Spain, emerged during the Paleolithic period. These art forms document the emergence of the human capacity for abstract mental processes and their revelation of the first forms of myth. The figures drawn on these cave walls may have been the first attempts to portray male and female. It may have also been in these caves that young boys were initiated into the mythology of the hunt; they were told the myths of their relationship to the animals, which were considered to be sacred and even superior to the hunter. The caves have been likened to the maternal womb, in that they contained the mysteries of the creation of life still unknown to Paleolithic men. This image is fortified by the caves' complex and labyrinthine passages, so like the womb's mysterious access. The mythic themes of this period were the cycle of birth, death, and rebirth or regeneration; man's relationship with animals; the procuring and increase of food; and the transformation of children into adults.[14]

So it is no accident that the earliest sculptured works of art, the stone carvings of Ice Age man, were of the Great Mother. It is generally agreed today that these carvings, whose distribution extends from Spain to Siberia, have a religious or cultic character. These figures of the female deity therefore stand at the very center of the earliest human culture. The Great Mother, who gives nourishment, shelter, and security, is the mistress of life and fertility. Her cult, of which the little we know is drawn from inferences from its archaeology, is the earliest expression of the emergence into consciousness of mankind's experience of the power of motherhood over life and fate.

The Matriarchy

With the passing of the Ice Age about ten thousand years ago and the end of Magdalenian culture with its first forms of art, the agricultural revolution began, signaled by the appearance of cities and towns. The archaeological discoveries of southeastern Europe dating to the Neolithic-Chalcolithic period of 6500–3500 B.C.E. have revealed an unusually rich and unique culture, which has come to be known as Old Europe. While there were similar cultural developments in Anatolia, Mesopotamia, Syro-Palestine, and Egypt, the archaeologist Marija Gimbutas does not believe they were as distinct as those of Old Europe:

> Between c. 7000 and c. 3500 B.C., the inhabitants of this region developed a much more complex social organi- zation than their western and northern neighbors, form- ing settlements which often amounted to small town- ships, inevitably involving craft specialization and the creation of religious and governmental institutions. They independently discovered the possibility of utiliz-

ing copper and gold for ornaments and tools, and even appear to have evolved a rudimentary script.[15]

The archaeology of this area reveals one of the clearest examples of a matrifocal, matrilineal culture, which is thought to have persisted for at least twenty thousand years, spanning both the Paleolithic and Neolithic eras and beyond. Because of the development of agriculture and the domestication of both plants and animals, nature took on a previously unparalleled significance, giving rise to the worship of the goddess of vegetation, fertility, and birth.

The Paleolithic traditions in art continued into the Neolithic period, with a dramatic increase in the appearance of human forms. Not only that, but a clear preponderance of female forms was found in most of the three thousand archaeological sites of this area. The archaeology of Old Europe revealed literally *thousands* of figurines of the mother.

The culture was rich in myth and ritual honoring the various forms of the Great Mother goddess. She is depicted in various forms, representing her different powers: the Mistress of Water; the Great Goddess of Life, Death, and Regeneration; and the Pregnant Vegetation Goddess. In addition to the figurines an abundance of clay pottery, models of shrines, and various ritual practice objects were uncovered, as well as the famous Tartaria tablets of the Zinca area, showing what appears to be the first linear writing, about ritual sacrifice and burial practices. There is also evidence that human sacrifice accompanied by animal sacrifice was performed in open air sanctuaries as offerings to the goddess.

Symbols on pottery, in shrines, and on the figurines themselves are of images relating to the origins of life and to cosmogonic beliefs. Pictures of water and of the egg—both singular and divided—represent and affirm the archetypal maternal principle in its earliest biological forms. Images of primordial water and of eggs, reminiscent of the single-celled prokaryotes in their watery mass, exist in art from the Paleolithic era to the present as symbolic expressions of the archetypal mother, the source of all life.[16]

The social environment of this matrifocal culture has been portrayed by some recent authors as agrarian, peaceful, and, with respect to the sexes, egalitarian. One gets the feeling that these authors see this period in rather idealized and utopian terms in spite of the social, political, and religious disparity between men and women. While this disparity does not, in itself, necessarily imply that the women oppressed the men, such authors do not address the psychological effects that men may have experienced living in a culture dominated by images of the Great Mother. It is also interesting to me that these recent writers seem to minimize the darker, negative side of the mother, particularly with regard to the sacrificial aspect of her fertility rites.

Images of the Great Mother were often accompanied by symbols of animals sacred to particular goddesses, whose mythology elucidated aspects of them. The goddesses often came to be known by the associated animal: the Snake Goddess, the Bird Goddess, and so on. The animals also came to symbolize the goddess herself, as visible in numerous sculptures of the Neolithic period. For example, the Goddess of Vegetation had the pig as her sacred animal as far back as 6000 B.C.E., which also became the sacrificial animal during the later festival of Thesmophoria in ancient Greece. In the later Greek cult of Demeter and Persephone, the pig was also the primary sacrificial animal. Decaying small pigs were thrown into a ravine supposedly also swarming with snakes. The remains of the pigs were then distributed over the fields as "fertility magic." In India, the goddess of the dead has been worshiped as Durga, the "Unapproachable" or the "Perilous," or as Parvati. The temple festival of Parvati is a fertility ritual in which the pig, along with buffalo and goats, was sacrificed: "Under the sacrificial altar there was a deep pit, filled with fresh sand that sucked up the blood of the beheaded beasts; the sand was renewed twice a day, and when drenched with blood it was buried in the earth to create fertility."[17]

The Goddess of Regeneration, an epiphany of the Great Goddess, takes the form of the bee or butterfly through the sacrifice of the bull. Gimbutas cites a quote from Antigonos of Karystos (250 B.C.E.): "In Egypt if you bury the ox in certain places, so that only his horns project above the ground and then you saw them off, they say that bees fly out; for the ox purifies and is resolved into bees."[18] And further from Porphyry (233 A.C.E. to c. 304): "The ancients gave the name of *Melissae* ('bees') to the priestesses of Demeter who were initiates of the chthonian goddess; the name *Melitodes* to Kore herself; the moon (Artemis) too, whose province it was to bring to the birth, they called *Melissa*, because the moon being a bull and its ascension being a bull, bees are begotten of bulls. And souls that pass to the earth are bull-begotten."[19]

In studies of these regeneration rituals, little attention has been given to the significance of the *kuretes* (or *curetes*), the eunuch priests in service of the goddess who were either castrated by the priestesses of the Great Mother goddess, or who castrated themselves in order to be saved from total sacrifice. In later times the bull substituted for human sacrifice, its decapitated head a substitute for the phallus and ritual dismemberment. The bull's horns in this context came to symbolize the son's phallus. Erich Neumann points out that the fertility ritual in Crete was played out by the Great Mother and the youthful god, her son-lover, who was sacrificed for her fertility.[20]

This is a notably important historical period of the mother archetype, equivalent to the stage in which the ego is still unconscious, imbedded in nature. The point here is not to dwell on the sensational aspects of the mother cult, but to point out the tremendous power in both the positive and negative aspects of the mother goddess at this cultural stage. We also need to look at her in terms of the archetypal image she conveys, both as the goddess of life and fertility and also as the goddess of death who demanded such phenomenal sacrifice in order to ensure her fertility.

In this period the archetypal mother's enormous power as a collective image in the male psyche culminates in a ritual sacrifice that directly involves her relationship to her son, as lover. From the psychological point of view, her power as an archetype reflects the evolution of collective consciousness or collective unconsciousness up to this point in time. In addition, this archetypal situation corresponds to a stage of the steadily emerging individual ego and the development of masculine consciousness. As Neumann points out:

> The overwhelming might of the unconscious, i.e., the devouring, destructive aspect under which it may also manifest itself, is seen figuratively as the evil mother, whether as the blood-stained goddess of death, plague, famine, flood, and the force of instinct, or as the sweetness that lures to destruction. But, as the good mother, she is fullness and abundance; the dispenser of life and happiness, the nutrient earth, the cornucopia of the fruitful womb.[21]

We see from this that the archetype of the mother has developed two primary aspects: the Good Mother and the Terrible Mother. From this historical point on, each aspect appears as images in myths, fairy tales, and the dreams and fantasies of individuals—images that remain generally unconscious. Furthermore, with the passage of time, the negative pole has tended to become increasingly repressed; we are more often aware of the mother in her positive aspect. Men who have had poor experiences with the personal mother are likely to experience the negative pole in their dreams and fantasies. This can be confusing since the mother, while negative in the man's personal experience, is unlikely to be as negative or evil as she appears when her archetypal image is constellated. She sometimes appears with her animal consorts, or sometimes as part-animal herself, further attesting to her archetypal nature. Sometimes, too, the animal may occur by itself, symbolizing the mother and emphasizing some particular aspect of the relationship.

One of the first dreams I had after entering analysis exemplifies this confrontation:

I am walking through a forest at dusk. There is a low misty fog swirling a few feet above the ground. I see a figure half-crawling, half-running to the side of me a few feet away. After a few moments the figure comes running toward me, and it then becomes apparent that it is my mother. She has an ugly, angry look on her face, almost savage, and appears to be part-wolf and part-woman. She seems much larger and stronger than she is. She grabs me and drags me back to the old house on Blackhawk Street where we lived in Chicago. Up in the house she ties me to a chair. On the stove is a thick green bubbling liquid of some kind to which she adds a large bottle of very strong hydrochloric acid. After she mixes this she pours it on top of me and it runs down my head, the side of my face, and my shoulder. Wherever the stuff touches me it causes me to decompose. After this, she plunges her hand down inside my chest and rips out my heart, taking it to the table and cutting it up. She then eats it. Then she runs from the house, but shortly returns and vomits the heart back onto the table. From the shelf she takes a bottle labeled "Mother's Oil" and pours it over the heart; it becomes whole again. At this point, her demeanor changes to one of being more positive, more caring, almost artistic. She then takes the oil and pours some of it on the great heart vessels and inside of my chest to reconstruct my heart, and she also pours some of it on the rest of me that has been damaged by the acid mixture. Then she unties me from the chair. After doing this she runs out again, but as she is running down the stairs tree roots break out from the walls and quickly wrap themselves around her, keeping her from getting to the outside. One large root breaks through and wraps itself around her neck, strangling her.

These images gripped and terrified me. Where did they come from? How was it possible to explain these distorted, ghastly, but then healing symbols of the mother when my personal mother could not be as evil or as blessed as this creature in my dream? There is nothing so wonderful, nor so awful, about a man's personal mother that will help him to understand the depth and magnitude of what the archetypal mother represents to him.

The imagery of this dream can be amplified by looking to the Lady of the Beasts, an early mother goddess, also known as the Goddess of Periodic Regeneration or the Bee Goddess, as well as to a later variant from Greek mythology, Artemis-Hekate. The reason for amplifying the dream is not to fit it into the clothing of the Great Mother or another archetype of the feminine, but to round it out by looking at historical and cultural parallels to its imagery and symbolism.

Artemis probably derived from earlier aspects of the Lady of the Beasts. In Roman myths she was known as Diana. Her origins in the mother goddess and fertility cults is supported by her association to the moon. At Ephesus in Asia Minor she was represented by the many-breasted goddess, Diana of Ephesians. And in Attica she was known as the Wolf One. Like Hekate and Selene she was also known as a moon goddess. Her domain was nature, wildlife, and the animals of the earth. She was a virginal goddess, the protectress of maidens, and a huntress. Her parents were Leto and Zeus, and Apollo was her twin brother. She was supposedly born with the "eyes of a wolf." Nor Hall describes her this way:

> Frequently Artemis-Hekate appears accompanied by hounds, or a terrifying three-headed dog. The goddess is a shape shifter: she and her brother both—the two lights of heaven, moon and sun, born out of utter darkness—are children of endless transformations. They inspire sudden changes, especially into animal forms. Artemis favored she-wolves, stags and bears. All-animal Artimis could be a dreadful goddess taking vengeance on man by killing, dismemberment, and devouring. Blood giving and blood letting, she rules deep in the untamed forests of the human psyche.[22]

The earliest function of this goddess for men was in the hunt and war: she raised their sense of competency and skill, as well as their independence and separateness from women. In this sense, she was an initiator of men, helping them develop the capacity for differentiation which in later times they used to free themselves from her power, through the journey of the hero. She is an archaic representation of the unconscious, which originally is both captor and initiator. Her function is taken in later times by the pubertal and initiation rites performed by the elder men of the tribe. In her original form she represents the totality of the world—water, earth, and sky—and so stands for wholeness, the container of the opposites in nature and the cosmos. In my dream she is not only the captor and the devourer, she is also the artist, magician, and healer. She mirrors both the destructive as well as the creative dimensions of the unconscious: "Precisely where man is a creature of instinct living in the image of the beast or half-beast, i.e., where he is wholly or in large part dominated by the drives of the unconscious, the guiding purpose, the unconscious spiritual order of the whole, appears as a goddess in human form, as a Lady of the Beasts."[23]

The initiatory experiences of shamanism can also serve as amplifications for this dream. Shamanism is thought to have developed during the Paleolithic and Neolithic periods—as early as fifty thousand to thirty thousand years ago in the Siberian hunter groups. It has been postulated that bones and skulls of animals were ritual offerings in the magico-religious tradition of the return of animals to life after death. Some writers have even interpreted the cave paintings at Lascaux, France as being the representation of a shamanic trance. The initiatory experience of the shaman (who often becomes a healer) is always precipitated or manifested by a crisis, illness, dreams, or ecstatic experiences. The initiation includes the following typical themes:

> The novice encounters several divine figures (the Lady of the Waters, the Lord of the Underworld, the Lady of

the Animals) before being led to the "Center of the World," on the summit of the Cosmic Mountain, where are the World Tree and the Universal Lord; from the Cosmic Tree and the will of the Universal Lord himself, he receives the wood to make his drum; semi-demonic beings teach him the nature of all diseases and their cures; finally other demonic beings cut his body to pieces, boil it, and exchange it for better organs. Each of these elements in the initiatory story is consistent and has its place in a symbolic or ritual system well known to the history of religions.[24]

All of the various descriptions of the initiatory ordeal have as the common theme "dismemberment of the neophyte's (initiate's) body and renewal of his organs; ritual death followed by resurrection."[25]

Although my dream illustrates a sacrifice which to the modern ego may seem primitive, vicious, and bizarre, a central function of the mother archetype is to assist us in our need for sacrifice and transformation. The feminine is our first initiator, either in the form of the mother or the anima, man's inner feminine nature. The coagulated unconscious, so badly in need of awakening, needs to be sacrificed, taken apart. The dismemberment portrayed in the dream is not far removed from a symbolic castration in which the heart, the seat of feeling and emotion, is torn out, devoured, and then healed. In this way it corresponds not only to death but to a symbolic death that is the precursor to rebirth. We also observe symbolic representations of this in the various alchemical writings, in a process known as *divisio, separatio, solutio* ("division, separation, solution").[26] My dream came at a time when inner transformation was crucial for further personal growth. On a more personal level, my "heart" was in fact in need of transformation. (It was not just coincidence that at that time I was experiencing what I thought were "heart problems" and feared that something was physically wrong with my heart.)[27]

Interaction between Mother and Anima

The dream of my mother demonstrates some of the emerging aspects of the inner feminine and presents the possibility of initiating a "new consciousness" through a sacrifice-like experience. In order to understand such a dream's psychological and emotional meaning, it is critical that the individual is able to separate out archetypal mother images from the personal experience of the mother: to know which is the "inner" and which is the "outer" mother, although these two may overlap.

The mother, as the symbol of the unconscious and the underworld, is also the percursor of the anima, which is the archetype symbolizing a man's connection to the unconscious. Here is another fascinating parallel to the shaman's initiatory journey, in which the shaman is assisted by a female helper, or *ayami,* who assists him much like a fairy or nymph assists the hero on his journey. The ayami may sometimes take the form of a celestial wife, and their marriage is celebrated in the heavenly sphere. (The ayami later appears in the Christian tradition as Lilith, Adam's first wife, and, in the Jewish tradition, as the serpent of the Garden of Eden.)[28] She may also, at times, be an obstacle, trying to keep him at a certain level of his journey or displaying jealousy toward his earthly wife. The ayami, as tutelary spirit, provides the indispensable spirits needed by the shaman to complete his journey. In this sense she functions like the anima, man's companion on his spiritual journey, and, hence, like the mother, a crucial figure in the individuation process.

One of a man's greatest developmental tasks is to achieve a healthy separation from the original bond with his personal mother. He must also develop an awareness of the importance of the image of the archetypal mother in his psyche. Unlike the daughter, the son lacks a primary identification with his mother, especially as he begins to psychologically emerge from her. In adult life, remnants of the original attachment/separation problem are conveyed by a man's internal anima image.

The Archetypal and the Personal Mother:
"Joint Custody"

As an archetypal structure, the mother dominates the early primal relationship even before the personal mother is known. The child already has a disposition to experience all that is generally known as the *maternal*. The personal mother, as carrier of the archetypal mother image, symbolizes for him both the mystery and power of endogenous creation. The human infant is unique in its helplessness—the young of no other species is so utterly physically dependent for so many years. This physical dependency on the mother is matched by a profound emotional attachment and dependency, which, in turn, is later offset by his struggle to separate from her. Next to the all-powerful mother, the emerging male ego experiences itself as small, impotent, and fearful; it is plunged into an alien world that, apart from the protection of mother, may be highly unpredictable.

Eric Neumann refers to this early stage of being one-with-the-mother as corresponding to the "elementary character" of the feminine archetype. It also corresponds to the pre-ego phase of the individual, and to that undifferentiated period in the evolution of consciousness. It is probably close to our most basic experience of paradise, for although even this protective, nurturing containment may not be a perfect state of being, the primordial union with mother likely receives the projection of paradise and bliss. As Jung describes it:

> The mother-child relationship is certainly the deepest and most poignant one we know; in fact, for some time the child is, so to speak, part of the mother's body. Later it is part of the psychic atmosphere of the mother for several years, and in this way everything original in the child is indissolubly blended with the mother-image.[29]

As a boy emerges from this mysterious container of the mother, his first experiences of otherness are stimulated, perhaps, by the encounter with his mother's breast. How the breast is experienced—as "good" (nourishing) or "bad" (withholding), or as alternating good and bad—determines to a large extent his perception of the natural world and the safety or threat it may come to represent to him. This initial perception also determines the success of the mother-son bond, which in turn is the basis for his capacity to develop a basic trust of both his mother and the world. The positive, negative, or even ambivalent quality of his experience is later filled out by the personality and behavior of the personal mother—by her feelings and attitudes toward her child as well as toward herself. Also, her experience of her own mother exerts a powerful influence on the quality of mothering she is able to give. In other words, every mother also has her own introjected mother that is based on her personal experience as well as her experience of the archetypal mother.

Splitting Without Separation

As a boy emerges from his initial experience of total containment by the mother, he experiences himself as alien to her. There is little in him, as a physical creature, that he can identify as being like that of his mother. He comes to recognize his mother as being "other" than himself. The painful awareness of his essential difference from his mother is magnified by his eventual knowledge that he does not have the capacity to create and contain life or nourish from his body. No matter how he tries he cannot find within *himself* this power and mystery of the maternal; he must learn to somehow create and nourish in an entirely different way.

Awareness of this deficiency gives rise to feelings of envy of the breast and of the womb. I believe this accounts for a major difference in the psychology of men as compared to the psychology of women. Much of the later exogenous overdevelopment of masculinity comes as a protest against the power of this first experience of otherness—a specialness that men can't find in themselves.

This envy of the feminine is often repressed in the boy's earliest life. It takes the form of not wanting to be a "mama's boy" or to play with girls' things, of wanting to be a "big boy," and all of the myriad self-imposed as well as socially imposed injunctions to disown any proximity to the feminine. This early repression creates an emotional and psychological dilemma to the extent that the young boy disassociates himself from the mother and any vestige of the feminine, particularly the acknowledgment of his dependency upon her. This results in a splitting from his own inner feminine, which is further ruptured by the cultural stereotypes that are apportioned to him from childhood on. He is permitted, and even unconsciously encouraged, to be more aggressive; he is supposed to be more independent and accomplish this much sooner than his sisters; he is encouraged to think clearly without being swayed by his feelings (and there is even some question about whether he should *have* feelings); he is encouraged to build things, do chemistry experiments, and behave rather recklessly. All these puerile preoccupations continue into adulthood, summed up under the trite homily "Boys will be boys."

It is highly likely that the concept of penis envy so often used to account for women's sense of inadequacy and inferiority is a masculine protest to diminish the significance of their envy of the breast and the lack of a symbolic breast within themselves.

The repressed feminine and maternal often reemerge in the dreams and fantasies of men who have been courageous enough to look at the spontaneous unconscious images their psyche generates in analysis. A male patient of mine once had the following fantasy:

> I was at home, holding my daughter on my lap, and I noticed that as she seemed to be going off to sleep I had this impulse to breast-feed her and so opened my shirt. I noticed to my surprise that I actually did have breasts and that I could nurse her. This filled me with such a sense of delight and warmth that I felt a new

sense of relationship with Cindy that I had never had
before. I wondered why God had not given men breasts.

Immediately following this dream he began to berate himself
for having such a "perverse" and "crazy" idea, thinking that there
must surely be something wrong with him. However, he could
accept the feeling quality of the experience as very special; it
added to his capacity to provide something for his daughter that
he felt otherwise unable to provide.

Another male patient dreamt that he was pregnant: "There is a
feeling of fullness, and I know it will be many months before I
deliver."

These dreams and fantasies cannot be taken literally as the
desire to have a child or even to nurse, but as instead conveying
a need to incorporate some of the endogenously creative aspects
of the mother from which men have become psychically split.
Dreams and fantasies provide mental compensation for the man
who feels that the only creativity he experiences is what he makes
outside of himself. This is often so even for the man who, by all
standards of society, has been successful and creative, but who
lacks a sense of *inner* creativity. Outer productivity and success
are actually a source of depression for him. He has the feeling
that "nothing matters" and a sense of inner emptiness. What he
yearns for is a more spiritual sense of accomplishment—an
awareness that what he has created is undeniably something of
his own making. Such a man is possibly overly identified with the
mother. Because he experiences the mother as the only source
of creativity, he sees creativity as very much disassociated from
the masculine. This sometimes results in what is known as
pseudohomosexuality.

The early split from the inner feminine may also help explain
why men experience difficulty going into analysis, for analysis is
symbolically a reentry into the mystery of the maternal unconscious. For a man disassociated from all imagery of the mother,
nothing seems to grow inside, and he can't understand how this

process will help. After all, he feels he should be able to help himself: "real men" don't need to rely on others to solve their problems. Men also experience a particular difficulty during analysis as compared to women: when a woman looks deep inside herself she is often concerned about *what* she may find there; a man's greatest fear is more often that there will be *nothing* there.

All men, whether they are conscious of it or not, have a secret awe of the maternal and the feminine—an awe that is composed of reverence and respect, but also fear. We envy her creativity and hate her power; and, as something still unconscious within ourselves, we also fear for her lack of wholeness. In spite of this, the hero's journey begins with the wish to leave mother, to find a suitable masculine identification for himself, and go in search of the Holy Grail. This struggle for consciousness cannot be carried out purely on an external level, for man's deepest need is to create a transformation inside of himself. When a man attempts to address his inner problems on an purely exogenous basis, it not only won't work; the consequences may be tragic.

Lack of Separation and Relationships

It is a cultural fallacy that men are emotionally independent; they are often far more emotionally dependent than women. This dependency, though very real, is often disguised because it is unresolved. Men often develop denying and/or counterphobic behavior as a defense, since even for boys emotional dependency is not easily allowed in our social and family systems.

Problems of unresolved dependency often have little to do with the man's partner, but rather are residual effects of the primal mother-son relationship. A man who lacks a healthy emotional separation from the mother often becomes confused about what his partner can and can't do for him, and what he needs to do for himself. Because the mother has not been adequately separated from his inner image of the feminine, he then projects this fusion of anima-mother onto his wife or partner.

Much as women sometimes say that men need to be "mothered," by doing so women interfere with men's development as well as their own. The psyche demands that a man accomplish separation from the mother himself, with the help of the anima. A woman who needs to foster a man's dependency may be struggling with the discomfort of her own masculine otherness. Her animus and her view of men as dependent may be part of her own projective fantasy about her sense of masculinity.

What is probably most confusing to a man in his attempts to understand his relationships to his mother as well as to outer women is the role that the archetypal mother continues to unconsciously play. This powerful image exerts its effect on his psyche in a way that tremendously exaggerates the way his mother or other women appear to him. In fact, it is rare that the real women could be either as "good" or as "bad" as the influence of the archetypal mother makes them appear. Even after the personal mother has been left behind, and even after she has died, the archetypal mother remains as a potent goddess image. This vestigial image is what Jung calls the mother *imago,* the image remaining well after the personal mother has come and gone.

When these images of the good or bad mother are accompanied by highly charged feelings in relation to the actual mother, a woman in authority, or a man's wife, we say that he has a mother-complex. The mother-complex most often originates out of a man's struggles with his personal mother, but it also has at its core the image of the archetypal mother. Thus the imagery in men's dreams is often mixed; for instance, the dream about my mother not only brought up an issue I had to face in regard to my own mother, but also conveyed this issue in imagery appropriate to the archetypal mother.

The mother-complex can cause a man to behave in ways that are incomprehensible, even to him; it creates a rather automatic and autonomous pattern of behavior because it is usually unknown to the ego. Although the effects of the complex may be known, they are often rationalized as being caused by something in the environment, such as someone who just happened to "push the wrong button"; indeed, the complex may arise because it is activated or triggered by something someone says or does. When the complex becomes so activated, the ego loses control, and a man may behave as though something has "gotten into him."

The complex seems to withhold a certain amount of psychic energy from the ego, which may cause a loss of energy, resulting in depression or other physical and emotional symptoms. When a man uncovers his complex, or complexes, in analysis, psychic energy that has been bound is freed for the other activities of his life. Uncovering the complex also allows him to better understand the unconscious factors controlling him and to develop a deeper spiritual awareness. This process is often painful and emotionally laborious; it may be easier to describe than to accomplish.

Uncovering the complex involves a regression to mother imagery, which in analysis may mean reexperiencing the infantile parts of oneself in relation to the analyst. A man must return to the mother so that he can *consciously* separate from her—and incorporate in a symbolic way her capacity for birth, death, and rebirth.

Since an encounter with the inner mother is always tainted with the unconscious, it is often accompanied by a natural feeling of resistance, especially for a man with a mother-complex. There is, however, also something positive in the wish or need to regress to the mother. As Jung states:

> The "mother," as the first incarnation of the anima archetype, personifies in fact the whole unconscious. Hence the regression leads back only apparently to the mother; in reality she is the gateway into the unconscious, into the "realm of the Mothers." . . . For regression, if left undisturbed, does not stop short at the "mother" but goes back beyond her to the prenatal

realm of the "Eternal Feminine," to the immemorial world of archetypal possibilities where, "thronged round with images of all creation," slumbers the "divine child," patiently awaiting his conscious realization. This son is the germ of wholeness, and he is characterized as such by his specific symbols.[30]

So, according to Jung, the positive aspect of regression to the mother is that it involves the mother as "the first incarnation of the anima," introducing the possibility of a journey into the unconscious, to possibilities of further growth. These new possibilities are symbolized by the archetype of the "divine child."

Freud, on the other hand, saw regression as a basically destructive force that arose out of a developmental fixation on the mother. We will elaborate on the significance of these differing points of view in chapter 4, "The Oedipal Wound."

Summary

The matriarchal period, with its earth-cultivating, sedentary way of life, can be characterized by its worship of growth and sacrifice to ensure fertility. Its prevailing archetype was that of the Great Mother. The Good Mother embodies the positive endogenous tendencies of the Great Mother: she creates life, nurturing and cultivating it within herself as well as within the family. The other extreme, the Terrible Mother, expresses the negative endogenous tendencies of the Great Mother: she takes life, suffocating and devouring.

Individuation for men requires an honest encounter with the unconscious, which may include facing uncomfortable insights. To do so a man must develop an attitude of reflective awareness that transcends previously overdeveloped ego attitudes of either emotional apathy or one-sided intellectualism. The individuation process is often initiated by a confrontation with the terrible aspect of the mother, who symbolizes in many ways the very nature of the unconscious itself. A man must face the mother in all of her power, mystery, and awesomeness as she is portrayed by the unconscious.

If a man has not separated adequately from his mother, his anima image remains in a state of fusion with his mother image; this fusion creates endless problems in his relationships with women. The need to achieve an adequate sense of emotional independence from the mother is a developmental task that in primitive cultures was accomplished, with help from the father, by rites of pubertal initiation. Unfortunately, the modern man has few external rituals or rites of passage to help him separate from the archetypal and personal mother; thus he is faced with the difficult task of attempting this separation largely by himself.

□ 3 □

Myths, Initiation Rites, and Masculinity

Initiation represents one of the most significant spiritual phenomena in the history of humanity. It is an act that involves not
only the religious life of the individual, in the modern meaning
of the word "religion"; it involves his *entire* life.

—MIRCEA ELIADE

Mythos

AS OUR LANGUAGE REFLECTS, we have always been trying to
identify, define, classify, and label our experience. Myth (from the
Green *mythos,* meaning "word," "story," or "fiction") represents
our earliest attempts to make sense of what is essentially unknown
or unknowable. Myths explain or describe, through the form of
the story, the meaning of what has been projected onto nature or
onto people. On the other hand, *Logos* (from which come *logical*
and *logistics*) represents the "word" whose validity can be argued
or proven; in Greek philosophy it refers to reason, the controlling
center of the universe.

Mythos, or the creation of myths, is an endogenous form of
explanation. Logos, an exogenous form of explanation, arose
later. Logos eventually came to dominate, with science emerging
as the supreme Logos. It is no accident that Logos is more often

associated with masculinity, while mythos is the irrational realm relegated more to the mysterious beginnings of life, the mother, and the feminine. Joseph Campbell, in fact, has said that he believes mythology may be a sublimation of the mother image.[1] As far as it is a "story," the myth describes some outer life experience, but it typically concerns itself much more with the inner aspects of life, that is, with the *meaning* of the experience.

The Emergence of Myth

The first burial practices (by the Neanderthals) reflect a budding human sensitivity to life, death, and the imagining of an afterlife. Through them we can infer the beginnings of mental abstraction as well as of myth in rudimentary form. The emergence of burial practices also seems to coincide with a further movement toward a spoken language. Language may have evolved as a side effect of attempts to construct reality, or, more properly, the mythology of the group: "Language is a means of constructing mental imagery. We need language more to tell stories than to direct actions."[2]

It appears that encephalization was the physiological substrate for the development of language, which progressed alongside increasingly sophisticated levels of social interaction among early humans.[3] Diversified food gathering behaviors and the early division of labor created by increasing demands on the mother to care for her "premature" offspring developed an early economy of mutual benefit between the sexes. This mutuality also brought about greater interdependence and a closer knit, socially more complex group. Men, although now more on the periphery of family life, came to hold a valuable position as providers of what was more difficult for the newly burdened mothers to obtain for themselves. These factors were the foundations of kinship. An increasingly complex language system continued to develop, serving the communicative needs of these behaviors as well as providing the means of expressing the emerging mythic dimensions of human experience.

Language and myth have had a parallel development in that one is in need of the other. Myth requires language for the expression of its imaginative processes. As Albert Cook expresses it:

> The system of myth has an inseparable relation to the system of language, and we owe it to Levi-Strauss, on the one hand, to have shown us how complexly the myths of a culture can be read as a sort of grammar of implied ideas. On the other hand, the form of myth, even as Levi-Strauss analyzes it, cannot be wholly free of the form of language. Myth is not only analogous to language; it must inescapably enter language in order to be transmitted.[4]

In early burial practices we see the emergence of a rudimentary conception of the sacred, expressed as a possibility of the "divine" (as opposed to profane) nature of human experience. Myth evolved as an expression of a nascent consciousness as well as a manifestation of an attempt to order the cosmos, but at this point without the benefit of reflection. Here, as well as in the beginnings of Paleolithic art, we see the beginnings of the psychological process of projection. These initial forms of projection were (unlike the later conception of projection as a psychological defense) attempts to exteriorize the contents of the unconscious. Thus, early art and language, as well as myth, are synonymous with the emerging consciousness of humanity.

Projection, in this sense, is one of the primary means of creating awareness of that which is unconscious. Myths, then, are the embodiments of these collective projections. Early belief systems were undoubtedly so intertwined with projection that there was little, if any, separation between myth and reality. In this sense consciousness of the Paleolithic and Neolithic periods was a *mythic* consciousness.

Boys' Pubertal Initiation Rites

Initiation rites can be seen as ritual enactments of myth. Their importance was apparent to our "primitive" ancestors in that, even without the benefit of reflective consciousness, they somehow knew that the transitions between important phases of life needed to be marked and celebrated in a ritualistic fashion. The rites of passage for boys were almost always kept secret from the women of the tribe, who had their own rituals; women unfortunate enough to witness them could be severely punished, put to death, or committed to silence for the rest of their lives. This secrecy contributed to the numinosity of the event and underlined the sacredness of what was to transpire. It also emphasized an important aspect of the rites: separation of the boys from their mothers.

While pubertal initiation rites have been studied for many years, yielding much speculation about their function and meaning, their exact origin remains a puzzle. Mircea Eliade has found elements of these rites that indicate they began with the hunter groups.[5] There is no available evidence for rites of circumcision during the Paleolithic period; the earliest initiations for boys probably followed closely on fertility rituals.

Pubertal initiation rites were obligatory, primarily to ensure the passage from childhood to adulthood, and also create group integrity. Other rituals of initiation into secret societies or shamanic practices were more individualized, oriented to an individual's experience within the context of a special group. Most pubertal initiations and initiations into secret societies involved males; there is much less known of female initiations. Girls' rites seem to have been more individual since they took place when the girl began to menstruate; boys' rites were more often carried out in group fashion. According to Bruno Bettelheim, boys' rites were originally performed by women, whereas they are now performed only by men.[6]

These initiation ordeals for boys often were emotionally and physically painful, involving trials of both psychological and physical endurance. Bones were broken, teeth were knocked out, and the penis was circumcised, subincised, and otherwise mutilated. Sometimes the initiate died. The emotional and psychological trauma lent the initiation elements of shock, surprise, and suspense. At different points in the process the boy was told the myths of the group and instructed to maintain secrecy, especially from the women. Often the initiate had to experience periods of isolation, in which he was treated as a regressed child or infant, as if he were being reborn. Sometimes he was left to survive on his own in the wilderness. These rituals were basically directed toward achieving a new sense of self for the initiate—often an entirely new identity, along with a new name. As rites of passage they were meant to ensure the successful transformation from boyhood to manhood. Most frequently the ordeal was to establish the boy's independence from his mother and sometimes to overcome the parent-child relationship altogether. Abandoning the child to nature and beasts of prey proved him to be a self-sufficient and totally independent individual.

These rites are still practiced in several parts of the world, though they are less physically severe than those of the past. The initiations now carried out by men on pubertal boys involve castration, subincision (lacerating the ventral side of the penis from the glans to the scrotum), and circumcision. In the current Australian aboriginal rites the initiators are the future fathers-in-law of the boys from another intermarrying tribe.

Psychoanalysts have been interested in rites of circumcision ever since Freud postulated that their importance was to instill the fear of castration as a means of reinforcing the incest taboo, thus placing initiates within a patriarchal context. Initiation rites of pubertal boys—and their absence in modern life—are of particular interest to us here because of the rites' role in the archetypal aspects of masculine development. They contribute to our understanding of the male's relationship to the mother and add part of the background in our present task of integrating the feminine in male consciousness.

The earliest forms of pubertal initiation, in the Paleolithic

period, did not involve mutilation, and Freud's destructive interpretations of puberty rites pale in the face of the more positive
functions of these rites as primitive attempts to develop greater
consciousness. Their relation to the castration rituals stemming
from the period of mother worship was also ignored by Freud's
interpretation. In *Totem and Taboo,* Freud admits his inability to
relate these rites to the mother cult: "I am at a loss to indicate the
place of the great maternal deities who perhaps everywhere
preceded the paternal deities."[7]

It is in mother worship, particularly worship of the goddess of
fertility, that we see the first evidence of the castration of men.
Bettelheim, in his outstanding review of puberty rites, *Symbolic
Wounds,* indicates that the mutilations may have been initially
carried out by the mothers or other women of the group and
only later taken over by the men. As we saw in the discussion of
the Great Mother, the *kuretes,* or eunuch priests in the service of
the goddess, were either castrated by the priestesses of the Great
Mother goddess or they castrated themselves in order to be saved
from total sacrifice. The strict use of the stone knife as the
instrument of castration and subincision in the Neolithic mother
rites and in puberty rites speaks to the archaic origin of the
source of these practices.

Castration was also known to occur as a punishment as far back
as the second millennium in Assyria. The practice of castrating
boys and selling them as slaves has a long history; such slaves
were part of Muslim harems until quite recently. Among the early
Christians, there were men who voluntarily castrated themselves
to avoid sexual sin; there was even a sect, the Valessii, who
believed their castration to be in the service of God. The theolo-
gian Origen (c. 185–254 C.E.) was perhaps one of the most
celebrated of these. In medieval Italy, pubertal boys were castrated to retain their soprano voices for the papal choir, a practice
in use until 1878.

In the myth of Cybele the *galloi,* or initiates into her priest-
hood, castrate themselves and bring their genitals to her chamber;
they are then given women's clothing to wear from then on. Their

"womanhood" represents a permanent sacrifice to the mother goddess, to whom their lives are dedicated. In contrast to the earlier Great Goddess fertility rites, their castration is a voluntary act which can also be seen as fulfilling some wish to incorporate the feminine within themselves. In the myth, Cybele's son, Attis, is finally driven insane by his mother's love for him, which causes him to castrate himself. From a psychological perspective, this suffocating mother-love represents the son's regressive longing for his mother and his inability to separate from her. The ritual sacrifice of the phallus is not merely a giving up of one's masculinity, it is also a symbolic sacrifice to ensure rebirth, that is, the creation of a new life apart from the mother. In this sense, castration represents the son's need to be separate and, at the same time, to retain for himself some aspect of the feminine and the maternal. The gallois' transformation into "women," on the other hand, can be seen more as an attempt to identify with the mother, as if by failing to separate one could achieve complete identification with her.

In a ritual of Malekula, male initiates are connected by a symbolic phallus, which symbolically enables them to recreate themselves:

> All those previously initiated lie down on the ground, head to feet, in a long line leading from the "mother-drum" set up in the dancing-ground to the neighboring initiation-lodge in which the novices are, with huge rolls of leaves symbolizing penises stretching from one man's genitals to the other's so as to form a continuous symbolic phallus reaching from the mother-drum to the novices. This is a male "umbilical cord" by means of which the female influence from the mother-drum is symbolically transmuted into a male one for the psychic benefit of the novices who are thought to be impregnated by it, so that they themselves become pregnant of psychic (male) matter, called *ta-mats,* that which has "died" to the mother-principle and has been reborn into a new male psychic one.[8]

Circumcision can be seen as a remnant of the castration sacrifice to the Great Mother—a symbolic castration that was, at a later period, taken over by the father, who had come to replace the mother as the initiator of consciousness in the son. For Bettelheim, circumsion was a male extension of fertility magic, a rite directed to ensuring procreation; he sees it as unrelated to a patriarchal idea of instilling fear of castration and protecting the incest taboo, as suggested by Fraud. In addition to helping a boy to develop a firmer sense of his masculinity and sexuality, circumcision may also have developed as an expression of men's desire to create a likeness of the female vulva in themselves. This is even clearer in the more severe mutilation known as subincision, in which the underside of the penis is opened with a stone knife and the blood is collected and drunk by the men or the women, or sometimes put in a special fire. This flow of blood was likened to the menstrual flow in the female. Since, unlike circumcision, this procedure was voluntary, and in fact sometimes repeated, it can be seen as an attempt to gain some of the power of the feminine through emulation. The ritual of subincision was seen as having the effect of changing men into "manwomen."[9] Also, in *Thresholds of Initiation,* Joseph Henderson conjectures "that archaic man, in thus simulating a biological likeness to woman, is seeking to take on her ability to experience death and rebirth literally—an experience forever closed to men, who can experience death and rebirth only as a ritual or mimetic rite.[10]

Menstrual blood was experienced by primitives as having special and magical qualities and was often used in healing rituals, where it was smeared on the body of the sick. The blood of the subincision wound was also believed to be healing and was sometimes given to a woman to drink when she was ill.

The relationship between intercourse and conception was unknown in Paleolithic and even Neolithic times; even among the present-day Australian aboriginals, it is still not understood. This lack of understanding may well have supported the belief that men could obtain the power of maternal and feminine—including the capacity to create life—through rituals designed to make them more like women. This envy of the feminine is a central theme in the psychological work of men in analysis.

Joseph Campbell, in *The Power of Myth,* tells of a rite of a men's society in New Guinea that illustrates how these rituals operate as rites of death and rebirth. In this rite boys are initiated into their first sexual experience by having intercourse with a girl who is dressed as a deity. The ceremony culminates when the last of the boys is still in embrace with the girl and the log house they are in is capsized, killing them both. They are then eaten by the other members of the group in a celebration of death and resurrection. The original unity of male and female is sacrificed; the offering acts as the nourishment of the group. Campbell relates this ritual to a form of the early planting-society myth of death, resurrection, and cannibalistic consumption.[11] The symbolic aspect of this ritual also has elements similar to those seen in the sacrifice of the mass of the Catholic Church, as well as in the sacrifice of the fertility goddess cult.

Initiation rites serve to satisfy three distinct and related functions for the pubertal boy. The first is an exogenous need to achieve separation and differentiation from the mother and to align his identity more with the father, which is accomplished through the symbolic death and rebirth aspect of the ritual. The second is an endogenous need to define his place within the group—to identify his role, obligations, and responsibilities. And third, these rites fulfill both an endogenous and exogenous need to incorporate the feminine within himself, in a way that allows him to be separate from his mother, sisters, and other females in his group. This represents man's earliest sacrificial initiation into the mystery of the feminine and his earliest attempt to integrate the anima. He must free himself first from the "terrible" aspect of the mother—symbolized by the dragon, whale, alligator, or other beast—which, as we have seen, represents his containment in the unconscious. In this way his feminine image can be rescued from its immersion within the mother. This is also why in some puberty rites the boy "enters" the belly of the alligator, after which his body is scarred with teeth marks (by the men) attesting to his rebirth and return to life. A central motif supporting the notion of incorporating the feminine is that the symbolic Great Father, as initiator of the son, is himself androgynous. So the father, in providing a container for the initiation of the son, acts also as a mother substitute.

> The transition from Mother to Father, as archetypal figures representing masculine and feminine qualities, can be more effectively understood as the expression of an existential condition for which the symbol of bisexual union represents the attitude of wholeness or integration necessary to maturity. It is a desirable, permanent acquisition, not just a phase of development to be outgrown.[12]

This coincides with the boy becoming an adult and transferring his identity from the mother to the father. With the emergence of his sexuality, there is also a transfer of his emotional energy from the mother to his wife or partner, who then becomes the carrier of his anima. This transfer is essential for the transformation of the boy into partner of the woman and always involves a sacrifice of part of his relationship to his mother.

The Myth of the Hero

The *hero's journey* is a form of initiation that attempts to provide access to a higher level of awareness by challenging the initiate with some task that involves eventually sacrificing different levels of ego dominance. The journey ultimately helps form a more healthy sense of masculinity. Completing the prescribed tasks inculcates a continued sense of competency and self-assurance, particularly as to the direction and meaning of one's life.

The hero's journey is portrayed in such stories as Apuleius's *Golden Ass* from the second century C.E. and *Parsifal* from the twelfth or thirteenth century; in various vision quests; in certain fairy tales; and in Greek myths.

The Parsifal myth is perhaps one of the most relevant, as it is one of the last great myths of masculine development. There are several variants of the Grail legend, but each of them has the common theme of a fatherless adolescent son, Parsifal (or Perceval), who leaves his mother and home to become a knight of King Arthur's court. He starts out as a naive youth who rather foolishly attempts to attain knighthood without any preparation whatsoever. Within the story there is also a young woman in King Arthur's castle who has not smiled for years; the legend has it that the first person to make her laugh will be knighted. Through his foolishness, Parsifal causes her to laugh, and so he is knighted by King Arthur. At the same time Parsifal expresses the desire to have the armor of the Red Knight, the most fearsome knight in King Arthur's court. He is told he can have it if he succeeds in besting the Red Knight, which he also does, killing him by throwing a dagger that hits him in the eye. With this armor Parsifal sets out on many journeys. He is roundly successful in his knightly adventures, though he never kills again, only defeating many other knights and sending them to the court of King Arthur.

An important character of the legend is the Fisher King, who is ill and close to dying, and whose land is barren and deteriorating as a result of his condition. Apparently, the Fisher King was wounded early in life—a wound from which he cannot recover until a naive youth comes to the Grail castle and asks a question that will heal him. In the course of his travels Parsifal meets Gournamond, a godfather who instructs him in the art of knighthood and chivalry. He counsels Parsifal to seek the Holy Grail and to ask the question that will heal the Fisher King: "Whom does the Grail serve?" Gournamond also instructs Parsifal to neither seduce nor be seduced by a woman.

Before he goes in search of the Grail Parsifal decides to return to search for his mother, only to find that she has died of a "broken heart." After this, he resumes his search for the Grail and encounters Blanche Fleur, whose castle is in a state of siege. She appeals to Parsifal to save her castle, which he does. They eventually spend the night together, but he remains true to Gournamond's advice to be chaste. Eventually, Parsifal stumbles into the Grail castle for the first time, but because of his naivete and the fact that his mother told him not to ask too many questions in his travels, he forgets to ask the most important question. This failure causes him to leave the Grail castle and return to his knightly ventures. His outer adventures, however, do bring him the recognition of King Arthur, who requests that he be sought out and brought back to the court for a celebration in his honor. He is found by Arthur's knights in a "love trance" induced by seeing three drops of blood in the snow, reminding him of his beloved Blanche Fleur.

In the middle of King Arthur's celebration, Parsifal is suddenly faced by a hideous, dark old shrew who accosts him with his inadequacies and failure to ask the healing question. Following this, Parsifal spends many more years in knightly quests that are accompanied by an increasing sense of futility and meaninglessness. He is finally brought by a band of pilgrims to a hermit who, like the hideous woman, confronts him with his inadequacies and rebukes him for not asking the right question in the Grail castle. The old hermit directs him again to the Grail castle, where he finally heals the Fisher King by asking, "Whom does the Grail serve?"[13]

The primary purpose of this myth is to facilitate a further development of consciousness. Myths in which a fatherless young man sets out on a journey to find something of great value, to recapture something that was lost, to find a new land, to solve a riddle that leads to some form of revelation, or to bring about some cure or healing of himself or his father are archetypal patterns of masculine development. These patterns act as metaphorical models of certain life experiences that need to be lived and integrated by individual men to facilitate the development of their consciousness and, eventually, a greater spiritual relation to life. This occurs through that part of the individuation process known as the *transcendent function*, a merging of the conscious and unconscious elements in such a way that there is a further constellation of the higher self. This emergence of a higher sense of self can be gained only through an initiatory ordeal in which the less mature attitudes of the ego are sacrificed. In this sense the initiation of the hero follows closely on the initiation of the pubertal boy, in that the journey involves a descent to the underworld not unlike the return to the maternal womb; in the hero's journey the return is portrayed as a dangerous mission, often expressed as needing to overcome some evil, such as by slaying a dragon, from which he returns victorious over bodily mortality.

The myth of Parsifal arose at the time when the Christian emphasis on the perfect spiritual man was at its height. Parsifal comes on stage as a hero, but also as a naive youth who is breaking his relationship to his mother. Initially seen by the knights of King Arthur's court as a fool, he finally becomes a true hero when he saves the wounded Fisher King, restoring harmony and fertility to the wasteland.

Myths portraying the hero's journey yield a model for understanding some of the psychological tasks of men. For example, the hero is often fatherless. Parsifal, according to Emma Jung, was about to return to his mother when he came to the Grail castle for the first time. Rather than doing so, he encountered the sick Fisher King, the father in need of healing. The need to find the ailing father and heal him is a fundamental element in male psychology, and this need is reflected on the cultural level as well. As the prevailing cultural symbol of the higher self *and* as father, the "king" is in need of healing. This is as true now as it was during the thirteenth century. There are also other images of the father in the story of Parsifal; Gournamond, for example, represents the positive pole of the archetypal father. When the outer father is either emotionally or physically absent the archetypal image may emerge in a man's psyche to assist in his initiation process. Both Gournamond and the hermit help guide Parsifal back to the Grail castle.

Parsifal meets several anima images in his travels, and these also help him to eventually see the true objective of his mission: to ask the right question in the Grail castle. Blanche Fleur is an idealized anima whom he loves, and by maintaining a chaste relationship with her he allows her to function as a "soul-mate."

By regarding her as a part of himself, rather than as an outer woman, he makes a connection with the deepest emotional part of himself. Even the dark shrew, as the negative pole of the anima, functions to wake him up, making him aware of his shortsightedness and the wounded parts of himself, much like the ayami, the tutelary guide, does for the shaman.

As indicators of individuation these initiatory motifs are still found in contemporary men's dreams and fantasies. We see them also represented in literature, such as in James Joyce's *Ulysses* and T. S. Eliot's *The Waste Land*.

A dream I had during my own analysis illustrates some of the features of the hero's journey:

> I am on a small boat going to some foreign land across an ocean. When I arrive the place is in a state of chaos; many buildings are completely destroyed. The buildings are a combination of contemporary structures and ancient ruins, like one might find in Greece. It seems that there might have been a military coup there, with a new power of some evil sort having just taken over the country. I go to a hotel and get a room, but as soon as I am in my room I become afraid that perhaps I should not have come here, that perhaps I have put myself in danger. Just then there is a loud banging on my door, and I am sure that the police or military have come to get me. At the same moment another door which seems to lead to an adjoining suite opens slightly and I decide to try to escape through it. As I enter the other room it is completely dark and I can barely make out what is in there, but soon it becomes clear that the room is in an incredible disarray: things are scattered all over. I then become aware that there is someone lying on a cot in the corner of the room. As I approach this figure I can see that it is a very old and perhaps dying man. When he sees me he seems to recognize me and immediately says he has been waiting for me. He says that I need to go and find "Casa Buena" and bring it there and that I need to go immediately as I am in grave danger. I leave

the hotel and am on my way back to my little boat, passing many still-burning buildings. In one of them I see in the embers what appears to be a jewel, so I stop briefly and pull it out of the ashes. In fact it is a very large ruby. Just as I put it in my pocket I notice that the military is chasing me, so I quickly run to the pier and am able to get into my boat and cast off before they get to me.

This dream contains several of the elements of the hero's journey. In some ways it seems particularly related to elements of the myth of Parsifal, involving, as it does, a journey to a wasteland where the hero finds an ailing old man suffering from some condition from which he needs to be saved.

Exaggerated Hero Myths

An example of a contemporary exaggerated hero is represented by the Rockys and Rambos that populate so many of our movies. One recent movie, *Cobra* (note the name!), features a policeman who is cold, unemotional, withdrawn, schizoid, possessed with destruction, and who, by the end of the movie, has murdered at least forty-six other men and one woman! His crowning triumph is to hang his antagonist on a meat hook. Practically all the while, a beautiful, passive woman, who has nothing to do but be protected by this caricature of masculinity, hangs on to his arm; of course by the end she falls in love with him, and together they ride off into the sunset, supposedly to live happily ever after.

This movie is not unlike many others being shown in American theatres. Sometimes the name doesn't even change, just the numeral. There must be a tremendous amount of unconscious support for this kind of imagery of masculinity in our society. If men did not care to see a myth with this kind of hero, they would not be spending so much of their money to perpetuate this sadism in entertainment. Where does this support come from?

Cobra, Rocky, Rambo, and the like are examples of a particular hero archetype very popular in our culture at present. An archetype, as we have seen earlier, is not an individual person but a representation of a generalized *image* of a person whose personal characteristics fade in the presence of the predominant characteristics of that image. In this case, he is a cultural archetype of masculinity and, as such, an extreme form. We could never get to know this character as an individual, as a person, but only as a collective image. Cobra, Rocky, Rambo, Chuck Norris, or the "nicer" predecessors of these archetypes, such as Gene Autry, the Lone Ranger, Batman, or Superman, are all cultural heroes. If you've seen one, you've probably seen them all. One might be more or less "cool" than another, more or less violent, but they are all unusually strong, independent, and clever; they are the "good guys" who rarely have a fault that doesn't also become part of their character.

In certain ways, *Cobra* is no different from other myths and fairy tales; they all tell similar stories with similar themes, with common beginnings and endings. The surface theme is always that the hero really is a "good guy"—however misdirected his causes may sometimes be and no matter how violent he himself becomes—who is battling evil of one sort or the other. His goal is to overcome this evil and the distress it has caused over the land—or in the city or the police department—and to somehow restore order and peace. His other goal is to rescue the maiden in distress, to relieve her suffering, difficulty, or oppression, and to win her hand in marriage (or, these days, maybe to just go off and live together).

"Cobra masculinity" represents a form of a primitive masculine identification in which the anima is immature and undeveloped, so that the hero's feminine qualities are powerfully overshadowed by an exaggerated degree of masculinity. The corresponding outer woman associated with this type of man is also not much of a "whole" person; her masculinity is overshadowed by stereotypical, exaggerated feminine qualities. She, too, is more of an archetype than an individual woman. She rarely seems to have a mind of her own, much less a stable set of values that exist apart from his. She is malleable, ready to be shaped into the woman he wants her to be, whether that means mother figure, doting lover, or obedient wife. In other words, in this dyad there is a remarkable developmental similarity: his lack of anima development is paralleled by her lack of animus development.

Rarely in such present-day myths do we see any deep transformation of the character, and even more rarely do we see much spiritual development. The hero simply shows up in the next film with a new story line, often not much more imaginative than the last.

If we assume that the drama we witness is an inner one, and the characters are identifications with the hero archetype, we begin to see the source of the unconscious support for these supposedly inane fantasies. The hero's struggle is actually the nascent ego's struggle for consciousness; it is his symbolic attempt to free himself from the power of the parents, particularly the mother, and to incorporate the inner woman. A recurrent theme in this struggle is a lack of harmony, expressed as struggles between various pairs of opposites, such as good and evil, light and dark, masculine and feminine. These polarities are the substance, or *prima materia*, out of which consciousness is created.

Men's dreams often confirm that there is a hero archetype—a prince or a Cobra—in every uninitiated man, as well as an inner woman—a damsel in distress. It is up to the hero to bring about peace and to win unity with the woman.

The hero in the early myths was in search of a hidden treasure or a Holy Grail, and his job was to overcome a monster or slay a dragon—in some ways not unlike the story of the modern hero. And while these early stories portrayed the hero's difficult trial to incorporate the anima, he was not supposed to *actually* run off with the maiden, or even sleep with her, as so often happens in the modern version. The "marriage" of the early hero was a symbolic marriage to the anima; that is why, as in *Parsifal*, he must remain chaste. But in order for the hero to truly succeed he must first separate from the mother, find and heal the father, and eventually undergo a major transformative process. But Rambo and Rocky just keep repeating the same old struggle. Psychologically, they remain right where they always were: unconsciously still in the grips of their parents, always in search of new girlfriends. Of course, they would not at all like to hear this—because of their toughness they act like they really need no one. However, the protest is a little too strong. Since they have no awareness of the need to integrate the anima as an inner figure, the outer woman they rescue takes the place of their own feminine, and any possibility of inner development is sacrificed.

Masculine/feminine polarity is an inner psychological problem. It is one of men's greatest challenges to achieve union or integration and, thereby, greater consciousness. As inner attributes, masculinity and femininity are dynamic complements which *actively* seek each other for balance and integration; at the collective level they only mirror the dominant cultural archetypes.

This contemporary hero typifies what Jung referred to as the man dominated by the *puer aeternus,* the archetype of the eternal son. This archetype is typical of male adolescence, where its appearance is developmentally normal, but when carried into adult life it represent a *failure* to grow up psychologically. According to Jung, the *puer*—the "son"—is largely a product of the mother-complex; he seems unable to assume responsibility for his own life and fails to make a serious emotional commitment in relationship. The *puer* must always have an escape hatch—another relationship, another project, or another move—as a way of avoiding the business of settling down in life. He is described as living a provisional life as well as one of false individualism. Also, in one way or another, the *puer* often lives dangerously. Joseph L. Henderson attributes the arrested development of the *puer* to a failure of initiation; that is, it is not simply a matter of distortions in early parent-child relationships, but it is a failure of the individual to take the next natural step toward maturity.[14]

The exaggerated masculinity encountered in this type of man illustrates only one pole of the *puer.* The other pole is equally exaggerated in the feminine direction, resulting in a "darling boy" quality, still too closely and obviously identified with the mother. Although we see both poles in our culture, the over-masculinized type is the more frequent and the more "accepta-ble" image of masculinity. Like Parsifal, who at the beginning of his journey wore the homespun clothes his mother had given him under his armor, the uninitiated overmasculinized man does not reveal—either by his countenance or by his behavior—his lack of separation from the mother. It is precisely this overly defended exterior that belies both his lack of separation from the mother and a lack of a viable connection to the integrated masculine. All of this is evidence that there has been no initiation by an "androgynous" father, with the result that the son's way of coping with the world reflects an archetypal manifestation of what could be called the warrior. Obviously, there are less sensational forms of the warrior in terms of the varied preoccupations men have. What seems to set them apart from the initiated man is their seemingly endless and repetitive quest for power, money, and status. It is as if they are never sure of how much is enough, or whether what they have accomplished is finally "good enough." For so many men this is never resolved and they arrive at the end of their lives with a sense of futility in spite of all they have "done."

Relatively little emphasis has been placed on the father's role in the psychology of the *puer*. However, when, and if, the under-side of this warrior is finally exposed, as it sometimes is in analysis or through a major psychological breakdown, a deep emotional vulnerability suddenly springs from beneath his armor. And it is at this critical juncture that he is again most in need of a *good father*.

Loss of Ritual

Initiation rites mark the beginning of self-consciousness in the adolescent boy. Erich Neumann points out the significance of puberty in this regard:

> Self-formation and self-realization begin in earnest when human consciousness develops into self-

consciousness. Self-reflection is a characteristic of the pubertal phase of humanity as it is of the pubertal phase of the individual. It is a necessary phase of human knowledge, and it is only persistence in this phase that has fatal effects. The breaking of the Great Mother fixation through self-reflection is not a symbol of auto-eroticism, but of centroversion.[15]

In the modern world men's inner transformation is hampered because there are few remaining viable rites of passage for them. Important transitions through the periods of development from childhood to adulthood to old age and, ultimately, death, now go largely undefined. As a result, one sees today many youths involved in attempts to assert their power and rudimentary sense of masculinity. These demonstrations of adolescent bravado, which include feats involving risk and even death, represent the frustrated need to experience a more formal rite of passage.

Improperly incorporated masculinity may also manifest as compulsive sexual exhibitionism, as if one were attempting to reassure oneself that one has what is, in fact, missing. Exhibitionism, which is like the inverse of self-reflection, is another archaic remnant of a form of sexual display in which one's sexual parts are presented as an unconscious attempt to defy the power of the feminine. Although it is an attempt to "prove" one's masculinity, exhibitionistic behavior instead reveals a sense of being castrated and a very immature level of integration of the feminine. The exhibitionist unconsciously depends upon his viewer's reaction to reflect to him the presence and power of his genitals. The sense of being castrated conveys not only an uncertainty with regard to one's masculinity, but also a deep entrapment in the mother archetype and an inability to self-reflect. In another type of exhibitionism, this time pertaining to power, the hero repeatedly attempts to demonstrate different forms of his strength, as if proving something about which he is actually unsure.

Various forms of exhibitionism are attempts to have others

reflect back something of oneself that can, in fact, only be confirmed through self-reflection. Many men today need to move beyond the adolescent requirement that the world reflect them— through their accomplishments and heroic deeds, for example— to a more adult state of self-reflection, which offers an internalized sense of meaning, value, and place. The role of the father in facilitating this initiatory process is indispensable, because he represents a masculine model for his son. The common failure of the father to fulfill this role can result in a lifelong impairment of the son's masculine identification; in this way, it also influences the role he later comes to play as father.

For example, one of the men in my men's group tells of his disappointment in his father's failure to provide a badly needed initiatory experience:

> When I was just reaching puberty one of the other boys at school related how his folks had sat down with him and told him the "facts of life." Although I "knew" all about the facts of life, I was fired with excitement, and I could hardly wait until my folks did the same with me. I fantasized what it would be like to sit with my mom and dad and discuss this most taboo of subjects in an open and frank manner. If we could talk about sex we could talk about anything. I waited! At times when the three of us were alone and relaxed, I would send ESP messages to them saying, "Now is the time" or "It's okay" or "Please, let's do it." At times I would sense that they were planning to do it, and I would become excited and wide-eyed, only to be frustrated nearly to the point of tears. It never dawned on me to simply ask them to tell me. The urgency of our talking about this waned during my middle and late teen years, but it was all brought back while I was in college.
>
> When I was twenty my dad and I went to the high Sierra to climb Mount Lyle, one of the highest peaks in the range. This trip followed the wedding of one of my older sisters. My dad and I shared a few beers in a tent cabin that night. I was convinced that my dad was finally

going to tell me the facts of life. As things turned out, the subject did not come up, but I decided that it was all right since we were to spend the next four days alone. The next day we backpacked up the canyon and made base camp at the foot of the mountain. We were totally alone. That night we spread our sleeping bags next to one another under the stars and climbed in as darkness closed. The air was incredibly clear and the stars seemed especially bright, and again I was convinced that this would be the night my father and I would finally have our talk. I lay there sending the strongest ESP messages I could, just as I had so often when I was younger. We were quiet, and after a long silence my dad cleared his throat to speak. This was it! The time had come! He then said, "Sam, when I look up at those stars and see all the order in the universe I am absolutely convinced that there is a God." My heart dropped. His head was in heaven and mine was on the earth. I was bitterly disappointed.

The next day we began the ascent of Mount Lyle. About a few hours into the climb the route required that we cross over part of Lyle Glacier. We were prepared and had brought rope to tether ourselves together in case one of us fell into a crevice. The sun reflecting off the ice was so excruciatingly bright that we pulled our hats down and walked with our heads pointed down-ward and our eyes squinting. We must have continued in this manner for almost an hour. When we stopped to get our bearings, we realized that we had drifted across the glacier. We were so far off the trail that we could not reach the peak and descend to our base camp before dark. I burst into tears. When my dad asked me why I was crying I told him that I just wanted to reach the top of the mountain with him. As we descended the steep trail we were constantly slipping on the loss talus. This jarring aggravated my dad's arthritis to the point that he could hardly walk. I thought I might have to carry him down. It was the first time that I had ever seen him as weak.

Looking back it is now clear that I had chosen my folks' telling me the facts of life as an initiation ritual, a symbol of their acceptance of me as an adult, as an equal. I never experienced that ritual. The events of climbing Mount Lyle are particularly poignant. My dad and I were not communicating, and we got lost on the frozen ice of unconsciousness. We had an opportunity for a meaningful experience together but we lost it. And so I wept.

A few years later I got married. On the night before the ceremony many of my out-of-town relatives came over to the house after the rehearsal dinner to continue the partying. During the evening my dad and an uncle, both of whom had been drinking for quite a while, took me aside. Dad said, "Son, I never sat down with you and told you the facts of life, but I am sure you know all about it. I would like to give you some advice: Women like to have their breasts fondled, and be sure to always clear the bathroom sink when you are finished using it." I was shocked! Squeeze their tits and wash the basin! I was angry, I was dumbfounded, and I felt betrayed. After all these years the subject was finally broached, but it was done while he was drunk, it wasn't one-on-one, and what he said was trite. The experience cast a pall on the rest of what should have been for me a special evening.

I wish the story had a happy ending but it does not. I suppressed all of this during the next several years. When my oldest children, both girls, were just at puberty I said to my wife that we should sit down with them and talk about sex. She glowered at me and said, "I have already taken care of that." The message was clear: You're late, it is none of your business, keep out. I did nothing. Some years later, after I was divorced and had been in therapy for some time, I related this whole experience to my daughters and told them how sorry I was for not talking with them about sex, so that it and other topics would be easy to discuss. My oldest daughter looked at me and said, "She said what? That is not true. When I began having my periods Mom gave me some tampons in a very perfunctory way and that was it. I so wish you had talked to me about sex then. I really needed to be able to talk about it." My heart dropped and I was overwhelmed by myriad emotions. The cycle had continued for another generation. I can only hope that my children will heed my experience and theirs and break the cycle.

In the past, the father was an important element in the initiatory experience of the son. Modern life presents fewer possibilities than before for this kind of experience between father and son: daily activity is more regimented, there is less contact between fathers and sons, and together they have fewer experiences with nature and the cycles of life.

A poignant portrayal of a boy's natural initiation into manhood by his father can be seen in the novel *A Day No Pigs Would Die,* a story about a twelve-year-old boy, Robert, and his family, who live on a farm in New England at the turn of the century. Robert's father makes a sparse living by slaughtering pigs. One day a neighbor gives Robert an unusual gift, a pig of his very own. Robert grows attached to Pinky, and while he hopes to raise it for breeding, more importantly it becomes his pet. As the pig comes of age, it becomes evident that it is infertile, and Robert's father tells him that the animal must be slaughtered because they cannot afford to feed a pig that will not earn its keep through breeding. At this same time Robert's father reveals to his son that he is ill and will not live much longer; Robert must think about assuming responsibility for the farm and the care of his mother and aunt. But first he must assist his father in the bloody slaughter of his pet. He momentarily hates his father for killing the pig, but he also feels a deep love when he sees him break down and cry. After Pinky is slaughtered, Robert kisses his father's bloodied hands. The following morning, Robert awakens to the unusual quiet of the farm and finds that his father has died during the night in the barn.

While this initiation is not a prescribed one, its elements are similar to the early rituals, in that it contains the elements of sacrifice through a ritual death and rebirth. Robert must give up an important attachment of childhood to become a "man" and take on the responsibilities of adult life. The sacrifice entails a literal transformation of consciousness, not just the accumulation of new information about how to live one's life.

The contemporary loss of initiation rites creates a danger to the boy's separation needs because of the lack of clearly defined boundaries between himself and his mother. The lack of ritual may cause him to develop his own methods of separation which, if carried too far, create a defensive posture in which men deny their need to incorporate aspects of the feminine. This form of splitting, in turn, often results in a man's disavowing his own feminine qualities altogether.

Over time, and especially in developing societies, most rituals and myths have become gradually diluted and eroded by attempts to erase signs of "primitivity" from our consciousness and move toward a more rational approach to life. Myths came to be seen as "old wives tales" by the critical *Logos*—the rational, logical, and, by the time of emerging science, masculine point of view. Science, as a major form of exogenous development, became the supreme Logos, attempting to dispel the earlier mythical notions as foolish and unfounded. Current attempts to unravel the mystery of myths have taken the form of scientific investigation, as found in formalism or structuralism.

The emergence of Christianity was also partly responsible for the eradication of these earlier rituals, since many of them were seen as pagan rites and antithetical to the dogma of monotheism. At the same time, such Christian rituals as the sacrifice of the Mass, confirmation, baptism, and the various sacraments, are some of the few remaining religious rituals of modern times; the same is true for some of the rituals of Judaism, such as the bar mitzvah. In Judaism, circumcision is still practiced as a religious custom, but not as initiation. The symbolism of many of the Christian sacraments, themselves rooted in ancient rites of passage, contain such ideas as symbolic cannibalism, as seen in the eucharistic ceremony of consuming bread and wine representing the body and blood of Christ.

Early Christianity rebelled against the early findings of science, protecting its own myths as "truths" from the "heretical findings" of science. In the seventeenth century, for example, Galileo was decreed a heretic by the Catholic Church for finding that the sun rather than the earth was the center of the universe. The creation myth as well as other dogma of scripture were for centuries considered to be ultimate truth as well as historical reality. That which conflicted with teachings of scripture was considered not only to be untrue; anyone holding contrary views was banned, excommunicated, or murdered by the Church.

Unfortunately, the numinosity and sacredness of many remaining rituals have been diluted by attempts to make them more "relevant" to modern customs. An example is the abandoning of the Latin liturgy and the addition of pop music during the celebration of the Catholic Mass. It is also not unusual to see churches today hosting such events as Casino Night and bingo parties. This is a misunderstanding of the purpose of initiation, since the function of ritual is to provide some level of transformation. These attempts at relevance create empty rituals, since they lose the mystery that facilitates a change of consciousness. The purpose of ritual is not to provide information, but to initiate a change in consciousness acquired through an esoteric *experience*.

The Logos approach to understanding myth is a reductive methodology—an attempt to reduce meaning to the lowest common denominator. These attempts to invalidate myths from the logical perspective miss the point because myths are neither historical accounts nor scientific findings; rather, they represent symbolic collective statements, in stylized form, of unconscious projections of that which is unknown. Jung, in numerous contexts, has pointed out the difference between a *sign* and a *symbol*. A sign refers to something like an object or an idea that stands for something basically known, while the symbol is the best approximation of something essentially unknown. The symbol, like the myth but unlike the sign, does not "stand for" the thing it represents; rather it points in the direction of the unknown without defining or reducing it with any degree of finality. Modern-day artists and poets who express their work in symbolic terms are some of the few remaining myth-makers of our culture.

Summary

Consciousness originally emerged from a nonreflective, nonrational, mythic dimension of experience; the first evidence of this emergence is in the burial practices of our earliest human ancestors. In these early rituals we see the projection of rebirth contained in the symbolism of death. The mythic dimension was later augmented by the more masculine counterbalancing pole of Logos—the logical, rational component of consciousness increasingly associated with the ego—which defined, labeled, and classified experience according to its own criteria of what was "real."

It is difficult to accept Freud's assertion that pubertal initiations were patriarchal attempts to instill fear and anxiety in the young men of the tribe through the threat of castration. It seems much more plausible to believe that they were modeled on the fertility rituals of the Great Mother cults, retaining the themes of sacrifice, death, and rebirth, with emphasis on the need to separate from the mother and incorporate parts of the feminine, while moving toward a more positive identification with the father.

Most rituals of initiation have been abandoned through the gradual estrangement of the mythic dimension of consciousness. As a result of this estrangement, modern men have come to rely on a rather one-sided quality of consciousness that primarily emphasizes rationality and outer life. Nevertheless, we see support for the dynamic tendency of individuation in the psyche's retention of a remarkable capacity to portray the imagery and emotions of initiation ordeals through dreams and fantasies. The anima can assist in masculine initiation by providing specific images of death, dismemberment, and rebirth—representing the sacrifice of an overly exogenic ego orientation. But in order to access this rich imagery of transformation men need to be open to the unconscious.

Uninitiated men face the danger of remaining caught in the mother, either by continually hoping for validation and approval from their parents, or, in the form of protest, by endlessly repeating the heroism of the warrior archetype without inner transformation. Men may have to devise contemporary initiation rituals for themselves and their sons in order to compensate for the lack of rites of passage and to reemphasize the importance of the father-son relationship in developing a more individuated masculine consciousness.

For Freud, the Oedipus myth was the psychological prototype of the father-son relationship. However, we must look closely at the myth to see that Oedipus is a "fatherless" hero: his travels and eventual tragedy are prefaced by abandonment by the father. This becomes a key point in our understanding of the Oedipus myth, and particularly in our understanding of incest, as we shall see in the next chapter, "The Oedipal Wound."

□ 4 □

The Oedipal Wound

It [Oedipus complex] revealed itself to me as a piece of my self-analysis, as a reaction to my father's death; that is, to the most important event, the most poignant loss, in a man's life.

—SIGMUND FREUD

The Importance of Freud in Male Psychology

FREUD'S THINKING, particularly in regard to the Oedipus myth, has exerted a profound influence on the way in which men are thought about, and on the way in which they think about themselves. His theories of seduction, incest, penis envy, and castration anxiety, as well as his attitude toward the role of the father, are important to our understanding of the psychology of men. Because any psychological theory bears, to some extent, the psychic imprint of its founder, in this chapter we will attempt to look at Freud's thinking in the context of his own personal attitudes and biases.

Any assessment of Freud and his theoretical formulations must acknowledge the fact that it is easy to be critical from the vantage point of almost one hundred years of intervening history and psychoanalytic experience. Indeed, the significance of any formulation is revealed partly by its endurance over time. Survival of a theory can also be supported by an archetypal core that transcends the time surrounding its creation. From the Oedipus myth, Freud derived his theory of the *Oedipus complex,* which describes a child's sexual wish for the opposite sexed parent combined with jealousy and murderous rage toward the parent of the same sex. Elements of the Oedipus myth (which is almost three thousand years old) provide an archetypal core that has served to nourish this theoretical formulation. That same archetypal core has acted as a magnetic center, attracting personal projections and biases, including those of Freud, which only time and experience will either confirm or invalidate; in the interim, however, these tend to become institutionalized as a dogmatic assertion of psychological truth. The central theme of the myth itself has stayed with us for so long because it describes a dynamic that is still operable in the psyche, one that has yet to be fully understood and psychologically assimilated.

It is difficult from the perspective of the present to appreciate the unique flavor of early psychoanalytic formulations, which took place in the Victorian milieu of the turn of the century. This is perhaps particularly true of the *seduction theory,* originally one of Freud's most central ideas, which was derived from his clinical work with (mostly female) hysterics who claimed to have been molested as children. In his original formulation he declared that the underlying cause of all neuroses could be found in the patient's exposure to sexual trauma in childhood by a parent, relative, or caretaker. This theory, originally posited by Freud as the cornerstone of understanding the etiology of neuroses, both hysterical and obsessional, was a radical statement both to Victorian society and to the emerging profession of psychoanalysis.

When Freud presented the seduction theory to his peers in 1896, it was rejected and even ridiculed as a "scientific fairy tale"; to Freud, this was a deep narcissistic blow.[1] Nearly six years later, he formally recanted his position almost entirely; although as late as 1924 he still continued to maintain that the etiology of certain disorders was to be found in the seduction of the child, most often by the father. He later claimed that, rather than actual physical trauma of a sexual nature to the child, it was the child's *imagination,* based on his or her own infantile sexuality, that was the main source of these neuroses.

In 1900, Freud began his analysis of eighteen-year-old Dora, who was a hysteric. This case is important in that he applied to it the later formulation of his theory, with disastrous consequences: when Freud interpreted an incident in which Dora was actually molested by a friend of the family as her sexual "wish" for her father, Dora walked out on him and terminated the analysis, much to his chagrin and surprise. He attributed her quitting to "an act of revenge, animated by the neurotic desire to harm herself."[2] More likely, this clinical failure was primarily due to the lack of empathy Freud had with his young patient, particularly since both the man who molested her and her father had denied the allegation and attributed it to her sexual fantasies. Now, Dora was not only disbelieved by her father and the man who molested her, but also by her analyst. But the importance of the failure of this case goes beyond Freud's lack of empathy and refusal to acknowledge the family friend's incestuous wish for Dora; its greatest importance lies in the fact that Freud mishandled it because he gave in to pressure to back away from his original seduction theory.

Following the rejection of his seduction theory, Freud's examination of his own dreams as well as a closer look at his family implicated both his father as well as himself in harboring incestuous wishes.[3] In a letter to a friend, he admitted that he was not free of incestuous wishes toward his daughter and that this revelation *confirmed* the correctness of his original theory.[4] But only four months later he also backed away from this position. It was during his self-analysis that he also came to acknowledge a "passion for his mother and a jealousy of his father." According to one biographer, Ernest Jones:

> Four months after this, however, Freud had discovered the *truth* of the matter: that irrespective of incest wishes of parents towards their children, and even of occasional acts of the kind, what he had to concern himself with

was the general occurrence of incest wishes of children towards their parents, characteristically towards the parent of the opposite sex [italics added].[5]

In his support of this changed position Jones's own credibility is open to question inasmuch as he was removed from a prominent position early in his career after being accused of inappropriate conduct with children he was evaluating.

The transition from Freud's theory of the sexual innocence of childhood to his theory of infantile sexuality was slow to take hold, even in him; as late as 1900, in *The Interpretation of Dreams* we continue to see references to the child's freedom from sexual desires. It is only in the third edition of the book (1911) that we find a footnote correcting his original belief.[6]

Freud stated that he wrote *The Interpretation of Dreams* in response to his father's death, in October 1896, but that he did not realize this until the book had been finished, in 1899. His father's death was a traumatic event for him, "the most poignant loss" for which he was to grieve for many years. Along with his grief he felt a strong sense of guilt, which he cited later in a paper on "survivor guilt." Exactly a year after his father's death, Freud indicated in several letters that he found his father "innocent" of the idea of sexual abuse and that these ideas were projections of his own. So Freud again recanted this central idea, in this case his father's incest wish. As with his seduction theory, this retraction also followed a rejection and abandonment, this time by his father, through death. He stated in his letters that his father's death reactivated many buried childhood memories, which became a large part of his self-analysis. It was also in *The Interpretation of Dreams* that he began to expound on the Oedipus myth, which seems connected to the emergence of more of his unconscious feelings about his father.

The specific question we are faced with is whether the appeal of the archetypal core of the Oedipus myth was related to Freud's suppression of his own incestuous wishes as well as his father's. He needed to account for the incest wish but he also needed to not find it in the parent, particularly in his own father. This dilemma seems to have been largely resolved by his embracing the Oedipus myth and by the particular, if not peculiar, way in which he interpreted it. Before returning to an examination of Freud's relationship with his own father, we will now review the origins and the background of the myth itself.

Historical Background of the Myth

The play *Oedipus the King* was written by Sophocles in 430 B.C.E. The earliest known version for the material of *Oedipus* originally came from Homer's *Iliad* and *Odyssey,* supposedly dating back to the eighth or ninth century. *Oedipus* was considered to be virtually the greatest and most perfect of the Greek tragedies— the medium through which many of the important and universal themes of classical Greek civilization were expressed. The Oedipus story spoke to an archetypal concern of people of this early historical period, and it still has a powerful appeal for the modern reader.

In the Oedipus myth, Laius and Jocasta, the king and queen of Thebes, were warned by the oracle of Apollo at Delphi that their newborn son was destined to kill his father and marry his mother. Horrified at this prophecy, and to prevent the oracle from coming true, Laius pierced his son's foot with an iron pin, to be used to tie him to a stake in the mountains. Laius then gave his son to a shepherd, telling him to abandon him in the mountains to die of exposure. Taking pity on the innocent child, the shepherd instead gave him to a herdsman from Corinth to raise far from Thebes. The herdsman in turn gave the child to Polybus and Merope, the childless king and queen of Corinth, who raised him as their own. They named him Oedipus, which translates as "swollen-foot." As a young man, Oedipus, in response to rumors that Polybus was not his own father, consulted the oracle at Delphi, where his fate was restated. Since he believed that Polybus and Merope were his real parents and he did not wish to harm them, he then left

Corinth. His travels took him back to the vicinity of Thebes, which was being devastated by a monster, the Sphinx. At a crossroads, he ran into Laius, who was on his way to Delphi to try to find a way to rid Thebes of the Sphinx. This crossing of paths was the fateful meeting that was to fulfill the first part of the original prophecy. Arguing over the right of way, Oedipus and Laius fought, and Oedipus slayed Laius. Oedipus then went to Thebes, where he met the Sphinx, solved the riddle she posed, and slew her. He was proclaimed a hero by the citizens of Thebes, who also made him king, since Laius had been killed, presumably at the hands of thieves. As the king of Thebes, Oedipus married Jocasta, fulfilling the second part of the prophecy; together they had four children. Following a rather brief period of prosperity, a plague then descended on Thebes—Apollo's punishment, Oedipus was told, for allowing the murder of Laius to go unavenged. Investigating the murder, Oedipus discovered that he himself was guilty, and he also found out who his real parents were. Overcome with guilt and shame at having committed two of the worst possible crimes—patricide and incest—he blinded himself with a brooch. His wife-mother, Jocasta, hung herself.

Freud's Relationship with His Mother

Freud saw Jocasta, Oedipus' mother, as the object of the son's sexual desire, in spite of the fact that in the myth there is no mention of Oedipus' sexual need for his mother, especially as a child. However, the roles of Jocasta and other women in the myth are relatively minor, with the exception of Oedipus' daughter, Antigone, whose name Freud often used for his own daughter, Anna, thus striking a parallel that Freud must have felt between himself and Oedipus. (Anna, like Antigone, stayed with her father to the end of his life.) Freud's relationship with his mother was also significant; that the mother is largely conspicuous by her absence is as true in *Totem and Taboo* as it is in the Oedipus myth. We know little of Freud's relationship to his mother, since he did not choose to analyze much of it. We do know that she was twenty years her husband's junior and that Freud found her quite beautiful. He was apparently the favored son, enjoying preferential treatment, particularly from his mother. One story has it that when the young Freud complained of being disturbed in his studying by his sister's piano playing, the piano was removed from the house forever. Both his mother and his father seem to have indulged their son in the fantasy of a future fame, and this, coupled with his mother's favoritism, must have catered to his sense of grandiosity.

There are only two known dreams that Freud had about his mother, both recorded in *The Interpretation of Dreams*. Erich Fromm interpreted one of these dreams as representing Freud's intolerance for a lack of immediate gratification from his mother, and the defensive posture he took in relation to these needs, which he expressed by assuming the role of a father. The other dream—an anxiety dream from his infancy—Fromm interprets as relating to fear of the loss of his mother through her death.[7]

Freud did admit in a letter that as a child of two he had had the opportunity to observe his mother naked and had been somewhat aroused by it. However, we find later that he was more like four years of age when this happened. In any case, even Ernest Jones, Freud's close friend, colleague, and biographer, mentions his belief that Freud never fully confronted, and certainly did not resolve, his unconscious feelings for his mother. Freud's other friend and personal physician, Max Schur, alluded to Freud's "complicated pre-genital relationships with his mother that he never analyzed."[8]

Some of his critics maintained that Freud did not analyze his own sexuality as he did that of his patients. This accusation was met with an angry defense by Freud, who rejoined that to have done so would have "required unwelcome disclosures about his relations with his father."[9] Even if Freud was right in saving this disclosure, we must conclude that what was good for the gander was not good for the goose. A recurring flaw in Freud's self-analysis, however noble and difficult it was, was his violation of one of the most cardinal of his own rules: the resistance in analysis must be ferreted out. We now know that self-analysis is in many ways virtually a contradiction in terms; as Freud himself stated, to overcome resistances there must be a positive transference established. In analyzing oneself, who can act as the healthy container of the positive transference? It was probably inevitable that Freud's self-analysis was incomplete, suppressive, and highly selective.

Freud's Attitude Toward Women and His Anima

Closely related to the fact that Freud seemed to be so unconscious of his relationship to his mother, his attitude toward women was characteristically negative. That he felt threatened by women and that he had a mother-complex seems obvious both from his theoretical formulations about femininity and from his conventionally Victorian stance about mothers and women in general. It is rather surprising that a man so committed to unconventional points of view, and particularly an explorer of the unconscious, would adopt the conventional masculine "anatomy is destiny" bias toward women. His theory itself manifested the bias so obvious in his personal views of women. Simply put, he did not consider women to be the equals of men—psychologically, morally, politically, or economically.

This attitude is clear from Freud's early courtship of Martha, in which he is portrayed by his biographer as rather insecure about his masculinity, very jealous, and demanding of his bride-to-be, insisting that she abdicate to his wishes on some of their most significant concerns.[10] Once married, Freud alluded little to Martha except in passing references to her in her capacity as mother.

For Freud, the differentiation of the sexes resided simply in anatomical differences, which his theory of sexual development (posited in the 1920s) conveyed most explicitly. His *phallic stage* of psychosexual development defined the female as basically an inferior version of the male, that is, as a male lacking a penis. Once he posited this female deficiency theory (what I call his *phallocentric* theory), the remainder of his thinking followed rather predictably, if not simplistically: because males had something that females didn't have, females were subject to envy of this missing part, hence *penis envy*. And since boys had something females didn't have (but perhaps once did), this inspired their fear of the future loss of it, hence *castration anxiety*.

As further embellishments of the Oedipal drama, these ideas led Freud to posit even more serious differences for the developing young boy and girl—differences he held to be responsible for the emergence of feelings of inferiority in girls and anxiety in boys. Most notably, he stated that these differences caused a divergence in superego development, with girls, of course, being the losers; because of their less severe transition out of the Oedipus complex, girls tended to develop a "lesser moral character." (Ironically, Freud was at the same time surrounded by males who were murdering Jews by the millions.) Freud's emphasis on the "natural" inferiority of women was a notion that has had unfortunate consequences for men as well as for women, since anything that is perceived as inferior is likely to be repressed. In men, this causes the inner feminine to be contaminated and to appear wounded.

Freud underemphasized or ignored the positive aspect of the maternal and feminine, to the mutual harm of both males and females. Our perception that he largely ignored the emotional significance of his relationship to his mother is reflected in his formulations on female sexuality as well as in his acknowledgment in his later years that he really understood little of the psychology of women, referring to them as "dark continents." He confessed to his friend Marie Bonaparte that he had been "doing research into the 'feminine soul' for thirty years, with little to show for it."[11] The particular feminine soul he did not study, but thoroughly avoided for all of his life, was his own anima. The consequences of the undeveloped anima in Freud's life is reflected in his theoretical psychology as well as in his clinical work.

And its lack of development is felt as deeply in his psychology of men.

Given his mother-complex, Freud may have been protesting too much about the "inferiority" of women, as his own anima was contaminated by this attitude. Wouldn't it make just as much sense to posit that males feel envy of the mysterious female cleft, as well as of the mother's breast that can nourish and sustain life, and perhaps even that men suffer from some fear of their own lack of potential to create life from inside themselves?

A major consequence of the lack of Freud's development of anima was his lack of differentiated feeling in regard to women. Reading his works and his biographies one readily gets a sense of Freud's intellectual passion, or his Logos, but not much sense of a real depth or refinement of his feeling in relationship, his compassion, his Eros.

Freud and the Father-Son Relationship

Freud overemphasized the negative father. In his theory, a son could expect retaliation from his father because of the boy's incestuous wish for his mother. This idea of the castrating father reaffirms the notion of the primal negative father who will cut off his son's penis unless he turns his attention away from his mother. The introduction of this savage element into the father-son relationship has contributed to our view of men—and particularly fathers—as jealous brutes.

Freud generated a negative exogenous masculine psychology, largely out of his personal psychodynamics and experience. Freud's relationship with his father was a contributing factor in his choice of the Oedipus myth to portray the father-son relationship, as the myth depicts a father-son relationship characterized by abandonment and ambivalence. While Freud's father didn't abandon him physically, there is evidence that their relationship was characterized by ambivalence and competition.[12] A particularly striking incident from Freud's childhood is recounted in *The*

Interpretation of Dreams, in which he relates urinating in his parents' bedroom out of defiance. His father's angry response was, "That boy will never amount to anything." Freud later recalls: "This must have been a terrible affront to my ambition, for allusions to this scene occur again and again in my dreams and are constantly coupled with enumerations of my accomplishments and success, as if I wanted to say: 'You see I have amounted to something after all.' "[13]

Freud's adolescent admiration for particular heroes, especially military ones like Hannibal, who not only made an impact on the world but changed the course of it, conveyed his envy of them and his own need to be seen as a trailblazer. Although Freud was certainly an iconoclast and a rebel, he suffered an extreme vulnerability to criticism: to criticize him was to fall into his disfavor. He could also be rigid and dogmatic, a quality vividly clear in *Totem and Taboo,* in which his ideas were as mistaken as they were eloquent. Yet, in spite of overwhelming anthropological and ethnological information contradicting his thesis, to the end of his life he insisted on its correctness. Freud was often described as an authoritarian personality by many of his associates; the fact that so many of his followers defected points to his father-complex, with its core image of an angry, violent, and negative father.[14] This internal archetypal negative father became the dominant image for his theory of the primal horde and the patriarchal father who, using the threat of castration, controls his son's wish to possess the mother.

Another effect of Freud's split from his anima is felt in the father image that his psychology projects. The image of the negative, castrating father who harbors fear and resentment of his son belongs to an archetypal pattern that has been set down at least since the end of the matrilineal family. This is the negative exogenous manifestation of the masculine split from its natural counterpart, the feminine. Freud's interpretation of the Oedipus myth served to perpetuate that split, resulting in its becoming dogmatically institutionalized in psychoanalysis as the prototype of the father-son relationship.

Clinical and theoretical applications of Freud's interpretation of the myth have been increasingly destructive to both men and women, and they have had the effect of preventing the masculine myth from evolving into a myth of individuation. In the myth of Parsifal, which is much more a myth of individuation than the Oedipus myth, we see the final redemption of the son: the cure of the Fisher King by the fatherless son. This resolution is a culmination of the father-son relationship in the realization that the father and son are one. As the stage of masculine development following separation from the mother, its goal is the atonement of the father-son relationship. In order for the father to help his son master this stage successfully he must himself have completed his own emotional separation from the mother, but he must also have retained an integrated part of the mother in himself. Unless he has done so, the relationship with his son will undoubtedly continue to be contaminated, that is, he will abandon his son once again. In this sense, the abandonment of the son or the killing of the father can be seen as a symbolic abandonment, or killing, of oneself.

Freud would have it that the primal father wants all the women for himself and is therefore in competition with his son; conversely, the son is in competition with the father because he desires the mother and wants her for himself. Freud's interpretation suggests that this is the natural psychological situation between son and father. However, competition is a problem that is created when the father abandons the son. Abandonment follows when the son is a carrier of an important projection of his father: the son wishes to regress to the mother. In that case, it is *not* that the father wants all of the women for himself, he just wants one— his mother. But his wish, born of his own lack of separation, is carried by his son. Competition is a consequence of the abandonment, not a quality intrinsic to the relationship.

At the forefront of the Oedipus myth is the prophecy that the son would grow up to kill the father, which is what caused Laius to drive a pin through Oedipus' foot and instruct the shepherd to abandon him. In other words, it was the father's abandonment

and intended murder of his son that initiated the tragic course of
events we see in the myth.

A Reinterpretation of the Myth

The archetypal core of the Oedipus myth can be used to account
for and describe significant aspects of the father-son relationship
as well as, by extension, the psychology of men. It is helpful to
understand the myth in the historical context of the rise of
patriarchal social and psychological structures in early civilization.
When the patriarchy emerged out of the matrilineal period, which
had been dominant for at least twenty thousand years, the Oedipus myth arose as a cultural expression of a danger inherent in
the split from the Great Mother culture. The myth symbolically
revealed, through the theme of a regression to incest, the danger
of a precipitous split in which the archetypal feminine could be
disassociated. This danger was inevitably as valid for the individual as it was for the culture. The fact that the myth is still with us
is evidence that it remains to be consciously assimilated.

The Oedipus myth is, and has been, a projective fantasy of all
generations of fathers and sons. The "son" Oedipus represents
the *symbolic* son—the father's inner child who has not sufficiently
separated from the mother and who harbors within both the wish
as well as the fear of a regressive return to the all-embracing
maternal womb, that is, to incest. By a "regression to incest" I do
not mean to reduce the wish to only a biological or emotional
need for the mother. It is a *regression* precisely because it
represents a "going back" to recapture something of an internal
psychic nature that is missing—something that the individual as
well as our culture requires in order to move forward. Jung's
view is that incest involves a regression backward to the unconscious, to the anima, to the mother, and eventually to the child
archetype. "The 'mother,' as the first incarnation of the anima
archetype, personifies in fact the whole unconscious."[15] The *senex*
(old man) and the *puer* (eternal son) are aspects of one polarity,

each in need of the other in order that development continue and not remain stuck in the past—in *mater,* the "mom."

Freud treated the competition between father and son for the mother as a "natural" part of their relationship, when it is more likely generated out of the fact that the father himself has not succeeded in separating from his own mother: there are two "sons" competing for mother's attention and affection. Seen this way, competition becomes psychologically more understandable: father and son each feel envy for the other based on their unfulfilled relationship. If our fathers abandon us, what are we to do? We need them to help us effect separation from our mothers. Our fathers tell us not to be "mamma's boys," but yet they are rarely physically or emotionally present to facilitate our new identity as men and whole fathers in our own right. Our fathers' emotional abandonment of us makes a sham of our attempts at separation. For if our fathers have not separated from *their* mothers—particularly if they have not retained a high positive regard for the feminine in themselves—how are we as sons, and also as future fathers, going to acquire a positive masculine identity and also retain a healthy integration of the feminine for ourselves? The psychological manifestation of this abandonment by the father is a man's *Oedipal wound.* The Oedipus complex underestimates the psychological suffering and damage men experience in being abandoned by their fathers. The present phallic-dominated image of masculinity is an immediate conse- quence of this woundedness. We inherit this unconscious image from our fathers, and we carry it into adult life. The image, or self-identity, is at best only "half-man," deprived as it is of the best of what is masculine and at the same time split from our feminine, since she has been relegated to an inferior side of ourselves. The fear of the father, the king, that his son will one day slay him makes sense in that our rage at father for abandoning us makes us want to kill him, both literally and symbolically. But instead we turn our rage against our brothers, against other men, against ourselves, and also against the women we try to love. That is the effect of our Oedipal wound.

The abandonment theme, then, represents the antithesis of increasing awareness between father and son and remains a primary problem; today the father-son relationship, of all kinships, has the least developed level of emotional differentiation. And one of the most profound effects of the Oedipal wound is its contribution to the incest problem.

Reexamining Incest

Without understanding the meaning of incest in its symbolic and unconscious dimensions, as well as its literal enactment, we will not be able to see its deep significance for the psychology of men. Incest has been a powerful and persistent taboo, beginning with the formation of kinship groups and continuing into the present day. It has been virtually universal, and its violation is typically accompanied by tremendous psychological and social consequences. And yet it has remained such a psychological mystery that we can infer it likely represents an archetypal structure deeply imbedded in the history of human relationships. As such, it must have great importance for the history of consciousness and for the health of the developing individual, as well as for the psychological and emotional integrity of the group. It is intriguing that this taboo is not attributed, as far as we know, to the commandments of any god (or goddess); in fact it seems to be prereligious.[16]

Freud explained the origin of the incest taboo as a need to combat the child's secret sexual desire (particularly the son's) for the opposite sexed parent. To support his theory of the Oedipus complex, he offered the idea that exogamy arose because the primitive family was a patriarchy dominated by a father who was, in effect, a jealous brute. In *Totem and Taboo* he postulated that the original social group was a primeval horde headed by a patriarchal and jealous father. According to this speculation, the father had access to all the females of the group, and as his sons matured sexually they were forced out of the group. The expelled brothers joined forces and slew and ate the father, thus putting an end to the father horde. As a result of their guilt for killing the father they developed a taboo related to the killing of a totem animal that symbolized the father.[17] According to Freud, the dynamic underlying the taboo is similar to the dynamic of the neurotic individual with a compulsion. The compulsion is based on a wish that has become repressed through fear of some grave consequence, thus creating neurotic ambivalence. Freud makes the comparison that compulsions, like taboos, lack a motivation and are hence enigmatic, although cultural prohibitions are imposed from without by the elders of the group or clan. For Freud, the fundamental dichotomy responsible for the incest taboo is the ambivalence of love and hate toward the father:

> I want to state the conclusion that the beginnings of religion, ethics, society, and art meet in the Oedipus complex. . . . [And] the nucleus of all neuroses as far as our present knowledge of them goes is in the Oedipus complex. It comes as a great surprise to me that these problems of racial psychology can also be solved through a single concrete instance, such as the relation to the father. We have so frequently had occasion to show the ambivalence of emotions in its real sense, that is to say the coincidence of love and hate toward the same object, at the root of important cultural formulations. We know nothing about the origins of this ambivalence. It may be assumed to be a fundamental phenomenon of our emotional life. But the other possibility seems to me also worthy of consideration: that ambivalence originally foreign to our emotional life, was acquired by mankind *through the father complex,* where psychoanalytic investigation of the individual today still reveals the strongest expression of it [italics added].[18]

Freud further conjectured that because of competition between the brothers, a second taboo was established that prohibited mating within the group. For Freud, all of this explained both exogamy and the incest taboo. There is, however, no evidence that the primitive family was patriarchal; in fact, there is fairly conclusive evidence that it was matrilineal. Freud's line of reasoning was more likely a product of his own unconscious projection. Important to note is the differentiation between the incest taboo and the Oedipus complex, for the taboo has been validated as a universal theme and the Oedipus complex has not.

No one has ever discovered either the origin of the incest taboo or the reasons for it. Although Jung did not discuss incest with particular reference to men, his works contain a more cogent theoretical discussion of it than that generated by Freud. Like Freud, Jung also conceived of incest as innate in the individual. But unlike Freud he was most concerned with the theoretical nature and symbolic aspects of incest, not the clinical problems. He saw incest as an archetypal structure portraying the push toward union—not literal physical union, but *heirosgamos,* or spiritual union. By resisting the impulse to concretize the incest wish, the *libidinal* (psychic) energy is pushed from the instinctual toward the spiritual pole. This is why incest enactment, and even psychological incest, is so devastating: the perpetrator and the victim both remain stuck in the purely unconscious instinctual pole, unable to actualize the spiritual component of union in relationship. Jung defines the endogenous instinct itself as a natural urge and therefore not pathological. Robert Stein continues this idea in his book *Incest and Human Love:*

> The function of incest prohibition is to stimulate the sexual imagination and to bring instincts into the service of love, kinship and creativity. This means that essential to the psychological health and maturation of the child is that it experiences an erotic flow and connection to parents and siblings without fear, guilt or violation.[19]

Resisting the incest impulse is a highly conscious act which allows a man to become more aware of his mother, sister, or child as *other*—as someone with unique attributes, values, and needs rather than as an extension of himself. It also allows an eventual relationship to the anima as an inner reality and as a bridge to his spiritual life.

The differences between Freud and Jung regarding their views of incest were never resolved. Jung accused Freud of being too literal, and Freud accused Jung of being too symbolic, too mystical. Present-day psychologists are left with the legacy of their conflict.

Whether the "theoretical" aspect of Freud's seduction theory was true, whether it in fact was an honest report of his early clinical experience, and what his reasons were for changing it may never be known for certain. Freud's error was not in his original assumptions about the etiology of neuroses as residing in sexual trauma, but only in the extent to which he attempted to apply those assumptions. What we must now account for, nearly one hundred years after Freud, and what we must perhaps rely on as an indirect measure of the "truth" the seduction theory alluded to, are the steadily increasing reports of the sexual abuse of children.[20]

The National Study on Child Neglect and Abuse Reporting has collected data on the sexual abuse of children since the mid-1970s. Their first report, published in 1976, documented 6,000 cases nationally in which sexual abuse of minor children was confirmed. The 1986 reports confirmed 132,000 cases of sexual abuse of children—more than twenty times the number of cases confirmed ten years earlier. What's more, the majority (sixty-five percent) of perpetrators of sexual abuse in those cases were members of the child's family.[21]

Incidents involving fathers and daughters is to date by far the most common form of incest, accounting for as high as seventy-eight percent of the total reported cases, according to some sources. And incidents of brother-sister incest in families where there is father-daughter incest are also high.

The increase in the number of confirmed cases does not necessarily reflect an increase in the number of incidents; it is more likely an indication that more incidents are now being reported, due to increased public awareness as well as mandatory reporting laws affecting health care workers, teachers, and, most recently, clergy. Yet, one can safely assume that sexual abuse is still much more widespread than it is currently reported to be.[22]

Incest in Oedipus and in Life

I believe that if Freud had maintained his belief in the original seduction theory without applying it to the neuroses so globally, he would have been at a later point forced to look more closely and differently at the role of the father in incest. This may have led to a deeper examination of the function of incest not only in the family structure but with respect to its role in the evolution of human consciousness. It seems that a signal problem for Freud was his fear of being found wrong and of having his psychoanalysis collapse on that account. Perhaps this was an effect of his own Oedipal wound.

In *The Interpretation of Dreams* Freud clearly uses the Oedipus myth as a means of explaining the child's wish to sexually possess one parent, as well as the wish to replace, or do away with, the other parent. For Freud these wishes became the literal, natural counterpart of childhood instinctuality. This development in his thinking (or his change of position) was unfortunate for the psychology of men for several reasons.

For one, he defined the concept of incest as a primary sexual-biological urge of the boy for his mother. This is an overliteralization of the boy's desire for mother as a *sexual* wish rather than as a symbolic regressive longing for what she represents.

Second, the fact is that the motif of incest goes back at least as far as the earliest forms of human socialization and even, to a lesser degree, to the behavior of certain non-human primates. The taboo regarding it is generally universal. One does not have to account for incest with explanations related to "wishes" to possess one's parents sexually, as there is a natural abhorrence of actually committing incest, even while there is a fascination, which is sometimes even compulsive, with the symbolic aspects of it.

Clinicians have found incestuous relations in the family to be the most psychologically devastating for the victim. If Freud was right, and the child had an innate sexual desire for the parent, it wouldn't make sense that the enactment of incest would be so psychologically damaging for the child. If the incestuous "instinct" or "wish" was natural, it would mean that the child was instinctually masochistic, if not overtly self-destructive. In my experience as an analyst, imagery of incestuous sexual relations occurs only in those children who clearly have psychologically if not overtly incestuous parents. It is obvious in these cases that this imagery represents not the child's own innate desire but the child's unconscious perception of the parent's wish. A further clinical issue here is that a victim of incest incurs additional emotional damage if the analyst believes that it is the child's wish for the parent that leads to incest.

Furthermore, incest is a symbolic psychological foundation of the individuation process and an integral part of it: it represents the natural endogenous function of kinship libido. That is, it is the energy that forms bonds within the family group, helping to produce an identity within the family as well as to define the family as a unit from without. At the same time, when unimpeded by family members' literal or psychological neurotic incestuous fixations, this endogenous tendency is counterbalanced by an equal exogenous tendency to move away from the family in the natural processes of psychological differentiation. But Freud's perspective *sexualized* incest and separated it from the individuation process, in which it plays a critical developmental role. Freud reduced a man's wish for his mother to a sexual desire rooted in a primitive instinct. He did not acknowledge the relationship of this wish to his early attachment to her or to his later need to achieve separation from her—while retaining some aspects of the feminine. That he interpreted the primal father as a man who wanted to keep all of the women for himself can be seen as a common projection of a man who has not mastered separation from the mother. Freud's formulation followed on his particular definition of libido, or psychic energy, which for him was primarily of a psychosexual nature.

As we have seen, another problem created by Freud's position is that he seems to have forced himself (and others after him) to account for the universality of the incest taboo on the basis of the Oedipus complex, that is, as the *child's* sexual wish for the parent of the opposite sex. For this he devised the notion of an original *primal horde* and *patriarchal father,* which anthropological evidence tells us is simply incorrect.

Freud's notion of *castration anxiety* was derived from a peculiar formulation of the Oedipus complex, which states that a son fears his father's retaliation against him for his wish to have his mother for himself. For Freud, circumcision, subincision, and initiation rites of pubertal boys were expressions of symbolic threats of castration, rather than symbolic ways to incorporate an important ingredient of the feminine and to initiate separation from the mother. Having disowned the feminine in himself, Freud overmasculinized the dynamic of the Oedipus myth. His suggested resolution places a boy in the position of having to repudiate the mother and, as a consequence, a significant part of his own inner feminine.

It is this last point, the repudiation of the feminine, that has been so problematic for many men, since the splitting from the anima causes them to develop a counterphobic stance about their emotional dependency, as well as an exaggerated and overly heroic relation to the world. The lack of separation from the mother coupled with abandonment by the father, as well as the splitting from the anima, lies at the base of the incest complex. A man in this untenable psychological position is unable to form a stable relationship with a woman; at the same time he cannot succeed in forming an identity with the protective father who understands and reinforces the importance of boundaries. Since he cannot adapt himself successfully to being either husband or father, he turns to the anima as daughter or child and attempts to incorporate her in a literal and physical way, which leads to overt or psychological incest.

Summary

Psychology as we know it today has grown immensely since the era in which Freud first formulated his ideas, and yet many of his early ideas about the sexual origins of disturbed behavior retain their hold within psychoanalytic thinking. Most disturbing is the lack of emphasis on the critical importance of the father-son relationship. In particular, we need to rethink the Oedipal drama in terms of newly acquired information and experience from men's lives and attempt to find a more appropriate myth for the father-son relationship. The psychological and spiritual development of men requires that we address the incest problem in its sexual, psychological, and spiritual manifestations by looking more deeply at both the symbolic *and* the literal meanings of incest, which means going beyond Freud's narrow, and I believe incorrect, view of incest. The inextricably related problem of abandonment by our fathers and the need to heal the resulting Oedipal wound has lain fallow in the recesses of our psyches. If men are to move forward on the journey of individuation, the issues of abandonment by their fathers, the Oedipal wound, and the problem of symbolic as well as literal incest must be addressed.

Unlike the myth of Parsifal, the myth of Oedipus is a story of the downfall of both the father and son, rather than their redemption. By slaying his father and actually marrying his mother, Oedipus ultimately returns to an unconscious incestuous relationship with her. He takes his father's place by killing him and, in doing so, does not redeem his own masculinity or his fatherhood. Rather than being the confirmation that Freud would have had it be—that is, of the universality of the wish on the child's part for incest with the mother—the myth is rather a confirmation of the importance of the need for the son's differentiation from his mother and his deep emotional need for his father. The tragedy is not that Oedipus killed his father and married his mother, but rather that the father projected his own incestuous wish on his son and, thus, abandoned him. Sons today, even as fathers themselves, remain deeply wounded by this. This can only be corrected by healing the father-son relationship. We now turn to look even more closely at this relationship.

□ 5 □

Sons and Their Fathers

The fathers have eaten a sour grape, and the children's teeth are
set on edge.   —JEREMIAH 31:29

The Rise of Kingship and Male Deities

THE BEGINNING OF PATRIARCHAL CULTURE was marked by the rise
of male deities and sacral kings, who eventually came to replace
the goddesses of the mother cults. These male gods were an
expression of the emergence of the father principle, which had
been underdeveloped in the earlier periods of both biological
and cultural evolution. The father, who had played the role of
impregnator and hunter on the periphery of the family, began to
emerge from his subordination to the mother-principle. His place
became increasingly removed from the earth, as he made his
domain in the mythological realm of the sky and the heavens.

On the psychological level, the father—as patriarch, king, and
then god—remained on the "outside" looking in, ruling the
family but removed from its interior. For over twenty thousand
years he had been excluded from the family by ignorance of the
role he played in procreation, by exogamy, by his emotional need
to differentiate himself from the mother, and by being increasingly valued primarily for what he could hunt or otherwise
produce from outside of himself. This early history of the mascu-

line set the stage for what was to become an extremely patrilinear system of kingship, eventually characterized by a preeminence of outer-directed social, economic, and spiritual values. As a secular, as well as sacral, power, the king took it upon himself to bring his own order to the cosmos through the development of his spirit and Logos. He also attempted to embody the fertility of the mother through new masculine celebrations and rituals of annual renewal. The goddesses became gods, and the fathers became the new rulers of the heavens *and* of the earth.

Up until the emergence of Greek civilization, society was largely endogenous: it fostered a sedentary, agricultural way of life in which religion was largely a worship of the mother and her earth. During this time the oppression of the masculine was not an issue, since the mother culture was not a *reaction* to the masculine principle; at the same time it is not difficult to imagine that the mother culture was not as egalitarian as some would have us believe. But when society and the family came to be dominated by the patriarchy there was a shift to exogenous tendencies in the extreme. What then erupted as the patriarchy was an *enantio-dromia*—a flipping into the opposite—with splitting from the feminine as the chief characteristic.

In the new culture, with its increasing awareness of the role of the father in procreation, the family was eventually ruled by the father principle. The mother, once the revered Great Goddess of Fertility, in time became "just" a mother, who only bore the children, cooked for the family, remained in the home, and basically stayed out of the newly emerging technological world.

The patriarchy was not necessarily a reaction *against* matriar-chy; it was more likely the consequence of naturally emerging factors inherent in the evolution of males. The patriarchal age has been a surprisingly short period compared to the matriarchal dominance lasting at least from some time during the last Ice Age up to the civilization of Crete. It was this emerging patriarchy that gave rise to images of the archetypal father in the culture of the West.

The Archetypal Father

In the same way that the archetypal mother exists in the psyches of men, so too does the archetypal father. As a result of the deep influence of the archetypal father, the personal father—like the personal mother—is seen as being much more than himself. The archetypal mother, as we have seen, is the symbolic representation of fertility, procreation, nurturance, and the endless cycle of life and death, birth and rebirth. The archetypal father "embodies reason, knowledge, inventiveness, and the power to mediate between the family and the world outside. . . . [He] is the initiator of change and diversity. On the conservative side, the lawgiver and the disciplinarian; on the progressive side, he is the master of initiation and the embodiment of the hero myth."[1] But some theorists have held that the father image is more determined than the mother image by the particular culture in which it occurs, so that it is more subject to change that reflects that culture.[2]

Like the mother, the father archetype has two aspects: the Good Father and the Negative Father. Unfortunately, we hear more of the negative father than of the positive father, in both life experience and in mythology. Greek mythology has characterized the archetypal father in a series of images ranging from the extremely negative one of Ouranos to the more positive one, Zeus.

Ouranos, the Sky Father, is the *devouring father* who forces his children to return to the mother's womb. This imprisonment of the son in the mother has the effect of destroying the son's potential for consciousness, since entrapment in the mother is naturally an unconscious or preconscious state. As a "stage" of consciousness, Ouranos himself represents perhaps the most undeveloped level—a disembodied masculinity split from the feminine. His realm and domain is unlimited sky, far removed from earth and the mother.

A son caught in the devouring father archetype stands little chance of being his own person in the outer world, as he is dominated by his father's values, ideas, and feelings. In this sense, his consciousness remains unborn: "Ouranos, in psychological

experience, 'results in conventionality through gross unconsciousness,' which means that 'this is the way it's always been
done.' "[3]

A son who is thus abandoned by his father remains a "mother's
son" until he embarks on a hero's journey to free himself of his
father's (and mother's) negative power and influence. In the
hero's journey the man must eventually abandon his search for
father's approval and seek an experience of self that transcends
the personal father-son relationship.

Kronos, the first son of Ouranos, who was able to escape with
the help of Rhea and castrate his father, is also a devouring father.
Under this less severe form of the negative father:

> Consciousness, if finely tuned to the prevailing values
> and attitudes of the outer collective, be it secular society
> at large, a church group, a political party, or whatnot,
> . . . seeks to twist all interests, passions, and spontaneous
> ideas to the service of conscious goals. . . . Everything
> goes to build the ego; the children of the unconscious
> are meant to support an edgy and insecure ego.[4]

Zeus, who is a bit of a devouring father, at least bears his
children and generally takes care of them. He is the father of
Athene, goddess of wisdom. Through him, the lineage of Sky
Fathers moves to greater development of conscious will:

> Zeus, too, betrays traces of the devouring father, . . .
> [but] Zeus bears many children whom he does not
> devour. Generally he is fond of his children and takes
> care to look after them. . . .
>
> If the strategy of Ouranos is locking the children in
> materia and away from spirit and that of Kronos is
> swallowing them in spirit and cutting them off from
> instinct, the strategy of Zeus is incorporating the anima
> in spirit and thereby depriving her of fertility, of the
> capacity for becoming pregnant with revolutionary chil-
> dren. Because he has integrated the anima in this way,
> Zeus can afford to tolerate his other children. . . . Athene

restrains impulsive aggressiveness, encourages reflection and strategic thinking. . . . Athene is her father's daughter, the eternal virgin, the anima of spirit, life turning toward reflection.[5]

Joseph Henderson indicates that these archetypal father myths "may be used to illustrate the stages of ego development from its emergence toward the end of the period of mother-child dependency to its culmination at the crisis of late adolescence when the young person approaches the threshold of maturity."[6] These stages of ego-consciousness lead the individual to the journey of the hero, often beginning in adolescence as the struggle to psychologically free himself from the archetypal parent images. If the individual is successful in that journey there may be an encounter with the archetype of the old wise man, who is the symbolic prefiguration of the self, the individual's deepest spiritual nature.

These images of the archetypal father help to explain why in such a powerfully exogenous society as the patriarchy there are still such strong endogenous tendencies, particulary toward incest. The "inner work" of men may lag far behind their intellectual and professional achievements. The mythology of Zeus presents the possibility of the emergence of self-reflective consciousness, of giving birth to the capacity for "restraining impulsive aggressiveness, for reflection, and for strategic thinking." This is the emergence of Athene, the *anima of spirit.*

As we saw in the last chapter, the Oedipus myth as promulgated by Freud has left some important questions about the father-son relationship unanswered. The myth itself, which arose at the time the patriarchy was emerging from the matrilineal period, portrays the patriarch as a symbolic negative father who abandons his son. The critical issue of a man's abandonment by his father—an issue neglected to a large degree even by psychoanalysts—is central to an understanding of the father-son relationship. The effect of this abandonment has been to deprive the son of both the idealized image of the father as well a a powerful emotional attachment to him.

Since Freud, psychoanalysts have maintained that a successful resolution of the son's wish for his mother will occur when he is able to form an appropriate identification with his father. And indeed, we *are* in need of separating from our mother. But in the process of attempting that separation, where is our father's help? Supposedly, according to Freud, the son's turning away from the mother is accomplished by the threat of castration by the boy's father. If this is true, what sort of father-son bond does that awareness enhance? The formulation, based on Freud's interpretation of the Oedipus myth, that the father abandons his son to prevent his own murder and to prevent his son from taking his wife also seems remarkable in view of the fact that the son in the myth is still an infant. What of tenderness and love between father and son?

How does the Oedipus myth actually characterize the father-son relationship? What we can learn from the myth in this regard is not so much that the hostility and competition between father and son is a natural condition, but that this unfortunate affliction is a consequence of the father's failure to form an adequate emotional attachment to his son and to provide him with masculine nurturance—the positive endogenous component. That is, the affliction arises out of the father's physical and/or emotional abandonment of the son and father's resultant unconscious fear of his son's retaliation. This retaliation is projected upon the son because the father himself is the holder of rage toward *his own father* for his abandonment. In this way the Oedipus myth represents the tragedy of a repetitive cycle of abandonment-rage-abandonment of sons by their fathers.

One example of a negative father constellation can be seen in Sam, who, when he came to me for analysis, was living out the self-defeating pattern of a son attempting to establish an emotional relationship with his father by trying to please him. He was on the verge of alcoholism and a divorce, and he was deeply confused as to exactly what was wrong in his life. In an outer sense he was quite successful: he was very well educated and respected in his profession. On the other hand, he was depressed and he felt emotionally unfulfilled in his relationship with his wife and distant from his children. In general, he was highly dissatisfied with his life. Sam was a man who always did what he was "supposed" to do. As an adolescent he never rebelled but was cooperative and always eager to please. He modeled himself so completely after his father that his choice of college, his profession, and even the company he worked for, were his father's. Unfortunately, this profession was not the one best suited to his psychological temperament. Also like his father, he was becoming an alcoholic. His childhood was typified by constant and exaggerated attempts to win his father's approval. When his father suggested he get a paper route, he got three of them. He did all the things a boy could do to win a father's love, but he never felt he had achieved that goal. His mother, also an alcoholic, was never particularly invested in his career, but always "just there."

Most of Sam's relationships with other men were characterized by an attitude of submission and fear. Even though he appeared to be self-confident, he was constantly vigilant about measuring up in other men's eyes, and often he would adopt mentors in his field, hoping to gain their approval and respect. Somehow this never seemed to work for him; he was continually left disappointed and depressed. He then turned to alcohol to blunt the pain.

In a sense Sam's father was more of an archetype than a human being. He was so emotionally disconnected that he was unaware that Sam was even trying to please him. One outstanding characteristic of Sam's father was that he always had to be right, no matter how small the point and regardless of the content of the discussion. This characteristic, practically of itself, is enough to diagnose Sam's father as embodying the archetypal *senex* father.

The Personal Father

A boy's personal father takes his place beside the mother as the second pillar of the boy's psychological and emotional world. His influence, while profound, only fully begins when the son is emerging as an independent ego, around the age of three years. Prior to this, as we have seen, the boy is largely contained within the maternal world matrix: his primary identification is aligned with the mother. As he begins to experience himself as different from mother, his need for an identification with a person more like himself takes on greater meaning and importance. He seeks this identity and new emotional relationship from his father.

In a sense, the father is first introduced to the son by the mother: her conscious and unconscious attitudes toward her husband as well as to her own father shape the image of father before the actual father can shape himself to his son. The mother's love and respect, resentments and hostility, or ambivalence are all conveyed to the son. Whatever strong emotions her husband, or even the image of her husband, conjures up for her are transmitted consciously or unconsciously to him.[7]

Of course, the son's experience of his father also depends on how active a role the father plays in family life, and specifically how he regards himself in relation to his son. For example, he might allow himself more direct expression of positive feelings for his daughter, and he might allow himself to express angry feelings more openly toward his son. Fathers sometimes rationalize this bias by saying that the son doesn't need as much tenderness as the daughter, and/or that the son is more capable of handling anger and is less likely to be hurt by it. A further and even less tenable rationale is that the son "needs" to be treated that way because he has to learn "how the world is out there."

However, as the son relinquishes his rather exclusive relationship to the mother and turns to his father, he extends his emotional needs from the maternal/feminine pole to the paternal/masculine pole. At this point, the quality of the relationship with his father is a strong determinant of the son's emerging experience of himself as a male and of his capacities to relate to more people than his mother with emotional depth. As we have seen in the Oedipus myth, if the father fails to form an appropriate emotional attachment to his son, the result is hostility and competition between the two, which may have the effect of destroying the relationship as a partnership. When this happens the son later in life, as the hero, must seek to redeem his father as a part of himself. We will return to this in the last chapter.

While the mother may be said to facilitate the infant's relationship with the inner world, the relationship with the father facilitates the son's introduction to the outer world. The degree to which the father has developed his own exogenous (world-directed) versus endogenous (family-directed) roles, and the importance of the qualities and meanings he attaches to his sense of masculinity, will exert a lasting impression on his relationship to his son. This orientation of father is crucial to his son's experience of father-attachment versus father-abandonment.

The boy's grandfather provides another critical influence on the father-son relationship, as the grandfather's experience with his own son—now the father—is transmitted through him. In other words, the father-son relationship is to some degree already partially determined by the quality of the *previous* father-son relationship, as well as by the quality of his mother's relationship with the maternal grandfather. The father who was not emotionally nurtured by his own father is, paradoxically, unlikely to be more nurturant to his son. Oftentimes, the analyst can trace the pattern of father-son relationships back several generations.

The son has a natural craving for attention, love, and nurturance from his father. If these natural feelings are accepted by his father, the bonding between them can be established in a healthy and mutually satisfying way. If, on the other hand, these feelings become contaminated and rejected because of a previous pattern of father-son relationship or for other reasons, the son will experience them with shame and humiliation and even come to believe that having these feelings is a sign of abnormality, particularly if, in later life, they arise in relationships with other men.

In effect, men learn to relate to other men on the basis of the quality and style of their relationships with their fathers.

One sees this manifest as early as adolescence. For example, a fourteen-year-old patient of mine was relating a particularly painful experience that occurred with another boy at school, and I asked him if he had told the other boy how this incident made him feel. Looking at me incredulously, he said, "No! I didn't want him to think I'm a wuus [sissy]." Clearly, this attitude was going to powerfully determine his future relationships with other men. Another older male patient in my men's group once related how a group of men from work had spent a three-day golf retreat together and, at the end of the trip, he was amazed to realize that nothing of any emotional or personal nature had been discussed among them. By contrast, one can easily imagine that a group of women on a similar outing for three days would end up knowing each other's life history!

The following clinical profiles illustrate some of the ways the son experiences his father as abandoning him. These cases are combinations of actual clinical experiences and what is known from available psychological research.

The Authoritarian Father

Clifford, forty-eight years old, is a highly successful corporate attorney. His father was also a very successful attorney; in many ways Clifford seems to be carrying on the tradition of his family name. He is a father who despises any sign of "weakness" in his son, which he defines specifically as a lack of rationality. He sees himself as needing to be in complete control of the family at all times, as though it were incapable of functioning without his guidance. He perceives it as his duty to provide the financial support and intellectual control of family life, but not to provide for the emotional needs of his children, and sometimes not even of his wife. Clifford sees his wife as being the provider of all of the family's emotional needs; he considers this to be the duty of the mother.

Clifford inculcates high standards of performance in his son, demanding competence in school more than in athletics or physical prowess. These expectations are often projections of his own high standards rather than what might be reasonable expectations of his son.

The authoritarian father perceives himself as the ultimate authority in the family and prides himself in having a high degree of rationality and intellectual control. He is often deeply split from his own feminine nature, to the point that he despises emotional displays, passivity, and intellectual "incompetence." His relationship to his son is characterized by intellectuality and disguised competitiveness. He wants his son to be just like him, and he is willing to sacrifice his son's individuality to attain that goal.

The Passive Father

Harvey is a passive father—almost the polar opposite of Clifford. He makes few, if any, demands upon his son, and he often appears to be uninterested in family life; instead his interests lie outside the family. He perceives the family as being there to provide for him, almost as if he was the son rather than the father.

Harvey is not very successful in his career or profession, since he always does the minimum of what is expected of him. He is often moody, irritable, and depressed, and he is rarely capable of mobilizing much emotional energy for himself. Harvey perceives the world as being a basically hostile, dreary, cold, and emotionally unresponsive place. He sees his lack of success and happiness as being due to "bad luck." He treats his partner more like a mother than a wife, expecting her to not burden him with many demands but wanting her to take care of his needs. His wife, more successful than he is in the world, complains of his lack of productivity, though she is resigned to his way of being. Harvey's mother was also depressed, passive, and unable to extend herself to more than meeting her family's most basic needs. His father abandoned the family when Harvey was quite young; Harvey's lack of any positive father identification is obvious.

The passive father is caught in a passive-dependent pattern. He is prone to alcohol and/or drug abuse, and may sometimes be prone to developing physical symptoms, if not overt diseases. His son, over time, may become similarly embittered toward life, or he may resent his father's passivity so much that he compensates by trying to provide a better life for himself. However, it is often very difficult to shake the passive father's basic cynicism.

The Macho Father

Joe is a machinist who was born and raised in a poor section of New York City. Although he does not physically abuse his wife and even considers it to be "unmanly" to do so, he is emotionally abusive toward her, disparaging her attempts to better herself by enrolling in classes at the junior college when their son entered high school. Joe prides himself in his streetwise knowledge of the world and delights in pointing out to his wife that she will never be as smart as he is.

Joe is virtually a coach to his son, constantly trying to make a "man" of him so that he won't be a "sissy" or wimp. He taught his son how to fight when he was eight years old and how to shoot a gun when he was fifteen. Joe has always taught him to take "disrespect from nobody." He is an atheist, and he hates homosexuals and religious "freaks." He takes pride in his job, never takes time off from work because of illness, and doesn't respect others who don't do a good job.

Joe's father was an alcoholic who physically abused both him and his mother. Although he often tried to protect his mother from his father by fighting with him, Joe deeply resented her for staying with him for so many years. When his father was finally committed to a mental institution because of brain damage secondary to alcoholism, Joe quit school and worked to support his mother and sister.

Joe's exaggerated masculinity results from several generations of psychologically undeveloped fathers, all of whom are split from the inner feminine. They attempt to pass on to their sons what they believe is the correct image of a man, but this image conceals their vulnerability toward women and ensures that there will be no emotional "weakness" in the son. Their mothers are often emotionally passive women who, in their childhood, deferred to domineering fathers. Men like Joe have deep unfulfilled emotional attachments to their mothers. The impossibility of ever having their needs met causes ambivalence and even hatred of women because their needs are so strong. Anything approaching softness or tenderness is anxiety-provoking, too reminiscent of their emotional dependence on mother to be permitted in their conscious view of themselves. The resultant stereotypical pseudomasculinity is therefore perpetually passed from father to son.

The Persona Father

Malcolm is a pillar of the community—very active in his church and a highly successful businessman. In high school and college he was both an honors student and a star athlete. By the time he was forty he was a millionaire. His greatest sources of pride are his financial success, his business reputation, his generosity to his church, and the integrity of his family. He has a beautiful, intelligent wife and two lovely children. From the outside, Malcolm appears to have all the rewards life could offer. But somehow he can never rest with his success; he is always trying to achieve more, build more, accomplish more. He seems compulsively directed to achieve even more than he could ever use.

In contrast to his father, Malcolm's son, Gary, is physically awkward, unmotivated, and prone to bouts of depression and self-deprecation. Although he doesn't berate him openly, Malcolm seems ashamed of the fact that Gary is incompetent in so many ways. Unable to match any of his father's expectations, Gary just seems to have given up trying.

Few are aware that Malcolm's father abused him physically. His father was also a very successful and respected businessman, but when his business started to fail and he became ill, he committed suicide. Malcolm's mother was seen as an "angel" who had given up her own career to meet the needs of her family. She was passive and helpless, a "darling mother" who could neither protest against her husband nor protect her son. As a result, Malcolm expected his wife to be like his mother—a "darling" with no life of her own. When she began to show interest in having a career, Malcolm became moody and threatened. When his wife began to develop her own interests, his own business started to decline.

The son of the persona father often tries to compensate for his father's compulsiveness and ambition. In this case the son unconsciously agrees to carry his father's shadow. The last time I saw Malcolm he said to me, "If you really knew who I was on the inside, I don't think you would like me." The next day he committed suicide.

The Incestuous Father

Bob was referred for treatment by the court because he had molested his pubertal daughter. An electronics technician who has been married three times, he considers himself an atheist with no spiritual orientation to life. Alcohol and sometimes drugs have been a problem throughout most of his adult life. He has always been rather socially isolated, with no close relationships with other men. His interests are confined to electronics, sports, and handguns. He tends to be rigid in his thinking, rather suspicious of others, and resentful of authority. His attitude toward women is licentious, with thinly disguised hostility and disrespect. He shows little ability to reflect on his own behavior, tending to blame others when things go wrong. While he is quite dependent on his wife and expects her to be there to take care of him, he denies her importance to him. His son, who is married with two children, belongs to a fundamentalist religion and is chronically depressed, though he doesn't show much of his depression to the outside world.

Bob's father was a cool, reserved, but authoritarian man who spent little time or energy on his son. He was also isolated, withdrawn, and depressed. His only encouragement to Bob was that he should do something that would "make a buck." His own attitude toward women was also hostile and demeaning. He tacitly conveyed to Bob to "do as I say, not as I do." Bob's mother tended to be passive, dependent, and mildly sympathetic, but ineffectual in regard to her son's complaints about his father.

The son of an incestuous father may flee to a religion in order to unconsciously create a defense against his father; religion or some other form of spiritual involvement may also be an attempt to find a positive relationship to a more abstract "father." There is an inherent need for the son to escape from the overly endogenous attitudes of the incestuous father, who may suffocate his children's psychological growth. If the son cannot escape this influence of the father early enough, he may manifest the same attitude in his relations with women—even with his own sisters. If the son does not become conscious of these attitudes before he marries, he may repeat the incest pattern with his own daughter.

The Sociopathic Father

Franco, formerly a highly successful executive in a large broker-age company, was referred for treatment by his attorney after being charged with embezzling a large sum of money from his firm. It is clear that his interest in treatment is to provide positive testimony for his defense; he wants a psychological evaluation to determine that he was not aware of the seriousness of his crime, which he claims to have done because of pressure to provide more for his family. He seems almost angry that he has been caught, even though he clearly understands the inappropriateness of his behavior.

With his own son, Franco was highly moralistic; he would burst into rage if his son doubted the sincerity or purpose of his father's "advice" or rules. He seemed incapable of expressing any feelings of warmth, compassion, or empathy for his son. Instead he would tell him, "That's the way the world is; if you don't get your piece of the pie, if you don't grab the brass ring, you can go thank yourself." His lack of conscience and compassion, combined with his opportunistic nature, turned his son against him irreversibly. At sixteen he ran away to become a "street person" and eventually a homosexual prostitute in San Francisco. At the age of twenty he was found in a cheap hotel room, dead of a drug overdose.

The son of a psychopathic father may not be able to influence the personal father. His lifestyle may reflect the unconscious masochism of a son who is desperately in need of affection and approval from his father.

The Absent Father

Michael's natural father died before he was three years old. All Michael ever knew of him was that he was a "good man," he provided well for the family when he was alive, and he would have wanted to have a good relationship with his son. Unfortunately, there were no other men to whom Michael could turn. His mother had a series of boyfriends but he had little to do with any of them. Michael, now ten, was brought for treatment because of increasingly poor performance in school and because he seemed to have difficulty forming friendships. In play therapy he is prone to contruct fantasy images of an all-powerful, all-good, loving, Superman type of person who always manages to escape the many perils that surround him. Even when this figure is "killed," he always manages to come back to life. At the beginning of treatment his mother thought this fantasy was unrealistic. Because she viewed it as a denial of his father's death, she wanted Michael to stop repeating it. With time she has been able to accept that this image is not of Michael's personal father, but of the archetypal good father, an image that had not "died" just because his father had died. She has also been able to see that this image is extremely important in helping Michael maintain an image of father that, however idealized, might promote the emergence of his own manhood.

The image of father in a boy's psyche is critical to his identity and developing sense of masculine self. It is usually the actual father that confirms or denies the qualities of this image. If the actual father does not measure up to an idealized image, the son attempts to adjust it to conform to the reality he is faced with. If the father's presence is negative compared to the idealized image, the son experiences this as both a betrayal and a lack or deficiency within himself. The father image then may begin to take on the characteristics of the archetypal negative father. If the personal father is not present, the *image* of father is even more essential to the boy's development.

Research on the Father-Son Relationship

We saw in the preceding portrayal of the different types of father-son relationships that there are whole generations of fathers who, as sons, sacrificed their individuality in order to please their fathers. These types of fathers, whatever their degree of involvement, tend to abandon their sons emotionally. These patterns perpetuate both the emotional alienation of men as well as the split from their internal feminine.

The evidence for poor emotional relationships between fathers and sons in the United States is staggering. Virtually every study reveals that the emotional quality of such relationships is poor, with fathers largely absent from their sons' lives, even if they are physically present in the home. The time that most fathers spend with their sons daily can be measured in seconds.

For example, researcher and author Shere Hite surveyed 7,239 men and found that "almost no men said they had been or were close to their fathers."[8] Another psychologist, Jack Sternbach, examined the father-son relationship in 71 of his clients and found that twenty-three percent had fathers who were physically absent; about twenty-nine percent had psychologically absent fathers who were too busy with work, uninterested in their sons, or passive at home; eighteen percent had psychologically absent fathers who were austere, moralistic, and emotionally uninvolved; and fifteen percent had fathers who were dangerous, frightening, and seemingly out of control. Only fifteen percent of the men in Sternbach's study had experienced "appropriate" interaction with their fathers.

This rather categorical lack of positive emotional involvement of fathers with sons in our culture is the major contributory factor to the sons' experience of the Oedipal wound.

The Wounded Inner Son

The father, although often disregarded by developmental theorists, is a particularly powerful influence in the development of the son's inner child. He is particularly important in contributing to the complexity and novelty of his son's early environment, through play and so forth.[9] So often the primary orientation of fathers is to the outer world, with its emphasis on productivity, success, and the meeting of professional and financial goals. Because of this they need to develop reasonable expectations of themselves in terms of balancing their success and accomplishments against the needs of their sons for recreation, family life, and more spiritually oriented values. In this respect, the father's demands and expectations of himself are also conditioners of his son's inner child: if they are inflated, unrealistic, and unbalanced, this carries over to the son. For the son, childhood itself ought to be a balance of positive self-regard and demands for performance from the father. When reasonable expectations are coupled with reinforcement of the son's limitations (based on the father's knowledge of them), the adult son's inner child will have similar expectations of himself. How realistic the demands are that a man places upon himself and how rigidly he feels he must adhere to them are often a direct function of his relationship to his father, which continues to operate in him unconsciously.

A man's inner son is often seen in dreams, fantasies, and memories of the past, particularly of childhood. Since the inner child is also part of a father's personal unconscious, he may project qualities of his own inner child onto his son (or daughter). The inner child also affects his relationships to his partner and other adults.

The inner child may be healthy or wounded, or somewhere in between. If the child is healthy we see the spontaneity and positive regressiveness characteristic of someone who is able to play freely, comfortably, and without self-consciousness. The healthy inner child is curious and inquisitive, with some awareness of the basic mystery of life. He allows a man to feel competent in work, giving him a sense of comfortable self-assurance rather than compulsiveness, as well as a sense of humor. The qualities of a healthy inner child lead to enhanced creativity, which allows a full exploration of a man's potentialities and a feeling of inherent goodness.

When the inner child suffers from the Oedipal wound, it is hard for a man to face himself in an emotionally honest way. He becomes afraid that there may be nothing of substance within himself, which makes him even more compulsively outer-directed. The wounded child can also make a man collapse into inertia, from fear of trying anything new. If a man was a victim of incest, he may compulsively perpetuate incestuous relationships in an unconscious attempt to become aware of his own wound-edness, which is often repressed.

The wounded child can cause a man to feel hurt, sad, angry, or abandoned when he least expects it, which may make him want to strike out, cry, or run away. Such powerful, irrational, and unbidden feelings can be very puzzling to an adult man, because he doesn't understand where they come from. What's more, most of his life he has probably been told to not be "childish," to control his feelings, and that "big boys don't cry." A general emotional staleness often results when these feelings of vulnerability are stifled and misunderstood.

Inner woundedness also fosters competitiveness in relationships and causes a man to sometimes take himself too seriously. He may tend to hold on to dogmatic attitudes and to behave in a compulsive manner. The wounded inner boy feels envy and anger at others' lightness and fun because he feels excluded or perhaps not worthy of the same. If the inner child feels rejected and unimportant, the man can become a nitpicking perfectionist who is compulsive in his work and who relies on tried-and-true methods rather than innovation and experiment to get things done.

A deep woundedness, such as that in men whose fathers physically or sexually abused them, may literally destroy lives. These men may lose the urge to live at an early age, spending the remainder of their lives in one self-defeating, masochistic endeavor after another. Extroverted men who are this wounded often act out their rage against society or against others and are often eventually imprisoned or murdered. Introverted men often lead lives of submission, silent suffering, resentment, and cynicism, and they often become physically ill or commit suicide at an early age.

The feelings of rejection, abandonment, and humiliation by the father do not go away because they are no longer available to the conscious mind; they linger in the unconscious and find their way into a man's life in indirect, subversive, and often self-defeating ways. Obviously, he cannot always yield to these feelings when they arise, but he needs to take note of them and then reflect on them either alone or with the help of someone who understands them as expressions of the inner child still crying out for recognition and acceptance. If a man can become aware of, and then accept, the pain caused by his father's lack of love, there is hope for his wounded inner child.

Letter From a Wounded Son

Mom,

My therapy has been invaluable. My therapist has helped me to see that I have a strong need to "overpower," beat, defeat my father (in a figurative, not a literal, sense). It is clear that I am still trying to overcome his "powerful" nature and thereby overcome my own feelings of weakness and helplessness in his presence. The images in my mind are always the same: first of all, him looking down at me, pulling his belt out of his pant loops, turning me around slowly, bending me over and spanking me—total weakness, total humiliation; then, him calling me over some time afterward, talking in a soft, caring voice, almost apologizing for my pain, but assuring me that he does this only because he is concerned about me growing up to be good.

Those two images explain a lot about the way I operate now—poorly in a love relationship; trying to still be a good boy; trying to achieve, to win acceptance (that never seems to come); trying to be totally different than my father in appearance, profession, lifestyle, thinking, *and* loving in order to "fight back" against his domineeringness and frightening power. Poor S. has to pay the price of my resentment for Dad. She has been a saint. Loyal to me every minute. Unfortunately, I cannot say I've been the same. I'm afraid of love. I'm afraid of intimacy. I'm afraid of her powerful and competent nature. I fear her strength like I feared Dad's strength. And I don't know how to accept her love. I don't trust that it really is love. I still think I'm a forgetful, lazy, unconscientious, unmechanical, cocky little boy who doesn't deserve to be loved and who won't be loved once he is finally found out for what he really is.

An exaggeration? Perhaps, but the scars are deep and the tears have flowed. I don't know whether S. and I will make it another year. I am the reason we will fall if we do. She stays true despite the hurt I've caused her. But I'm frightened to have anyone like my father in my life. Sometimes I think I'm sabotaging this love affair, just like Dad is sabotaging your marriage because of his feelings of powerlessness. And his feelings, just like mine, go back to his father (who was even more violent and powerful) and the fear of being weak, emasculated, and crushed. For him, to love you is to accept his weakness/powerlessness. It is to live with his father again. He is a traditional man—he hides his weaknesses behind his mask. He's a little boy pretending to be a man so he won't have to be humiliated by a powerful other ever again. He's afraid to accept his weakness because weakness was painful when he was a child. "Strength" only meant no more spankings, no more being yelled at, no more being the subject of father's rage, no more physical pain, no more being a "bad boy."

I don't know if I will ever outlive the scars I feel from childhood. But I have a chance because my dad wasn't as violent as his was, as scary as his was, as unwilling to play with me as his was. I had good times, too, though it is difficult to remember them. I'm sure that Dad will never outlive his scars. He tried to hide them, thought they would go away when he had kids and became powerful himself, but they didn't. And he is frightened to see a therapist who might help him. It would be an admission of his own weakness. In short, Dad will *never* be what you want until he has undergone a lot of therapy and is willing to talk and talk and talk with you about his feelings and why he has them.

Sorry to sound such a pessimistic note. But I think I'm right. And I don't think you can help him change unless he gets help himself. I feel sorry for him. Great sorrow. He is my antagonist, and when I pause from my struggle to overpower him, I know the loneliness of a self-conscious little boy who doesn't believe anyone could truly love him. He is a victim of years of male socialization in the M. family. And he is a victim of its pride because he cannot admit he needs help and then go out and get it. I could be totally wrong, but I don't think so. I don't think I've even scratched the surface of his boyhood—a boyhood he never talked about with us, a boyhood which I think scarred him for life.

We are sons of the same father. We are the victims of his violent regard for humanity, and we are the perpetrators of his crime. We cannot love and we cannot accept love. We must kill our fathers, and we must create their heirs to kill their fathers. We are doomed by the myth of being male, which has shaped our muscles, broadened our shoulders, and kept us animals. When most women discover our primitive simplicity they ignore it or run from it. How frightening to think that we rule the world. We command the ship, we give the orders—we will destroy ourselves.

The Healthy Father

A man who wishes to be a healthy father might begin by making a conscious decision to accept the responsibilities of parenthood. He could accept that his future son has a right to be born into a family where he will be cared for within the best psychological and emotional environment that can be provided for him. He could accept the significance of his role as father, even during pregnancy. He could participate in the delivery process as much as possible and be there to support his wife and to greet his son at birth. His emotional commitment to his son could continue until his son has reached a sufficient level of emotional and physical maturity to adequately care for himself.

Above all, the healthy father possesses self-awareness. He is emotionally and intellectually open, and he is honest enough to be able to reflect on his own attitudes, feelings, and behavior. He doesn't take for granted that he is always right, but he is willing to examine himself and, if need be, come to a more appropriate way of feeling and acting without being coerced to change by outside forces. In fact, he sees change as representing a healthy continuation of growth within the family structure. He is not emotionally invested in an exaggerated sense of masculine identification. He also accepts traits within himself that are traditionally considered to be feminine or even maternal—that is, he accepts his anima. A father who accepts his own contrapsychological qualities provides a model that will allow his son to be more accepting of his own feminine qualities and consequently more accepting of women.

If the father accepts his sensuality and sexuality as an integral part of his nature, his son is likely to do the same. This enables them to talk about the positive and negative aspects of sexuality as an important part of their manhood without diminishing or denigrating women.

The healthy father is also aware that he is not perfect, and that there will always be qualities in himself that he needs to work on to improve. He accepts these "darker" aspects of himself as part of who he is. By accepting his *shadow,* he spares his son the burden of having to unconsciously carry it for him. He also accepts his son's shortcomings as part of his personality, without assuming the right to impose his values on his son. He accepts his son's reasonable disappointments in him as a healthy expression of their differences. He introduces his son to the outside world in a way that helps him to develop a respect for the natural social and moral boundaries between himself and others.

The healthy father realizes the importance of developing honest communication skills with his son and ensures that he has time to do this. He is able to see his son as an individual and not as an extension of himself, even though he realizes his son will use him for a model well into his adolescent years. He sees some disagreements as his son's way of testing his perception of his father as all-powerful and invulnerable.

He allows his son to begin to break his dependence on him when the son begins to strike out in his own direction; he sees a certain degree of healthy rebellion as his son's way of experimenting with being his own person. He is able to understand and accept that his son may increasingly see him as less than perfect. But the flaws his son sees allow the son to resist placing unrealistic demands upon himself. They also allow him to see his own limits of physical and intellectual performance. Through this, he can develop a stable concept of what it means to apply himself fully to his tasks in life, as well as to know what "good enough" means for him.

In early adulthood, the son may turn away from the father to another mentor, often an older man in an area of mutual interest or profession—a transitional figure whom the son may idealize in place of his father. The healthy father may view this as a loss, but he also understands it as his son's way of starting to let go of the idealization of his father. In later adult life the son stops idealizing his mentor as well; while he may retain respect for him, he increasingly turns to himself as the ultimate validator of his life.

In old age, the father comes to portray the spiritual values developed over a lifetime of experience. By demonstrating them, rather than espousing values that have been mindlessly borrowed from a dogmatic theory or belief system, he continues to be a source of inspiration for his son. At the same time, the healthy father continues to encourage his son to explore and find his own values.

The healthy father-son relationship allows the son to increasingly see his father's humanness and natural vulnerability, as well as his strength. It also eventually allows him to separate his projections of the archetypal father from his own father, the man.

The following poem by Frederick Feirstein, entitled "For David, in the Middle of the 21st Century," conveys to me the feeling that a healthy father has for his son:

> David, when you are
> bald
> (Though I hope you're not)
> As you are now
> And rocking in a
> hammock,
> remembering
> Something that has
> no words
> Pick up this poem
> That has your father
> in it:
> I've just come home
> From travelling. I
> Shake out my
> umbrella.
> I lift you from the
> darkness
> And rock you like a
> pendulum.
> You tug at my shirt,
> fascinated
> By the blue and
> purple rectangles,
> So I take it off.
> You stuff it in your
> mouth, as you will
> My virtues and my
> faults. The sun blazes
> And holds us like a
> photo in the moment
> As you hold this
> As I once held you,
> David.[10]

□ 6 □

Man the Slayer:
The Dark Side of Masculinity

Man is the only species that is a mass murderer, the only misfit
in his own society. Why should this be so?

—NIKO TINBERGEN

Awareness of Evil

THE ANCIENT CONCEPT of the dark side of human nature is
recorded in mythology, folk legend, and fairy tales, as well as in
the religion and philosophy of both primitive peoples and classical civilizations. That which is dark and sinister within was
probably initially projected outward as a force in nature, as a dark
god or goddess, or later, in Christianity, as the devil.

This projection, or externalization of iniquity, has been one of
humanity's greatest problems. The projection process creates a
polarization of nature, turning its original cycle of life and death
into a "moral" problem of good and evil. On a collective level,
there has always been a remarkable intolerance in human beings
to recognize that adversity may reside within. When people
inevitably began to recognize that this dark side existed in
individuals, possession by evil spirits was blamed. This aspect of

human experience was originally conceived within religions as the *problem of evil.*

In the history of psychiatry and psychology, "evil" began to be viewed as disease, neurosis, or psychosis. We have now come to recognize the internal nature of psychological conflict, which expresses itself in myriad symptomatic forms, such as delusions, persecutions, psychosomatic diseases, and so forth.

Freud and his followers had established the place of psychoanalysis by the beginning of the twentieth century, but the prevailing influence of Freud's early training in neurology and medicine left its mark on the foundation of psychoanalysis as a strongly biological rationale for the basic dynamics of mental functioning. In the last hundred years this biological focus of human behavior has been often overused as a rationalization to explain the problem of evil as well as aggression.

Although Freud saw evil as residing within the person, he formulated this idea as part of the duality within the psyche that came to be known as the *death instinct.* His later *theory of drives,* formulated in *Beyond the Pleasure Principle,* posited that this duality consisted of a sexual drive and an aggression drive.[1] A polarity of masculine and feminine was inherent in Freud's theory of the "instincts" of sex and aggression. That the death instinct was part of his theory followed naturally from what Erich Fromm and others refer to as the *patriarchal tradition,* which perpetuated the view that women were an inferior and "crippled" version of men, that is, that women were castrated. This central point seems to have sprung from an unconscious splitting of masculine from feminine, as well as good from evil. As a result of this split a man is overidentified with the masculine pole of his psyche and disassociated from his own endogenous power.

Rather than being able to rest with a conscious sense of superiority, he is saddled with an unconscious sense of inferiority—a sense of inadequacy vis-à-vis the creative maternal and feminine. In this way he becomes impaired in his ability to promote life, to nurture, and to relate effectively and empathically with either men or women. The anima, then, even though it is projected, is best understood in this context as an incomplete, damaged sense of self.

How is this related to aggression? Freud's death instinct became a rationalization for "the evil that men do"—as if aggression and the drive for power and control were simply attributes of their sex. Another way of viewing the death instinct is to see it as a result of men's need for power, which is in turn a function of their exaggerated exogenic means of coping with the world, women, and themselves—or, stated another way, a result of their failure to incorporate the feminine in themselves. We can surmise that men then need women as a group to carry this deprecated image of femininity. In this way women may be said to be carriers of an anima image that is contaminated by the masculine *shadow*. Understood in this way, much of what is known as aggression in men can be accounted for. A historical instance of this collective projection can be seen in the persecution of witches in the Middle Ages, when millions of women were murdered for imagined or symbolic activities they were performing, especially for making "pacts with the devil."

My guess is that Freud never fully succeeded in justifying his dualistic instinct theory because he could also never fully resolve his own inner masculine/feminine split. His unconscious attempt at resolution, if one can call it that, was to project this incomplete sense of masculinity onto women, seeing them as "inferior men." Aspects of his personal life seem to portray this split: his rigid need to maintain authority in the face of challenges from those around him; his incessant preoccupation with death; the way he related to his daughter, Anna; and his projection of inferiority onto women.[2]

As a society, we seem to have lost the understanding that many of our psychic struggles are manifestations of an inner splitting and a refusal to acknowledge that there are undesirable elements within us all.

The Shadow

The Jungian concept of the *shadow* offers a fertile starting point for examining the psychological origins of men's violence toward each other and toward those they love. As Jung states: "Unfortunately there is no doubt about the fact that man is, as a whole, less good than he imagines himself or wants to be. Everyone carries a shadow, and the less it is embodied in the individual's conscious life, the blacker and denser it is."[3]

The shadow aspect of our personality consists of those parts of ourselves that we have learned through experience are not tolerable to others, especially to our parents. When these thoughts, feelings, and behaviors become unacceptable to us, we *split* from them. To fully understand the concept of the shadow we need to understand what splitting is and how it both helps and hinders us in our efforts to achieve the greatest level of self-reflective consciousness.

Splitting is a universal psychological phenomenon that takes place in the earliest stages of childhood, as the ego is being formed. It continues throughout life, functioning both as a defense mechanism and as a means of differentiating ourselves from others. As we saw earlier, the child experiences itself initially as part of the mother; its own ego only emerges as a separate sense of self around the age of three or so. Splitting from the mother at this point is entirely normal and assists in the development of a stable ego, or the sense of "I-ness." Another form of splitting occurs as we attempt to discriminate between different parts of ourselves, so that the sense of what is "I" and what is "not-I" is further clarified. While this splitting process helps establish the boundaries of the ego, it can also function defensively to split off the undesirable parts of the ego and relegate them to the unconscious, as shadow.

In general these are qualities that are not congruent with the more socialized, or *persona,* aspects of our personality. However, since no part of the personality is ever completely "lost," split-off parts become relegated to a less apparent, more unconscious level of the psyche. In other words, the more difficult it is for us to accept certain disturbing qualities in ourselves, the more likely they will be relegated to the shadow aspect of our personalities.

The splitting process becomes complicated by the fact that negative feelings that we repress or disown gain a particularly strong, though unconscious, emotional charge. The nature of the psyche is such that nothing of any emotional consequence remains truly unexpressed, even though we may be unaware of the form in which we are expressing it. So, even though these disassociated qualities are unconscious, their peculiar emotional charge causes them to "push" for expression. The expressed form of an unconscious emotional content may then arise as a *projection*. What we have disowned is projected onto others, who, consequentially, we will reject as being somehow "less than" or inferior to ourselves. These projections are always accompanied by strong, often negative, feelings, such as revulsion, disgust, anger, or fear—our previously repressed emotional reactions to our own unacceptable qualities. Our projections, then, are the ostracized elements of our own personalities. That is why when we encounter a carrier of some split-off shadow quality, we have such a strong and often irrational emotional reaction. The reaction itself often indicates that a *shadow* has been activated.

The Collective Shadow

The shadow becomes collective when it manifests in the attitudes and behavior of large groups, or when one individual comes to personify it, embodying the collective evil. Personifications of the collective shadow include Napoleon, Hitler, Mussolini, Lenin, Stalin, and Jim Jones of the People's Temple. What seems remarkable is that all of these men were initially motivated (at least superficially) by political, religious, or philosophical images of achieving a utopian ideal. They all viewed themselves as being facilitators of much-needed reforms that ultimately would benefit their group, if not humankind. But in each case there was also an equally powerful obsession to exclude (by whatever means) from this ideal state those elements that were considered to be incompatible, inconsistent, or antithetical to their point of view.

War is perhaps one of the best examples of a shadow problem carried out in a collective arena of mutual projection. Little individual consciousness is expressed in the preparation for, and engagement in, war. It is in war that men are again thoroughly split from the feminine and nature, both in the ways they act and in the ways they view their opponents. I don't think the dynamic is essentially much different from the antics and passions aroused by a football game, in which allegiance is based more on the city one lives in than the virtues of one's team. The issue is often one of a wounded narcissism trying to heal itself through forms of "justified" vengeance.

The history of civilization abounds with examples of the deplorable consequences of scapegoating, such as the persecution of witches, the Nazis' murder of the Jews, and the Spanish Inquisition, as well as other atrocities against minorities and women.

The splitting process often occupies a central and critical role in mass movements and belief systems, serving to maintain the group's identity, beliefs, and convictions. In this way, the group's point of view becomes compulsively dogmatic, arrogant, dictatorial, and increasingly intolerant of anything that departs from it. Whether this point of view is political, religious, or scientific, it begins narcissistically to exert a claim on what is "right," while also establishing a definition of reality that claims to know what is wrong, incorrect, immoral, and evil.

So where, then, does evil really lie? Perhaps, like beauty, evil is also in the eye of the beholder. There is no universal consensus of what is evil.

The Personal Shadow

On a personal level, the shadow can often be found in dreams, fantasies, and, of course, as projections onto others. When the shadow is projected, it may be carried by an individual or by a whole group of like individuals. The shadow is often experienced in terms of negative value judgments accompanied by strong negative emotions. The shadow is almost always identified from the perspective of how one would not like to be seen either by oneself or others, that is, as "not-I."

A man's shadow character is most commonly represented as a male figure, but there are many instances in which the shadow may also be represented as a woman with particularly negative qualities. In these cases the shadow may be contaminated by some aspect of the man's anima or his mother. This may also be seen in a dream where a woman the man knows personally and admires is in the company of "undesirables." In this case the man often can't figure out why this woman would be in such "bad company," because his conscious associations to her are so positive. The answer may reside in a number of possibilities. One is that the dreamer may be unconscious of some negative associations or feelings he has to the person and needs to block his awareness of them in order to retain his conscious more positive image of her. A second possibility is that the dreamer may have some unacceptable wishes or impulses toward this woman that he cannot allow himself to acknowledge in his conscious state, so he compromises by having the admired person be in the company of "these others," who carry some aspect of his shadow. In this second case the dream allows him to begin to become aware of the suppressed wishes or impulses in a form that at least initially keeps them at a distance. A third instance in which this dream situation may occur is if the dreamer has been regarding this woman in an unrealistically positive way; the dream may be performing a compensatory function to modify the dreamer's exaggerated perception. This dream situation is just as likely to be represented in this way if it is another man with whom the dreamer is concerned.

The shadow may also appear in a number of different guises, human or less than human. A man's shadow may manifest as a child, an adult male, or an old man, with each representing a different developmental level. In general, the more disassociated the shadow qualities are, the more primitive the representation is going to be. The shadow may have features that are primitive, animalistic, crippled, deformed, or even mutilated. Because the appearance of a shadow character in dreams varies, it is seldom recognized as a part of oneself and is more likely to be experienced as alien to one's conscious identity.

From the conscious standpoint, the dreamer will often be judgmental about the shadow character and will wish to disassociate from him. Frequently, this character will cause some trouble within the dream and will evoke strong negative feelings in the dreamer. For example, one of the men in my men's group had the following dream:

> An armored truck raises its guns and fires into the night sky. Half a dozen men flanking the truck do likewise. A glow in the air illuminates the truck and two soldiers are felled by machine-gun fire. All those in the truck scramble out and clumsily crawl through a nearby barbed-wire fence. Just then a group of soldiers on horseback riding through the hillocks arrives, surrounding their prey: Adolf Hitler and his escape party. Everyone who fled from the truck is shot several times, including two women. The soldiers then take a handheld electrical probe and place it on the temples of the dead group, searing their brains. Then a knife is thrust into the temples of Hitler and another man, and a portion of their cranial matter is dug out. As this occurs the dead Hitler's eyes look up peacefully and pleadingly.

This man's dream portrays the shadow in a quite primitive form. The dream was particularly upsetting for him because his strong persona and ego allowed little conscious violence or rage. His parents—both alcoholics—had forbidden the expression of anger in any form by any member of the family; as a result, his perception of anger was that it was a particularly malevolent and dangerous emotion. His dream presents the shadow in archetypal proportions, as Hitler. The shadow needs to be completely "killed off." So, Hitler, as the dreamer's latent rage, is killed, and he becomes both "peaceful" and "pleading." The peacefulness represents the persona's success in quieting the shadow, but the pleading quality may refer to the shadow's need for acknowledgment. The dreamer really needs to be more conscious of his rage and accepting of it; this will allow him to broaden his perception of himself and the depth of his feelings. It will also prevent the rage from being acted out in some unconscious form.

Recognition of the powerful feelings connected with the shadow does not mean that a man will need or even want to act on them. Rather, it presents an opportunity to accept them as part of the complex emotional repertoire that makes up his psychological life. With increased awareness and "ownership" of these feelings, he is able to recognize key emotional conflicts, often for the first time. On the other hand, repressing feelings that are unacceptable to the ego, or persona, creates psychological and sometimes physical symptoms, which the ego experiences instead of the repressed feelings. Continual suppression can affect a man's general energy level, often resulting in moodiness, irritability, depression, irrational fears, phobias, and preoccupations with death.

It also takes a lot of psychic energy—in the form of defensiveness, hypervigilance, and suspicion—to project one's shadow onto others and to then maintain a disassociated state of nonreflective consciousness. In such states there is often a rigid self-righteousness. "True believers" and those who are certain that they know the "truth" beyond doubt are upset by any departures from their perceptions primarily because another point of view threatens their image, their feelings of self-worth, and their basic beliefs.

If a man's ego is not strong enough to contain his split-off feelings, his basic defenses will not be adequate to maintain the disassociated state. In this case, there is a greater likelihood that he will attack the carrier or carriers of his shadow based on his perception that the other *is* as he is perceived to be, no matter how irrational or idiosyncratic this perception may be.

Cultural Contributions to the Shadow in Men

The shadow qualities of men are shaped both by behavior that is discouraged and by behavior that is rewarded or reinforced by parents and the culture at large. In this way, boys in Western culture learn to conform to behavioral patterns that are defined as "manly." For example, young boys are often rewarded for being aggressive with other boys; they are expected to be able to defend themselves and to not come home crying. A boy who does not defend himself—whether that is something he wishes to do or not—is considered a sissy and is often humiliated by his parents, particularly his father, and by his peers.

In the inner city of Chicago where I grew up, a boy's competence was not based on how well he did in school, but on how well he defended himself. To be "tough" was a virtue that was admired by one's peers. It conferred a degree of security and self-confidence—a much sought-after haven when one is exposed to violence on a virtual daily basis. (In my own childhood I witnessed a man shooting his wife and then dragging her body down the street.)

The first time I ever came home after a fight I had lost, when I was ten, my stepfather told me in no uncertain terms that I was to go back out and beat up the other boy, and if I didn't *he* would beat *me* up. As it turned out I did go back and beat up the other boy—not because I wanted to, but to avoid being beat up by my stepfather, who had already humiliated me for not winning in the first place. My stepfather had received a Purple Heart in World War II, as well as a case of shell shock that lasted many years of his life, and he told me that my time for war would also come. But even though he obviously had been traumatized by his experience he refused to discuss it, simply maintaining that when my time came, I would serve and do my "duty." Killing people in defense of my country seemed to be part of what it meant to be a "man," but it was a part that I secretly feared and abhorred, although I felt too ashamed to say so. In spite of those fears, as a teenager I became the leader of a gang in which every member except me was on probation. It was not until I was almost killed in a fight that I saw how unconscious my attempt was to have status in my family and my peer group.

When "my time" for war (Vietnam) eventually came, I couldn't go because of a severe hearing impairment. Even though I became involved in the antiwar movement, I initially felt guilty for not having gone. After I finally admitted this to my antiwar friends, I learned that they felt the same way; we all felt guilty, even though we disagreed with the war on moral grounds. We also felt tremendous compassion for our "brothers" who, for whatever reason, had to go.

In American culture boys are often given more positive reinforcement and less punishment for aggressive behavior than are girls. In fact, at two years of age both boys and girls hit, scream, and cry with nearly equal frequency, but by the age of four boys do more hitting and less screaming than girls. Girls generally become more verbally aggressive than boys, especially as they grow older, while boys become more physically aggressive.[4] Other research indicates that preschool rage and tantrum behaviors are predictive of adolescent and adult aggression for males, but not for females. Other studies in child development show that aggressiveness is reinforced through imitation; that is, children who early on witness parents and adults behaving aggressively increase their own aggressive behavior even without rewards for doing so.[5]

These studies show that men who witnessed violence between their parents were almost three times as likely to hit their wives as were those whose parents had not been violent. The sons of the most violent parents had a rate of wife abuse a *thousand* times greater than sons of nonviolent parents.[6] Several other studies have also found that witnessing abuse between parents is the most powerful determinant of becoming an abuser, even more so than if the man was a victim of child abuse. Also, interestingly, the most consistent characteristic observed among victims of wife abuse is that the women had witnessed violence between their parents while growing up.[7]

So we see that cultural and familial influences pattern individual male behavior in a fashion that men might not freely choose, had they the choice. For example, what is often collectively considered to be "manly" behavior prescribes an unreflective way of being in the world.

The following vignette appears in the psychological literature as an attempt to describe a young boy's problem; however, it fails to explain his relationship to the feminine, or rather what of the feminine is missing for him.

> B.J., age 5 years, referred to his combined sexual and aggressive impulses as his "robber" feelings; he described how he, as policeman, seemed to be in constant battle to keep the robbers in jail. As his immature superego seemed to function more to punish than to help him to be in control of his impulses, he usually felt that the policeman was out having coffee when most needed, but was sure to punish when the robbers took over.
>
> Failure to integrate sexual and aggressive impulses into a valued view of the self as "in charge" undermines self-confidence, heightens fears of punishment, and the projected aggression heightens castration anxiety. A defensive facade of masculinity characterized by aggressive sexuality and demeaning or chauvinistic attitudes toward women may emerge, an obvious element in the exaggerated "macho" character.[8]

Social and cultural stereotypes, as well as psychological stereotypes of men, often exert a collective effect on men's shadow problems. Many examples of this can be seen in psychological work with adolescent boys who have not yet achieved a stable sense of identity and who are struggling to define themselves in terms of the prevailing cultural stereotypes. These societal values powerfully influence a boy's sense of identity and reinforce gender-specific attitudes and behavior.

The role-playing that men do at work is a well-established pattern in the business world. Emotional vulnerability (an aspect of the anima) is a definite sign of "weakness" in this context, as women who have moved into the corporate world are quickly discovering. Signs of strong emotion, particularly crying on the job, are regarded as indicators of "low credibility" in the work-place.

Furthermore, men may speak of their sexual prowess and even overtly and covertly encourage each other to do so, but they cannot speak about impotence. The anima may make one "soft." One male patient of mine struggled for several sessions about whether to bring up the issue of his sexual impotence. When he finally did, I asked him why it was so difficult for him to talk about. He eventually decided that it was because he was afraid that I would think that he was unmanly. Yet another male patient, a successful business executive who had been injured in an automobile accident, hid the extent of his physical pain and limitations from his superior because he was afraid of losing credibility and status within his corporation. He was afraid of being seen as less than "man enough" to do the job. There are many other examples of socially conditioned attitudes that burden men and become part of the general male shadow problem. Emotional vulnerability, signs of physical limitation, and sexual impotence are only a few of the "weaknesses" that men hide because of shame, humiliation, and a fear of being perceived as inferior.

The Son as Carrier of the Father's Shadow

A man's shadow can sometimes also incorporate problems that come from his father's unresolved issues. (These issues may in fact sometimes go back several generations.) In such cases we say that the personality of the son is *contaminated* by the shadow of the father. For example, in my practice a boy with a particularly difficult shadow problem is evaluated in the context of his father's personality (which includes his attitudes toward masculinity) as well as the boy's intellectual abilities, emotional makeup, and life experiences. When a father does not "own" his own inadequacies and vulnerabilities consciously, these problems are often passed on to his son. The son may sometimes unconsciously live out his father's shadow, with the result that the father not only experiences some relief at seeing these qualities outside of himself, but he will also be critical of the son for not measuring up to the way the father "wants him to be." This, of course, places the boy in the untenable position of having to carry the shadow *and* anima qualities of his father, while at the same time being criticized and rejected for it. He is faced with the alternative of either rejecting himself or rebelling against his father. In both cases he loses. The son is often brought for therapy when he is carrying the father's shadow. But if the father can be treated instead of the son, the son's "problem" seems to clear up. Or if the son is treated without the father and improves, then the father's problem becomes apparent. (The ideal is to be able to treat them both, but unfortunately this is not always possible.) The mother obviously can also contribute to the son's difficulties by unconsciously communicating her own shadow problems to the child.

When a boy attempts to emotionally remove himself from the dominant influence of his mother, his father becomes even more important in the formation of his sense of masculine identity.

The Sociopath: Archetype of the Unrelated

The most devastating manifestation of a complete disassociation from the anima is when a man develops a sociopathic personality. This person has few friends and is very often in trouble with authorities and the law. His most salient characteristic is a lack of capacity for love accompanied by an equal inability to experience guilt or conscience. It is as if the most basic attributes of love and empathy are simply empty spaces in his personality. This defect occurs in men more than three times as often as it does in women, and it is even more frequent in men whose fathers are also sociopathic. As far as we know, sociopathic personalities are formed very early in life; by late adolescence the antisocial pattern of behavior has become well established, characterized by often frighteningly criminal and exploitative behavior and shallowness in all relationships. Its tragedy is compounded by the fact that it is also more prevalent among the poor.

The sociopathic personality amounts to an archetypal constellation of male negativity and is hence a ready carrier of the masculine shadow in our society, particularly when it occurs in a political, social, or religious leader.[9] Conscienceless mass murderers like Charles Manson, Richard Speck, and Ted Bundy are among its more sensationalized representatives. But sociopaths can also be found among respected businessmen, politicians, and other professionals, as men who are capable of charming their victims while they extort, exploit, deceive, and humiliate them.

Here, perhaps more than in any other personality disorder, we find the defect of relating to others as "objects." Their love is not perverted as it seems to be, it is simply absent. It is perhaps the antithesis of love: as Erich Fromm states the opposite of love is not hate, but indifference.[10] The sociopath's lack of love for others is not offset by a love of self, as the typically self-defeating nature of his life so frequently attests. His entire life seems to be a continual loveless act which, in one way or another, culminates in self-destruction.

Among personality disorders, sociopathy is still an enigma; we do not fully understand its cause. It remains one of the few disorders for which, so far, there is absolutely no cure, in spite of the fact that it is the most studied and researched of all personality problems. Perhaps one reason for this is the fact that sociopathic personalities find no need to be treated, because they feel there is nothing wrong with them.

The sociopathic person poses a dramatic challenge. Because if love, as Fromm has pointed out, consists of care, responsibility, respect and knowledge for the other, then how are we as individuals and as a society to regard the sociopath? Perhaps this dilemma is the existential test of the Christian dictum, "As you do unto the least of my brethren, so you do unto me."

Integrating the Shadow

For Jung, the acknowledgment of the shadow is an essential step in the individuation process; it is a means of reaching into deeper and often less accessible levels of the psyche, where the anima, as mediator of the creative unconscious, can be met.

> The shadow, although by definition a negative figure, sometimes has certain clearly discernible traits and associations which point to quite a different background. It is as though he were hiding meaningful contents under an unprepossessing exterior. Experience confirms this: and what is more important, the things that are hidden usually consist of increasingly numinous figures. The one standing closest behind the shadow is the anima, who is endowed with considerable powers of fascination and possession. . . . In the case of the individual, the problem constellated by the shadow is answered on the plane of the anima, that is, through *relatedness* [italics added].[11]

The integration of the shadow, then, is a constructive and expansive endeavor which eventually allows a man to develop increased degrees of personal emotional freedom, self-acceptance, and a greater degree of autonomy in his beliefs, feelings, and attitudes than he previously possessed. Accepting one's own dark side also culminates in a greater respect for others and a more empathic understanding of others' shortcomings and struggles. One of the greatest benefits in uncovering the shadow is that the general quality of human relationship is improved because we take a deeper responsibility for ourselves, thereby projecting less of our unintegrated selves onto others. This process moves us toward relatedness to our fellow human beings. In short, this process has the effect of increasing our capacity to love.

And it is to men's sense of love that we now turn.

□ 7 □

Men's Sense of Love

> Love has no purpose, . . . and that is why love is so rare these
> days, love without goals, love in which the only thing of impor-
> tance is the act of loving itself. In this kind of love it is *being*
> and not *consuming* that plays the key role. It is human self-
> expression, the full play of our human capacities. But in a culture
> like ours, which is exclusively oriented to external goals like
> success, production, and consumption, we can easily lose sight
> of that kind of love. It fades so far into the distance that we can
> hardly imagine it as a reality any more.
>
> —ERICH FROMM

THE SPLIT BETWEEN "MASCULINE" AND "FEMININE" has developed
over the course of human evolution, eventually becoming polar-
ized into what are viewed as almost "irreconcilable" differences.
These perceived differences are ultimately highly influential in
the way that men relate to women. If we accept these differences
as valid and innate, we are forced to conclude that men and
women are, indeed, very dissimilar creatures, and that the way in
which men relate is indelibly fixed in their nature.

Language itself has come to incorporate the split between
masculine and feminine; male behavior has come to be linguisti-
cally defined by an established evolutionary tradition of exogenous tendencies. Although the words we use may only represent

linguistic conventions, in terms of relationship they serve to reinforce behavioral stereotypes.

Words that are used to describe psychological characteristics of males in Western society include

> aggressive, assertive, authoritative, competitive, coura-
> geous, daring, decisive, domineering, independent, in-
> novative, self-reliant, vigorous, as well as blunt, boastful,
> bull-headed, combative, presumptuous, pugnacious, sa-
> distic and violent.

> At the same time, females are described as affection-
> ate, demure, dependent, emotional, excitable, gentle,
> illogical, indecisive, intuitive, passive, sensitive, submis-
> sive, tender, unambitious, as well as bitchy, fickle, sac-
> charine, secretive, superficial, undependable, vacillating,
> whiney, and wily.[1]

The question of whether these words represent innate differences in the sexes is rarely pursued; rather, we infer this to be so
from the use of language itself. If we overhear a conversation in a
restaurant during which one person is telling another that her
son's teacher is "innovative, independent, cold, aggressive," what
do almost all of us conclude as to the sex of the teacher? We
automatically visualize the teacher as male. However, if the
teacher is described as "affectionate, intuitive, dependent, submis-
sive," most of us are likely to imagine the teacher as a woman.

As far as the qualities we seek in human relationships go, there
are certain words and their behavioral equivalents that are regarded by most of us as desirable for our partners to possess. For
example, both healthy men and healthy women would wish to
have their lovers be affectionate, emotional, excitable, gentle,
intuitive, sensitive, and tender. On the other hand, neither would
want their lovers to be cold, cerebral, independent, dull, rough,
unperceptive, insensitive, and indelicate. It is clear from this that
both men and women desire that their lovers be more "feminine"
than "masculine."

I am not trying to portray here that male behavior is purely the product of linguistic labeling, but rather that linguistic customs powerfully reinforce the polarity between masculine and feminine, thus strengthening sex-typed behavior. Once accepted, these language structures operate unconsciously as conditioners of how men continue to learn to perceive themselves as well as how they are taught to relate.

The Mother and Narcissism

As we saw earlier, the early mother-child relationship is most often the primary determinant of the quality of all later experiences of love. The capacity for healthy human love is engendered by feelings of early infantile security based on an adequate mother-son bond, on having had "good enough" mothering, and on having experienced trust that our mothers, in the earliest stages of our development, had our best interests at heart. In describing the first stage of human development, which he describes as *trust versus mistrust,* Erik Erikson posits that the first and primary developmental task of emotional health in early life is the establishment of a basic sense of trust, which plays a critical role in one's perceptions of the world and the "others" in it.[2] The mother establishes for her son the sense that, by extension, the world is a welcoming, safe, and nurturing container in which he can grow.

A boy who learns that he can basically trust the world develops a secure center of self that is capable of withstanding the normal vicissitudes of life. He believes he "belongs" here—that there is a niche for him and, perhaps most importantly, he does not have to prove it. This perception leads, consciously or unconsciously, to the judgment that life is basically good and that there is a reasonable expectation that he *is* going to get his needs met, both by others as well as though his own resources. This also allows him to have confidence that he will not be unnecessarily rejected. This judgment, in turn (though none of this necessarily follows a neat or orderly sequence), results in self-generated behavior that is directed toward getting his emotional needs met.

This formative healthy attitude toward the world, oneself, and others is an essential psychological paradigm for the capacity to love as an adult. By internalizing his mother's love a boy can use this introject later in his capacity to both love others and empathically understand them. This internalized mother-love leads to what is sometimes referred to as *primary narcissism*—a high regard for oneself that is part of an enduring and healthy sense of self-worth and self-love. Without his healthy love of oneself there is little hope for a healthy love of the other. When mother-love is fraught with ambivalence and even hatred we perceive the other as we feel we were once regarded ourselves. This creates a paradox in that what was missing and is now longed for may be difficult to accept even when it is offered. In this case, whether we do so consciously or not, we try to make our current love experiences fit the model of the past. When mother-love is internalized as a healthy self-love, however, we are able to regard the other as truly "other" and not only as a reflection of a part of ourselves or as a vestige of our early experience. This is what Martin Buber referred to as the "I-Thou" relationship.

A so-called *secondary narcissism* may occur when the development of the primary love relationship is incomplete or unsatisfactory, for whatever reason. Secondary narcissism manifests as exaggerated feelings of self-worth or self-importance, sometimes bordering on grandiosity, which basically function as a defense against recognizing a diminished or defective sense of self-worth. This results in a perversion of love, both for the self as well as for the other.

Mothers who have "narcissistic injuries" themselves inevitably perpetuate these wounds in their sons. Unloved, rejected, and abused male children become the instinctively abandoning, unloving, and abusive fathers to their own children. In this way the cycle is repeated. John Bowlby, an English psychiatrist who has extensively studied attachment and separation processes in children and the effects of abandonment by mothers, maintains that many defects traditionally explained by psychoanalytic theory can as well be traced to problems of bonding in every life experience. He speculates that many degrees of pathological *detachment* occur in childhood and adulthood as defensive reactions designed to prevent the pain and humiliation of the possibility of future abandonment.[3]

The therapist often sees narcissistic woundedness in individuals who demonstrate an inability to either accept or give love. This is often apparent in children, who respond to rejection by refusing to accept love, or who sometimes even refuse to interact with others, as when adopted children react to the premature rupture of the biological mother-child bond by refusing to accept the love of the adoptive parents. In extreme cases, children respond to the loss of love by withdrawing into the self-stimulating behavior of autism or schizophrenia. Although there are no definitive studies that indicate men have greater vulnerability to emotional rejection, because of men's apparent emotional aloofness and frequent denial of hurt one gets the impression that this might be the case. One could see these tendencies as defensive reactions to the fear of abandonment.

The Role of the Father in Men's Sense of Love

The father is the second critical factor in determining a man's capacity to love. We could say that the mother is more instrumental in the development of a man's capacity to *receive* love, and the father is more instrumental in his capacity to *give* love.

Traditionally, a father's love for his son is conditioned by how well the son mirrors his father's values and conforms to his expectations. Unlike the love the son receives from his mother, which is usually unconditional, the father's love is earned through the son's successful mastery of his father's expectations.

Because of men's exogenic orientation, the father's expectations of his son are to a large extent determined by values having to do with productivity and success in the outer world. So, as mediator between the home and the world outside, the father sets objective standards and rules which his son is expected to meet. Sons learn early that they have to "perform" in order to keep their fathers' love flowing. This becomes a paradigm for how boys, and later men, relate to each other. The positive aspect of this as a model of relationship is that it may promote healthy competition and the development of competency. The negative side is that it fosters envy and rivalry between fathers and sons as well as between men. If the father is too authoritarian and doesn't create enough room for mistakes and experimentation, his son may rebel by disavowing his father's love in order to protect his sense of integrity. This model of father-son love introduces a destructive potential that becomes manifest when love and power become fused.

As we saw earlier, a signal developmental task for the young boy is to make the transit from a mother-identified to a father-identified son. He must eventually separate from his mother while at the same time retaining "parts" of her, which will later become aspects of his own sense of self. The father's role is of critical importance here because his attitudes toward his wife (as well as his own mother) will shape what aspects of the mother his son feels safe to retain. In fact, the entire repertoire of father's behavior toward all women is a determinant in shaping the quality of his son's relationships with women. We saw earlier in the boys' pubertal initiation rites the importance of not only separating from the mother but the need—through circumcision and subincision—to symbolically retain aspects of the mother as well.

As we saw earlier, the early psychoanalytic position is that it is the son's fear of retaliation from his father that causes him to finally relinquish the tie to his mother. I would propose that, rather than fearing the father's retaliation, it is the father's own repudiation of the mother (and women in general) that serves as a model for his son, who will then have difficulty maintaining a proper love relation to *his* mother. If a father has been unable to integrate a healthy sense of the feminine in himself, he will unconsciously transmit his lack of regard for the feminine to his son.

If the son's early experience of the mother is such that he is unable to incorporate the positive mother (and consequently the positive feminine) as part of himself, *and* if the father has also repudiated the mother and the feminine, this combination virtually ensures that the feminine will not be an integral part of the young man's self. When this is the case, he can locate the feminine only in the outer world—as an object he desires, but also as an aspect of self that is split off and devalued. This results in a fundamental ambivalence toward women: women are objects of desire, but, at the same time, objects of derision. Further, this ambivalence is at the heart of what many men experience as the lack of a well-established "inner life," which is so aptly symbolized by the mother principle. The father's acceptance of his own femininity models for his son a respect for women and, by extension, for the inner life, so that he does not need to exclusively rely on the masculine exogenic principle.

Expressions of Love

Love is one of the most confusing words in our language. It is interesting that men (in my experience) use the word much less frequently in ordinary conversation than women do, whether they are referring to people or objects.

Whenever I hear patients use the word *love,* especially the first time, I ask what they mean. Many simply say something like, "Well, you know, I *love* her." Others explain with synonyms, like *care about, want to be with,* and so forth. Often people don't think much about what *love* really means to them. Even more often, two people who proclaim that they love each other have not considered that even though they use the same word, each of them attaches very different meanings to it. They may be "in love" and have entirely different behavioral expectations of what that means.

In therapy I have often observed the painful disappointment and confusion that invariably results when a couple finally discovers that their behavioral expectations are at variance. A man's expectations of himself as a loving partner may strongly rest on the traditional idea of "providing for," so that he feels he *is* being loving by fulfilling those expectations. He is surprised, as well as hurt, when his partner expresses disappointment in his providence as well as his performance. A man typically counters his wife's accusations that he doesn't love her with reference to all the things he's *done* to make her happy. He may invoke the fact that he bought her a new car, that he makes a good salary, that he sends the kids to private school, and so on, but none of these satisfies his wife's sense of what it means to feel loved by him. Even the idea of "doing things together" may mean something different for each of them. A wife may want her husband to spend more time with her or the children. For him this is likely to mean *doing* something together, while for her it may mean doing nothing—just *being* together. A patient once told me that he had finally yielded to his wife's request for some time together. When I asked him how that was for him, he said he had suggested that they watch TV or go to a movie, but she hadn't wanted to do that; in fact she turned down all of his suggestions and they finally just stayed home and talked. Although she really enjoyed that, he couldn't understand how "doing nothing" could be so important to her.

Sometimes avoiding this kind of interaction reflects a man's discomfort with the intimacy that results from not having activities as distractions. But many men simply feel they must be doing something "productive" in order to feel that they are *really* doing something. One sees this even in how fathers and mothers greet their children after school. Mothers often ask, "How was your day?" Fathers often ask, "What did you *do* today?"

It seems that men often express love (both verbal and nonverbal) differently than do women. In one study, for example, while both men and women valued the sex act as an important aspect of love, men (by as much as four times) valued its importance with greater frequency than did women. It certainly seems that men more often value "sex for the sake of sex" while women seem to value sex as a way of enhancing intimacy. This is not to say that women do not also occasionally want sex for its own sake, but that, by and large, they seem to prefer sex in the context of sensitivity and tenderness. Women surveyed also emphasized the importance of fidelity and forgiveness twice as frequently as men. With respect to resources, males nominated the display of their financial and material resources as being important, again, four times more frequently than women. Both sexes valued marriage equally as an act of love, but women valued having children far more frequently than did men.[4]

Love and Psychotherapy

To a split-off overmasculinized consciousness, the material of analysis seems to be contained within the endogenous realm of the *terrible mother*—the realm of the irrational and forsaken, of dreams, fantasies, free associations, and the repressed memories of the past. It is also often the realm of the *wounded inner son,* who has been relegated to the shadows of the unconscious by the *abandoning father.* Submission to the inner work of analysis may mobilize a man's feelings of helplessness and hopelessness that he has learned to project onto the mother as well as onto outer women. Without a *good father* he may, in fact, feel weakened and emasculated by psychoanalysis. Because even the idea of analysis is so alien to his usual way of operating in the world, it may threaten his need to be in control. Men typically want to know how long it will take, what they are supposed to do, how they are supposed to do it, what the "rules" are, and so forth. They often experience the descent to the unconscious as a fall into the possibility of "emptiness and nothingness." For a man who has never fully separated from his personal mother, the analogy of returning to the womb, or to the *dark mother,* is entirely appropriate in this context. It is even more appropriate when we consider the significance of the abandoning father.

The difficulties a man has in his relationships with women are often what bring him to analysis in the first place. Here he may for the first time "meet" the inner feminine who can help him understand his outer problems. The fact that there is also the potential for a deep and emotional relationship with the analyst involves a confrontation with the problem of loving that is different from the ordinary way of being in love in outer life.

Compared to women, for whom it is more culturally acceptable to be "emotional" or "weak," men find it much more difficult to admit that they are in need of help, or that they cannot manage their emotional lives. For this reason men are more often deeply depressed or even seriously ill before they consider going into analysis, and even then it is seen as a defeat of their capacity to manage their own lives. The masculine task-orientation is inimical to analysis because so much of the analytic process is a slow, almost circuitous path involving a confrontation with the unconscious and the irrational realm of experience, which is often not amenable to conscious control.

The analysis of men by male analysts often poses a special problem revolving around the transference relationship, in which the peculiar qualities of the original father-son relationship become reconstellated. In this situation, the analyst receives the father projections of the patient (as from son to father), which are often initially negative, characterized by the same feelings the patient experienced in childhood. If he and his father did not experience a strong positive emotional bond characterized by trust and mutual respect, the negative pole of the father-son bond will be projected onto the analyst, who will then be seen as judgmental, mistrustful, competitive, and overly powerful. (Female analysts, on the other hand, are more likely to carry the mother projections, which are often positive in the beginning but later come to characterize the struggle with the *negative mother*.) In the beginning of the treatment, when a man feels confronted by his perceptions of the negative father, transference is often a determining factor as to whether he will remain in analysis. In the middle and the end of the treatment, transference can be a critical healing factor in that it provides an opportunity to experience the analyst as an endogenous, containing, and nurturing figure, which may contribute to the resolution of the patient's complex.

Men in analysis may be unwilling to relinquish power to the analyst, unless they can consciously decide that for the benefit of the work they will temporarily give up their struggle to maintain control of the relationship. Sam describes this problem and how he was able to consciously resolve it:

> In my first serious relationship after my divorce I came to realize that there is a giving and taking of power in any relationship, whether it be between lovers, parent and child, business associates, friends, or analyst and patient. I had given Julia a great deal of power with respect to me (as she in turn had given to me). She had the right to explore my body sexually; she had the right to expect that I would not have sex with other women since we had an exclusive relationship; she had a key to my house; and she had the right to expect an honest and full answer to questions regarding my hopes, my frustrations, my dreams, and my failures. But as our relationship moved into the second year I found myself becoming more and more resentful of her. It was not until after the relationship broke up that I came to realize that a major source of the resentment was that much of the power that I had given Julia I had given unconsciously—without reflection, without making a clear choice, without deliberateness.
>
> In my analysis with Loren I found myself resentful also. He could read me like a book. He could predict my reactions. I felt obligated to have material to discuss at our sessions. I felt guilty when I went for long periods without remembering dreams. I was even resentful when he delighted at my having an important insight,

an "aha" experience. My work with him had reached a stagnant place and I seriously considered quitting. Then during reflection one evening I had an "aha" insight: I had granted Loren an enormous amount of power over me but I had given this power unconsciously—without reflection, without making a clear choice, without deliberateness.

I resolved the problem in the following way: I reflected on the power that I had granted Loren and the power he needed for our work to continue. I examined my attitude toward him. I made a clear choice that I wanted him to have the power necessary to make the analysis effective. I then bought a crystal pyramid prism. It was perfectly clear glass with a few flaws in it. It reflected the sun's light and it played the light to a variety of colors on the walls of the analysis room. It was beautiful and felt very masculine to me. I brought the pyramid to Loren one session and presented it to him as a gift, telling him that this was a symbol of the power he had over me. It was something that I was lending to him, that was mine, and that I would retrieve one day. But I told him that I wanted him to have it and to keep it in the analysis room. Loren told me that the pyramid would find its place in the room. Sure enough the pyramid moved from place to place in the room for several weeks and then settled into one spot, where it has remained for over two years.

My attitude about Loren is remarkably different now than it was before. I feel no more resentment nor guilt. I view him as a professional whom I hire and who, by virtue of his insight, experience, and intelligence, can help me along on my process. Clearly, my action was a watershed event in my process work.

My own experience has been that in the beginning stages of analysis women are far more likely to act in a warm, caring, and "related" way than are men. They will often idealize the analyst and allow him to carry their projections of the good father. This initial positive transference can become negative transference when they begin to experience a deeper acceptance of the more assertive and aggressive parts of themselves. Men, by contrast, seem to learn to love more deeply when the initial negative transference in the analytic relationship comes to be replaced by increased vulnerability, tenderness, and warmth. In both cases there is an eventual balancing and integration of masculine and feminine qualities.

In the dynamics of men's groups and women's groups there is also a similar initial disposition as well as an eventual process of integration and balancing. Before the integration process could begin in my men's group, a splitting between the masculine and feminine took place within the group itself. This group was not a support group, but one that emphasized intensive psychological confrontation. There were only two "rules": the first was that the primary focus remain on individual interactions *within* the group, and that "outer" issues be saved for individual treatment sessions (all of the members were also in individual treatment); the second rule was that there could be no physical violence, no matter how heated a discussion might become. Both rules proved to be important. When the group started, there was an underlying air of competitiveness and bravado. The first display of tenderness was met by one of the men proclaiming, "If this is going to be a bunch of touchy-feely crap, I'm outta here!"

The familiar split between the masculine and feminine manifested right within the group as three of the men adopted a more "masculine" posture and the three others assumed a more "feminine" stance. There then ensued a mutual process of projection, as each subgroup began to project its shadow qualities onto the other. One of the manifestations of this split was to create an alliance within the two subgroups which was then covertly, and sometimes overtly, acted out against the other subgroup. It became clear that all six of the men had troubled relationships with their fathers who, while very different in many ways, were all generally characterized as unemotional, distant, and critical, and as having had high expectations of the men as boys. None of the fathers had had much of a positively sustained or emotionally developed relationship with his son.

The differences between the subgroups seemed to rest on the men's early relationships not with their fathers but with their mothers. The more masculine subgroup had mothers who also carried high expectations for their sons and who were invested in their sons' accomplishments and potentials. Sons who carry the combined expectations of both mother and father tend to be much more critical of themselves and more vulnerable to the judgments of others. Outer accomplishments, while initially sought, seem to offer little in the way of internal acceptance, as if no amount of success in the outer world will satisfy the need for high self-esteem. Some of these men unconsciously undermine their own success in order to not compromise their inner psychological integrity for the demands and expectations of their parents. When such men succeed in their outer world accomplishments, their inner world often continues to feel barren and empty of warmth and self-acceptance. In fact, outer success often has the effect of *deepening* their sense of inner emptiness and despair. This disparity between the outer world and the inner self was poignantly expressed, in our group when one of the most "successful" members committed suicide. In his suicide note he said, "When they cut me open, they'll find I was already dead inside."

We can see from this how exaggerated exogenic expectations and the "success ethic" claim the emotional lives of many men. The increasing disparity between their inner and outer worlds eventually leaves them in the grips of an overwhelming depression. This often happens when a man has focused too much on being a "good provider" but has not developed the relational side of his family life. He arrives at retirement feeling that whatever the good life was supposed to have been, he somehow missed it. Suicide rates seem to reflect this: while males generally commit suicide three to four times more often than females, in the sixty-five-and-over age group males commit suicide *seven* times more often than females.[5] If the most common stimulus for suicide is indeed "unendurable psychological pain" and the "common stressor is frustrated psychological needs,"[6] what dismal prospects must men feel they are facing when they reach the end of their professional and occupational lives?

The more feminine subgroup had mothers who were less invested in their son's accomplishments and who were perhaps more resigned to, or accepting of, the traditional mother role. These men received more overt emotional support and fewer exogenic expectations from their mothers. This seemed to contribute to their tendency to be more invested in relationship as a source of self-esteem, making them more sensitive to the approval of others. Even though they were also invested in outer world activities and accomplishments, they were also more invested, positively or negatively, in family life. They were interpersonally warmer and somewhat more easy-going than the more masculine subgroup. They also showed more emotional vulnerability and had an easier time forming attachments.

Men and Friendship

Men's therapy groups can provide an opportunity for men to develop relationships of depth with each other—an opportunity that is lacking in the outer world, where relationships with other men are often confined to the professional or business realm. American men usually have "safe" relationships with each other, in which business, sports, and the superfluities of family life are discussed, but in which little of an emotional or personal nature is shared. Emotional closeness between men is restricted by unarticulated rigid customs of behavior that are often thoughtlessly ritualized. A common example is the way in which men who are friends greet each other and say goodbye. Although women who are friends almost always hug and sometimes kiss each other, and men also hug and sometimes kiss familiar women, men typically keep each other at a distance by shaking hands. In our culture hugging between men is rare and kissing strictly avoided, except under special circumstances. Even then, there are always a few men who maintain their distance, or who stiffen at the prospect of being hugged.

Friendship between men is further burdened by the fear of phallic or genital relatedness, which is also known as *homopho-bia*—the fear of being homosexual, or the fear of homosexuals. Men are so accustomed to relating emotionally in a phallic way that they fear that closeness with men will "turn into" sexuality, as it so often does when they relate to women. Part of the difficulty is that men have few, if any, models of how to behave when they feel tenderness toward another man. We know only too well how to act when we feel angry or threatened by other men, and we know how to be competitive, intellectual, or boastful, but most of us are at a loss when it comes to expressing tenderness toward other men.

Stuart Miller, in his book *Men and Friendship,* expresses this dilemma as it once occurred in his own experience with a man he admired:

> Surely when one is in a significant relationship with another person, there is a play of excitement over our whole organism. We sense a diffuse thawing, a generalized pleasure. And we don't know what to call it. Not anymore. So, nowadays, we call it sex.
>
> But though it may, incidently, sometimes pluck those strings, it is more than and different from. It is not really desire—in the sexual sense—I feel for Wreston yesterday. It is love, tenderness—mixed with admiration, understanding, and even gratitude. But we have no ways of expressing such a mixture to another man anymore.
>
> So dumbly, my smile still on my face, I sit in my chair and feel what I feel. But I do not caress that tired head. And he could probably use it.[7]

Men need to learn that intimacy is not necessarily sexual, as women are also so often trying to tell us.

Homosexual and Homophobic Behavior

There is perhaps no culture in the world in which there is not some record of homosexuality. There are some cultures in which homosexuality is not seen as a pathological form of behavior, and there are even some cultures—like the Sambia of New Guinea—in which homosexuality is practiced by pubertal boys in the period between leaving their mothers' houses and entering marriage. This transitional homosexuality is institutionalized and practiced as part of the boys' becoming men.

The traditional psychoanalytic view of overt homosexual behavior has recently been criticized and reevaluated in mental health circles. There have been objections to the classification of homosexuality as a form of pathological behavior, which has enhanced its social stigma. Under pressure (particularly by gay activists) to view homosexual relationships as simply one form of human sexual relatedness, the American Psychiatric Association (in 1973) finally dropped the diagnosis from the categories of mental disorders listed in the diagnostic manual of the mental health profession, the *DSM III.* One of the results of this has been that many mental health professionals are now wary of attempting to deal with homosexuality as a psychological problem, for fear that they will be accused of harboring a "pathological" view of this behavior.

Even though homosexuality is no longer officially considered a pathological disorder, its causes are still in question.[8] Psychoanalysts generally continue to believe that the early environmental influences are the most significant, with the most common explanation being that a male with a homosexual orientation identified with an overinvolved and intrusive mother and, at the same time, was unable to form an adequate positive identification with the father, who was often overbearing, cold, distant, and uninvolved in immediate family life. This early life dynamic, psychoanalysts believe, results in the son's failure to resolve the Oedipus conflict: he is not able to separate from the mother and form a more

appropriate identification with his father. There are some psychoanalysts who believe that homosexuality is strictly inborn, but
they also knowledge that gay men seem to be longing for a lost
or incomplete attachment to their fathers. However, they speculate that the father is rejecting his son purely on the basis of the
son's homosexuality.[9]

The father's rejection of the homosexual son itself brings up an
interesting question. What is so dreadful about homosexuality
that would cause a father to reject his own flesh and blood? Might
this rejection, when it does occur, be based on the father's deep
fear of the feminine qualities in his son? Homosexuals in our
society are rejected, humiliated, and even physically abused because they are perceived to be "effeminate"—the more effeminate they appear, the greater is the likelihood that they will be
ostracized. On the other hand, because homosexuals are so
frequently stereotyped as "effeminate," "masculine" homosexuals
are more likely to elicit surprise in those who identify them. The
fear of homosexuality is so strong in our culture that young boys
who have been sexually molested by men often don't want to
report the abuse because of the fear of being seen as homosexual
themselves.[10] Men who have a homosexual orientation are particularly susceptible to the negative projections of heterosexual men,
especially men who have an overmasculinized sexual view of
themselves. It is interesting that women tend to be more tolerant
of male homosexuality than men are, and that men are more
tolerant of the imagery of female homosexuality than they are of
male homosexuality.

Although "acting out" against homosexuals is seen as a form of
homophobia, it might just as well be called *feminophobia,* since
it seems far more to characterize men's fear of the anima. Why
don't we hear of a correspondingly intense homophobia in
women? Women seem to accept both male homosexuality and
lesbianism more openly than men do, because they have a more
positive identification of femininity within themselves. As we saw
earlier, a man needs to separate from his mother in a rather
dramatic way in order to find his masculine identity. The problem

of separation for a woman is much less dramatic because of a preexisting feminine identity that she shares with her mother. I would speculate that men who react most against homosexuals have the greatest split from their own feminine nature, as well as the greatest fear of losing a masculinity that has not been grounded in a stable and secure father-son relationship.

But what is so fearful about the femininity perceived by homophobic men? From the standpoint of a fixated, overdeveloped masculine consciousness, femininity represents the opposite pole, which is also regarded as inferior. In short, homophobia is a rather childlike egocentric thought pattern that operates as a defense against being emotionally in need of another man. The homophobic man is projecting onto the homosexual man his need for the deep emotional attachment that was missing in his early development, as well as his denial of that need. The dilemma of so many men in our culture is that when they relinquish their primary emotional attachment to their mothers, their fathers are not there to take up the attachment and help them develop a masculine identity. As these sons become fathers, they also become phobic about the intensity of their son's emotional longing for them. This pattern in our culture has been enacted between fathers and sons for many generations.

Let's round this out with an example. Mike, a man I once saw in therapy, told me that in high school he and his "jock" friends would often cruise Hollywood Boulevard looking for homosexuals to beat up. Mike was an only son whose father was a very successful businessman. He described his mother as an "absolute angel" who had always been there for him, but who had given up her own successful career to be a housewife. Mike's father was extremely demanding of him; he was also emotionally distant and physically abusive. His father's expectations were at complete odds with what Mike wanted to do with his own life: Mike wanted to be a musician or an actor, while his father wanted him to be a businessman. His father threatened not to pay for his college education if he didn't go to business school. Mike went to business school, graduated, and then married.

Not long after he married, Mike began to have numerous affairs, maintaining that he could "screw constantly" if allowed to. When Mike was forty years old, his father committed suicide. The remainder of Mike's own adult life was marked by chronic dissatisfaction. He never felt he was successful enough (in spite of having become a millionaire) and was always on the lookout for new ventures that would make more money. His relationships with other men were always superficial, restricted primarily to business associations. Two preoccupations seemed to plague him: a concern that his wife, of whom he was extremely possessive, would stray from him, and a constant worry that if he started to get close to other men they would turn out to be homosexual. When he was fifty, he began to experience his wife moving away from him emotionally; tragically, shortly after, he committed suicide.

As is so often the case, Mike's suicide was not based on a lack of success but on an early lack of emotional fulfillment that persisted into later life. His failure to gain his father's love and approval and his lack of emotional separation from his mother, which was later transferred onto his wife, kept him from feeling that he was a worthwhile person, no matter how successful he became. His life became a "phallic quest," in which no amount of financial security or sexual activity could provide the emotional nurturance he craved. Mike's fear of homosexuality represented a defense against his denied emotional need for his father which, because it was so split off, became a phallic threat. As is generally true of the psyche, that which was split off returned in a negative and exaggerated unconscious form. Mike's rage at his father, with whom he unconsciously identified and whom he also rejected, was finally turned against himself. He shot himself in the heart.

The Phallic Orientation

Cultural mythology perpetuates the notion of the male as provider and the use of his sexuality as a tool. This notion, which I would call a *negative phallic orientation,* results in the tendency to view women, and the world itself, as objects of conquest. In the young boy, it can begin as a preoccupation with penis size as a measure of future potency. Later, sexual performance becomes a critical issue: a man feels compelled to "make" his partner reach orgasm as a criterion of his adequacy. The negative phallic orientation is conspicuous by its lack of *Eros,* the quality of relatedness. Without Eros, love is narcissistic, an unrelated performance.

Male impotence, as a psychogenic disturbance, represents a threat to many men's self-esteem and self-worth. This is because men unfortunately associate sexuality with power. Even the word *impotent,* with its synonyms of *weak, powerless, feeble, helpless,* and so on, is a reflection of the cultural bias that says a man is supposed to be powerful in his performance. We do not say that women are impotent—another linguistic reflection of presumed gender-based differences. In sexuality, as in other areas, men have been taught to value an exogenic orientation, with its emphasis on the *goal* rather than the *process.*

Penis-envy, castration anxiety, and other phallic concepts from early psychoanalysis have been "grandfathered" into current masculine psychology with little consideration for the effect of this imagery on the male psyche and the father-son relationship. As we saw earlier, Freud was responsible for the concept of penis-envy as applied to the psychology of women. In my own clinical work with women, imagery of the "envied penis" occurs most often in daughters of overbearing, domineering, and "castrating" fathers who were unsure of their personal, emotional, and spiritual strength. These fathers employed the peculiar patriarchal custom of projecting their inadequacies onto their daughters and, in turn, inflating their son's penile grandiosity. Freud, as much as I can understand him through his own writing and the writing that has been done about him, was essentially not psychologically different from those fathers. Although certainly an intellectual pioneer in the exploration of the unconscious, he remained a product of a strongly patriarchal society and family, and much of his psychology reflects that tradition. Its emphasis on penile grandiosity has projected the notion of penis envy onto women, and is to some degree responsible for the current phallocentric orientation of men.

An extreme manifestation of this orientation is rape. Rape does not have to do with reproduction, or with love for one's partner, even when it is "date rape" or spousal rape. It is an act devoid of Eros because it is so "unrelated" and hence is carried out in the worst sense of treating the victim as an object. It has nothing to do with the victim as a person; the rapist's unconscious aggression and hatred are directed against his symbolic mother. The rapist's inner feminine has been arrested at the stage of an angry and helpless child. His envy of his mother's breast finally mounts into a genital attack on the symbolic cold, withholding mother in order to take what he feels deprived of. The rapist could be seen as an endogenously helpless male attempting to overcome his inner sense of powerlessness through an exogenous use of strength against an all-powerful mother-object whom he perceives only through his projections. He is incapable of relating to his victim, or anyone else, as a person, because he has never experienced "I-Thou" relatedness.

Castration anxiety is another notion that has obstructed our understanding of men's negative phallic orientation to women. According to Freud, a boy turns his attention away from the mother out of a primal fear of the father's jealousy and vengeance. However, a father whose own anima has been reasonably well integrated can help his son to separate from the mother while retaining important aspects of his relationship with her. Through this relationship the son forms the ground for the capacity for emotional relatedness, known as *Eros*. In the father he finds embodied *phallos*—the creative energy of masculinity, which has a spiritual, as well as physical, component. As Jung says, "The father is the representative of the spirit, whose function is to oppose pure instinctuality."[11] James Wyly refers to *phallos* as "the energy with which one mobilizes individuality."[12] And, as Jung also points out, "A phallic symbol does not denote the sexual organ, but the libido, and however clearly it appears as such, it does not mean itself but is always a symbol of the libido."[13]

So, a positive phallic orientation is one in which Eros and *phallos* are embodied together, based on a secure sense of masculinity. A man then uses his sense of strength physically as well as emotionally, without an adolescent need to protest against the power of the mother, and without a need to overpower or possess the outer woman.

Relationship as Transformation

The "choice" of a love partner is always an attempt (however amiss the results may be) to fulfill a deep emotional as well as spiritual need. Whether we are homosexual or heterosexual in our orientation, this choice is far more determined by unconscious factors than by conscious ones; we are rarely sure why we choose the partners we do. A propensity that seems innate for both sexes and that exerts a powerful influence, even on our unconscious choices, is the urge toward individual wholeness or completeness. The search for an outer partner is always an attempt to gain a closer connection to what is missing within. And when the outer relationship fails, or seems to, we must be careful not to place too much blame on the outer person, since part of what we have experienced is the workings of our inner woman. As John Beebe points out, "Initiation by the anima means submitting to painful experiences of betrayal and disappointment when the projections she creates with her capacity for illusion fail to produce happiness. Accepting the pain of one's affects toward those experiences is a critical part of integrating the anima."[14]

A love relationship, with all its hope, pleasure, and pain, represents a striving at the deepest psychic level for a vital emotional constituent that is far beyond an individual's biological or even "sexual" needs. On the spiritual level, the experience of love ideally leads to *coniunctio,* that is, a union not only of the individuals themselves, but also of the masculine and feminine opposites within each of their personalities. In this way, the love relationship can act as a channel and container of potential psychological and spiritual transformation. It is this aspect of relationship that needs to be kept in the foreground of the awareness of both society and the individual. It is as Marie-Louise von Franz points out in the myth of Eros and Psyche: "Love with its passion and pain becomes the urge toward individuation, which is why there is no real process of individuation without the experience of love, for love tortures and purifies the soul."[15]

Epilogue

But where was this Self, this innermost? It was not flesh and
bone; it was not thought or consciousness. That was what the
wise men taught. Where then was it? To press towards the Self—
was there another way that was worth seeking? Nobody showed
the way, nobody knew it—neither his father, nor the teachers
and wise men, nor the holy songs. . . . They knew a tremendous
number of things—but was it worthwhile knowing all these
things if they did not know the one important thing, the only
important "thing"?   —HERMANN HESSE

CIVILIZATION BEGAN largely within a matrilineal and matrifocal
group, and only later, with increasingly complex tool-making and
metallurgy and the rise of kingship, was the patriarchy spawned.
Now, only a brief four thousand or so years later, it would appear
that the patriarchal age, with its Oedipal father, is on the way out,
and we are evolving toward psychological androgyny. The psychology of masculine consciousness is deeply in need of integrating the feminine parts of itself that have been split off during this
span of human history. This confrontation and attempt to integrate the feminine leads ultimately to the process of individuation
and the experience of the self.

The Self

For Jung, the meaning of life could be found in the realization of the self, which for each individual holds a different meaning and a different destiny. The driving force behind the individuation process is the archetype of the self. In this sense, the individuation process does not culminate in a life lived only for its own sake as has been determined by the ego, or even in a realization of the "divinity of life," but in an experience of the "divine" within oneself. And here is the heart of the matter: in the individuation process the ego—experienced for most of one's life as the center of personality—comes to the realization that it is not as absolute as it has seemed to be, and it is superseded by an experience of the archetype of the self. This archetype then acts as a balancing or centering force in one's life, moving one beyond the constraints of ordinary ego consciousness. One outcome of this is the capacity for self-reflective consciousness, which functions to direct our attention away from the ego as the center of awareness, values, and meaning, thus creating a new transcendent perspective of consciousness. Another possible outcome is that the experience of the self restores a balance to the experiences of ordinary consciousness, overcoming the ego's tendency to one-sidedness.

Symptoms, depressions, and inexplicable moods and suicidal crises may be viewed as a function of the self, which is unconsciously attempting to bring about a state of emotional, psychological, and even physiological balance.

Memories, Dreams, Reflections is a journal of Jung's own inner struggles from earliest childhood through his entire adult life, as well as a description of the means he developed for coping with them. Images of the self from his dreams, active imagination, mediumistic experiences, and his mandala drawings helped him consciously portray a process of unfoldment. Through this process he came to understand the psychological and spiritual dimensions of his life. In this sense Jung's life was perhaps the best example of his theory. In *Aion,* the volume of his *Collected Works* devoted largely to the image of the self, Jung says: "The self as the essence of individuality is unitemporal and unique; as an archetypal symbol it is a God-image and therefore universal and eternal.[1]

Jung's Concept of Individuation

Jung's notion of the *individuation process* was the cornerstone of his entire theory. He described this process as life itself: "In the last analysis every life is a realization of a whole, that is of a self, for which reason this realization can also be called "individuation.""[2] The individuation process is a human being's "progressive realization of wholeness" in life, expressed in the form of an ongoing encounter between the conscious and unconscious, the ego and the archetype of the self.[3] Jung posited that the self is the forerunner of the ego, and that the ego arises developmentally from the self to bring "order" to the totality of one's experience. The ego is the medium of conscious experience and is as essential as the self; without the ego there could be no observation or "recording" of life experience, and therefore no individuation process, and without it there would be no vehicle of reflection, no awareness of the content of consciousness. The ego also "creates" the self, as it were, and in this way there is a mutual interdependence of the ego and the self. Through conscious awareness and reflection on the contents of the unconscious as they are revealed through dreams, fantasies, and active imagination, the contents of the unconscious are "actualized," brought into being. So by observing the images of the unconscious, including those of the self, and our reflection upon them, the self becomes a lived actuality rather than an abstract potentiality. This is what I have called *self-reflective consciousness.*

For Jung, the individuation process implied a teleology in life— a movement from one point to another, a sense that life has a direction and purpose. Although the Greek word *telos,* or *teleos,* implies an "end," it seems to me that individuation may also be described as a natural unfolding beyond ego, toward an awareness of the self. Men's Logos orientation may have turned many of us away from this notion; we are now more oriented to exogenous linear processes, with a seemingly distinct beginning, middle, and end.

Turning Points

Self-reflective consciousness—the process of incorporating the unconscious into one's conscious life—is, I believe, largely what Jung alluded to when he spoke about individuation, particularly when he pointed out the need to sacrifice our rather primitive lack of self-reflection. Self-reflective consciousness is different from the passive registering of the comings and goings of one's life and the ego's narrow evaluation of them. It is an active process of paying attention to those unconscious contents of our psyches that arise by way of dreams, fantasies, and experiences—particularly "bad" ones. It is experiencing the tension between living life in its mundane literalness and searching for the archetypal patterns that reveal themselves as they operate from below, from the unconscious. We do this in order to see if, in fact, there is a "direction" unfolding before us.

This direction is symbolized by major emotional events, which are our *turning points*. We look at these events and ask ourselves simply, "What did that mean to me?" and "What does the unconscious have to say about this?" Once (at the midpoint of my analysis) I dreamed that I was making a circle on my chest with my fingernails, over and over again. When I woke up I was actually making the circle on my chest; in fact, I had made a definite circular scratch. As I was waking, I kept repeating one word—"circulare, circulare, circulare"—almost in synchrony with the movement of my hand. The meaning of the word was unknown to me; I was puzzled. I searched dictionaries and reference books and finally found the Latin word *circulatio* in a book on alchemy, which had numerous references to the process of alchemy being "circular," as in "the process of making the gold is circular."

According to Jung, alchemy contains a wealth of symbolism related to the process of individuation. My dream turned out to be quite a revelation because it told me that the individuation process is a dynamically *circular* one—just the opposite of a linear process. One's life actually occurs with *direction,* but the movement is circular, a spiral that moves up and down and around, as well as forward. For men, who seem to have lost a connection with nature and its periodic cycles of death and rebirth, the notion of the circularity of life may be an essential key to understanding life's meaning.

The meaning of our lives is revealed to us through a circular process in which we identify our unique turning points and then touch on them over and over again, in effect, circumambulating them. As T. S. Eliot wrote in the *Four Quartets:*

> We shall not cease from exploration
> And the end of all our exploring
> Will be to arrive where we started
> And know the place for the first time.[4]

If we take some time to look at the important turning points in our lives, perhaps beginning with our first memory, we can begin to see how our lives are related to the process of finding meaning. Such turning points may include the day we started school, a death in the family, a marriage, when someone left us, when we left someone ourselves, and so forth. We will find that each of these times has certain images and affects, or strong feelings, clustered around it. Each of these events has an archetypal core, which frequently involves a relationship with one or both of our parents.

Let me relate an example from my own experience. My first memory is of my father leaving my family when I was three years old. As he drove out of the driveway, my mother ran out to stop him, grasping for the side of the car. She fell, and the back wheel of the car ran over one of her legs. I remember sitting at the roadside with my mother, trying to comfort her, telling her, "Don't worry, Mommy, I'll take care of you." I never saw my father again. (Now you know why I eventually wrote this book!) This was the first turning point in my life. The archetypal core of this experience is made up of two images: the "abandoning father" and the "wounded mother." Both of these images had a powerful influence on the direction my life took. As I review other turning points, I see how they either relate back to this experience or constitute new archetypal cores.

We keep returning to these archetypal cores even though we rarely know we are doing so or that there is any relationship between them and our present experience. These cardinal experiences form the emotional, psychological, and spiritual fabric from which much of our later life experience is woven. Our lives represent elaborate tapestries within which these experiences are loomed: we follow the same patterns, using only different colors, new variations on the same themes.

The ego, with its sometimes deceptively simplistic outlook, does not allow us to reflect on these turning points directly because they were too painful. The unconscious, however, never forgets. And so it is often through our dreams, fantasies, and later experiences that these turning points are eventually revealed.

Unfortunately, in the extreme case, specific unconscious experiences that act as stumbling blocks to future development sometimes take the form of compulsions. These include the abuses which we suffer and then paradoxically reenact, sometimes against those we love the most. In spite of the tragic consequences that may result, this tendency confirms the irrefutable prospective nature of the psyche: compulsive behavior may be the only way that these experiences are able to reach consciousness.

Jung placed individuation at the center of one's life in terms of its importance to psychological and spiritual growth—in large part because this process had a deep validity for his own life. The task, as he saw it, was to find meaning through understanding one's individual experiences, as well as through realizing that the ego needs to be supplanted by an awareness of our essentially spiritual, as well as psychological, needs.

Men's Developmental Issues

Modern men are confronted with major developmental issues, related not only to childhood development, but to development in adult life as well. The path of individuation, at least for most of us, is strewn with the accumulated and unfulfilled demands of our early development as well as the complications they have created in adult life. The failure to acknowledge and work to resolve these critical tasks has a great influence on men's behavior and ultimately on the quality of their lives. On the other hand, the conscious acknowledgment enables men to grow psychologically as well as spiritually.

What then must men do? How do we approach the tasks ahead of us? The future of the masculine myth depends upon the commitment men are able to make to the development of a new set of values, which include:

1. self-reflective consciousness as a dominant effort and value

2. a conscious effort to separate from the maternal container, in order to gain a true sense of emotional independence

3. the recollection and integration of projections of the disowned shadow

4. a reorientation to a more competent fatherhood as a role equal to career and profession

5. a renewed relationship to the feminine as an *inner* reality

6. the establishment of loving relationships with other men

7. an increased awareness of the spiritual dimension of one's life, through relativizing the ego and persona.

Uniting Opposites in Masculine Consciousness

The present character of both "masculinity" and "femininity" has been created and shaped by evolving biological, historical, cultural, and psychological determinants. From the viewpoint of the evolution of consciousness, that character has never been fixed or static, but has always been dynamic and even "magnetic."

Now human survival itself may depend on the successful integration of the best of what we now know as masculine and feminine, within both men and women. There is a need to find in ourselves a New Father and a New Mother, as archetypal structures capable of giving birth to a more psychologically androgynous child within.

This integration is possible within collective consciousness as well as within individual self-reflective consciousness; it is accomplished by continually expanding, exploring, and reevaluating ourselves. Through a conscientious effort and renewed emotional honesty, men can perhaps begin to realign their values and create a new faith in themselves.

The present moment is an extremely important one for men, particularly as we try to redefine and reformulate both who and what we are. The challenges are great and so are the potential pitfalls. It is particularly important that we be aware of the ever-present tendency to split from ourselves and to adopt defensive positions that may amount to unconscious protests against the deep inner work that needs to be done in order to truly discover ourselves. It would seem that men must learn to develop, in the words of the thirteenth-century Christian mystic Meister Eckhart, "A rich potential for sensitivity, a magnificent vulnerability."

So, the new task for each man is to turn the outer struggle inward, which may even feel to him to be backward, to his real soul-mate, the anima. He needs to appeal to her as a guide to the underworld of his psyche, to where she seems to know the way.

Our hearts need to be open and unprotected, the most difficult art of being human, and especially of being a man. We need to avoid the propensity to find shelter in any absolute "truths," but instead be willing to circumambulate our experiences; we need to look steadily at our concerns, take our fears by the hand, and look deeply into our "dark hearts."

Notes

Introduction

1. Warren Farrell, *Why Men Are the Way They Are.*
2. B. F. Skinner, *Beyond Freedom and Dignity.*
3. Edward F. Edinger, *Ego and Archetype.*

CHAPTER 1. *Anima*

1. James Hillman, *Anima: An Anatomy of a Personified Notion;* Verena Kast, *The Nature of Loving: Patterns of Human Relationship;* and Andrew Samuels, *Jung and the Post-Jungians.*
2. C. G. Jung, *Memories, Dreams Reflections,* p. 187.
3. The gender identity issue is compounded by the fact that Jungian analysts have traditionally described the anima as the contra*sexual* characteristics of a man—those qualities that have been culturally defined as female. For the purpose of greater clarity, it has been suggested that we instead speak in terms of the contra*psychological* qualities. English analyst Andrew Samuels reevaluates the anima as follows: "Jung's use of animus and anima can be better understood by regarding them as archetypal structures or capacities. In that sense, anima and animus promote images which represent an innate aspect of men and women—that aspect of them which is somehow different to how they function consciously; something other, strange, perhaps mysterious, but certainly full of possibilities and potentials." (Samuels, *Jung and the Post-Jungians,* p. 212.)
4. Hillman, *Anima,* chapter 10.
5. *Webster's Dictionary,* Second College Edition. (Springfield, Mass.: Merriam-Webster, 1983.)

6. See James Hillman's idea of *anima-feelings* in Marie-Louise von Franz and James Hillman, *Lectures on Jung's Typology*.

7. Arthur Miller, *Death of a Salesman: Certain Private Conversations in Two Acts and a Requiem*, p. 138.

8. C. G. Jung, *Psychology and Alchemy*, p. 177n.

9. Marie-Louise von Franz, *Projection and Recollection in Jungian Psychology*.

10. James S. Grotstein, *Splitting and Projective Identification*.

11. Somerset Maugham, *Of Human Bondage*, quoted in *Cliffs Notes on Maugham's Of Human Bondage* (Lincoln, Neb.: Cliffs Notes, 1963), p. 58.

12. Michael Gazzaniga, *Mind Matters: How the Mind and Brain Interact to Create Our Conscious Lives*, p. 35.

13. Vance Packard's book *The Hidden Persuaders* (New York: Washington Square Press, 1980) dramatically documents subliminal perception and the profound influence it exhibits on human behavior, as in its controversial use in advertising. See also Wilson Bryan Key's *Subliminal Seduction* (New York: New American Library, 1972).

14. Paul Watzlawick, *How Real is Real?*.

15. Harry Guntrip, *Schizoid Phenomena, Object Relations and the Self*.

16. The mythological equivalent of this modern father is Ouronos, the Greek sky father whose domain is the distant cosmos of unlimited space. He either eats his own children at the moment of their birth or else forces them back into their mother's womb.

17. Monica Furlong, *Merton: A Biography*.

18. Ibid., p. 232.

19. Ibid., pp. 274–275.

20. By R.S.; reprinted with thanks.

CHAPTER 2. *The Emergence of the Great Mother*

1. See Roger Lewin, *Human Evolution: An Illustrated Introduction*.

2. Microfossils and molecular data seem to indicate that the first forms of life arose within a few hundred million years after the cooling of the planet. For the next two billion years or so the earth was inhabited by simple algae and bacteria known as *prokaryotes,* individual tiny cells without nuclei but containing a set of genetic material within a single loop of DNA. Reproduction was accomplished by simple division of one cell into two "daughter" cells with exactly the same DNA as the parent cell. This primordial form of reproduction was strictly asexual.

3. The Age of Reptiles spanned a period between some three hundred to sixty-five million years ago. Following these were, of course, the

dinosaurs, which in turn became extinct due to either climatic changes or (the more recent speculation) an asteroid hitting the earth some sixty-five million years ago. *Cretaceous extinction* gave rise to another evolutionary landmark: the Age of Mammals. It has been said that if it had not been for the Cretaceous extinction, dinosaurs would still inhabit the earth today, and if the mammals had not survived, there would be no humans on the earth today.

4. Prior to *Homo habilis* the cranial capacity of the closest potential ancestral line to later humans, the *australopithecines,* was only about 450–550 centimeters. In *Homo habilis* the cranial capacity increased to 650–800 centimeters. Then *Homo erectus,* which arose at least 1.6 million years ago, showed an increase ranging from 900 to 1100 centimeters. In *Homo sapiens,* it increased even further, to about 1360 centimeters.

While some anthropologists and paleoanthropologists have hypothesized that the increase in cortical growth resulted from the increasingly complex demands of social interaction, it would seem that to ascribe the phenomenal increase in encephalization to a single, or even a few, factors is reductive as well as misleading. The potentiality provided by this increase in cortical mass far exceeded any known needs—whether social, intellectual, or spiritual—of any of our ancestors. Even today, the portion of our cortical capacity that we actively utilize is estimated to be a mere fifteen percent of the total.

Over the years, anthropological attempts to account for the increase in brain size have generated several hypotheses. One, known as the *hunting hypothesis,* indicates that the aggressive demands of hunting behavior were what separated the *Homo* line from their hominid ancestors. There is, however, little evidence to support that there was much hunting behavior two million years ago: the first evidence suggesting organized and cooperative hunting behavior might be attributed to the *Homo erectus* period. A subsequent hypothesis, known as the *gathering hypothesis,* postulates that the female/offspring bond, which was strong in all primates, created the evolutionary change. A hypothesis put forward by Glynn Isaac, the *food-sharing hypothesis,* suggests that food sharing, with its resulting social activity, was a major factor in restructuring social and economic life of the hominids as compared to the apes. The most recent hypothesis, the *central-place foraging hypothesis,* seems to have overturned the food-sharing hypothesis and replaced it with the notion that the hominids of one and a half million years ago were not quite as "human" as it was originally hoped.

5. The loss of the heat cycle in females occurred during the transition from the protohominids to the hominids.

6. Human infants are born with a cranial capacity of about 350 centimeters, which corresponds to the birthing capacity of the human female pelvis. In contrast to all other primates, which double their cranial capacity postnatally, the human quadruples its cranial capacity after birth. If this did not happen humans would still be at the cranial capacity of *Homo erectus,* or about 700 centimeters.

7. See, for example, the study of Spitz and Wolf on infants raised apart from mothers and the "failure to thrive" syndrome that often resulted in the premature deaths of children deprived of mothering. [See René A. Spitz and Ken Wolf, "Anaclitic Depression," in *The Psychoanalytic Study of the Child,* ed. Anna Freud et al., vol. 2 (New York: International University Press, 1946), pp. 313–342.] We also know that this early deprivation has a direct relationship to the severity of emotional damage in the growing child: the earlier the disruption of the parent/child bond, the greater the psychopathological consequences. This is also seen in the psychological effects created by mothers giving their children up for adoption, even when the adoptive parents are as loving or as psychologically and emotionally ideal as parents could be.

8. It has been speculated that our ancestors developed *sexual/anatomical dimorphism*—a difference in the body size of males as compared to females—because of the intense competition among males for females. There is evidence of sexual dimorphism extending as far back as the later *australopithecines,* indicating that there was competition among males for females at that time. Sexual dimorphism is also found clearly as late as *Homo habilis,* indicating that competition was still strong. It is not until *Homo erectus* that we see a modification in body size. Here the male is still larger than the female, but the differences in body size more closely approximate the differences seen in chimpanzees and, to a lesser degree, reflect differences more like those of modern men and women. This would seem to indicate that the degree of competition among males for females was partly supplanted by cooperation among them. The modern male child at birth still has greater muscle mass than the female, a difference that persists throughout adult life. The male is on an average twenty percent larger than the female. Even in numerous species of primates these differences in size and weight are also found alongside the division of labor. Today there is no remaining biological reason for anatomical dimorphism among humans; it remains only as a remnant of our predecessors.

9. As seen in most species of animals and in the emergence of the hominids, polygyny in males was the precursor to monogamous relationships, or *serial monogamy,* as it is known today. Sociobiologists have speculated that polygyny was an expression of the male's need to maximize his "reproductive success," and they would argue that even today this background accounts for the difficulty males have in settling down in relationships—in spite of the fact that polygyny's biological determinants can be traced back as far as the *dryopithecines,* several million years ago.

10. Totemism can also be understood as fulfilling both endogenous and exogenous needs of the tribe or clan, in that the totem helps to define kinship, or membership in the group (an endogenous need), while also prohibiting the intermarriage of members of the same totemic group or "family" (an exogenous need).

11. The earlier anthropological theory that exogamy was a naturally selected advantage in that it reduces genetic defects bears no weight since there is little, if any, evidence supporting substantial deleterious effects of inbreeding. Those defects that do occur require hundreds of generations to become manifest. Other early theories that also posited explanations of exogamy included one by Briffault and Thomson, as quoted in John Jackson's book *Man, God, and Civilization* (Secaucus, N.J.: Citadel Press, 1972): "Exogamy . . . was the natural outcome of the matriarchal basis of primitive society. The men lived with the clan into which they married and were obliged to surrender their products to the members of that clan. Thus, the practice of getting husbands from other clans enables each to extend its diet by obtaining access to foods which it did not produce itself. The initial function of exogamy was to circulate the food supply." While this may hold as a socioeconomic reason, the issue is deeper than one of only circulating the food supply.

12. Gaston Bachelard, *Water and Dreams.*

13. C. G. Jung, *Symbols of Transformation.*

14. Joseph Campbell, *The Power of Myth.*

15. Marija Gimbutas, *The Goddesses and Gods of Old Europe: Myths and Cult Images,* p. 17.

16. See ibid.; Riane Eisler, *The Chalice and the Blade: Our History, Our Future;* and Monica Sjoo and Barbara Mor, *The Great Cosmic Mother: Rediscovering the Religion of the Earth.*

17. Erich Neumann, *The Great Mother: An Analysis of the Archetype,* p. 151.

18. Gimbutas, *Goddesses and Gods of Old Europe,* p. 181.

19. Ibid., p. 182.

20. Erich Neumann, *The Origins and History of Consciousness*, p. 47.
21. Ibid., pp. 39–40.
22. Nor Hall, *The Moon and the Virgin: Reflections on the Archetypal Feminine*, p. 118.
23. Neumann, *The Great Mother*, p. 278.
24. Mircea Eliade, *Shamanism: Archaic Techniques of Ecstasy*, pp. 42–43.
25. Ibid.
26. C. G. Jung, *Psychology and Alchemy*.
27. A man's physical body and its various organs often carry the unconscious projections of emotional issues he needs to integrate into his awareness. These symptoms can lead him to a deeper level of communication with himself if he takes the symptoms as signs of a need to sacrifice the rigidities and narrowness of his conscious attitudes.
28. C. G. Jung, *Alchemical Studies*.
29. C. G. Jung, *The Structure and Dynamics of the Psyche*, para. 723.
30. Jung, *Symbols of Transformation*, para. 508.

CHAPTER 3. *Myths, Initiation Rites, and Masculinity*

1. Joseph Campbell, *The Power of Myth*, p. 165.
2. Harry Jerison, as quoted in Roger Lewin, *Human Evolution*, p. 87.
3. Whether encephalization or increasingly complex social demands was primarily responsible for the development of language is not completely clear.
4. Albert Cook, *Language and Myth*, p. 3.
5. Mircea Eliade, *Rites and Symbols of Initiation*.
6. Bruno Bettelheim, *Symbolic Wounds: Puberty Rites and the Envious Male*.
7. Sigmund Freud, *Totem and Taboo: Resemblances Between the Psychic Lives of Savages and Neurotics*, p. 192.
8. John Layard, "Homo-eroticism in Primitive Society as a Function of The Self," *Journal of Analytical Psychology* (1959).
9. Bettelheim, *Symbolic Wounds*, referring to F. Bryk, *Neger-Eros* (Berlin: Marcus & Webster, 1928).
10. Joseph L. Henderson, *Thresholds of Initiation*, p. 98.
11. Campbell, *The Power of Myth*, part 4.
12. Henderson, *Thresholds of Initiation*.
13. Robert Johnson, *He: Understanding Masculine Psychology*.
14. Henderson, *Thresholds of Initiation*, p. 188.
15. Erich Neumann, *The Origins and History of Consciousness*, p. 89.

CHAPTER 4. *The Oedipal Wound*

1. Peter Gay, *Freud: A Life for Our Time.*
2. Ibid., chapter 6.
3. Ernest Jones, *The Life and Work of Sigmund Freud.*
4. Freud's letter to Wilhelm Fliess of 13 May 1897, from Jones, *The Life and Work of Sigmund Freud*, p. 322.
5. Jones, *The Life and Work of Sigmund Freud.*
6. Ibid.
7. Erich Fromm, *Sigmund Freud's Mission*, chapter 2.
8. Gay, *Freud*, pp. 505–507.
9. Ibid, p. 585.
10. Jones, *Sigmund Freud*, chapter 10. It is unfortunate that the letters spanning the five-year engagement period have never been released from the Sigmund Freud Archives.
11. Gay, *Freud*, p. 501.
12. Fromm, *Sigmund Freud's Mission*, p. 59.
13. Sigmund Freud, *The Interpretation of Dreams*, p. 216.
14. Freud's father-complex in many ways dominated his outer life, while his mother-complex seems to have dominated his inner life. If one tries to estimate his success in resolving these complexes, by examining what is known of both his personal and professional life, there are no easy answers to be had. Evaluations of this sort in themselves are rather formidable undertakings. But there is enough evidence from his life and the influence of his work to venture an opinion of the impact he had on our understanding of the psychology of men, and particularly of the father-son relationship.

    Freud's need for absolute authority in spite of his confessed uncertainty, his deep vulnerability to being wounded by abandonment and rejection, and his fear of being found deficient all seem to be components of his father-complex. His own split from the feminine and his unconscious need to denigrate women speak to his failure to separate from his mother and a fear of regressing to a mother-dominated state of powerlessness. His incestuous longing for his daughter attests to his lack of anima development.
15. C. G. Jung, *Symbols of Transformation*, para. 508.
16. The incest prohibition is fascinating from the evolutionary perspective because even males of certain species of monkeys (rhesus) and wild gorillas will not mate with either their mothers or their sisters even though they will mate with all other females of their group. This tendency is probably the instinctual antecedent of the later incest taboo as it is seen universally in humans.

17. Freud's special interest in totemism was directly related to his interest in the incest taboo. In the aboriginal group Freud referred to, totemism and the taboo coexisted; that is, members of the same totem group were not allowed to intermarry.

18. Sigmund Freud, *Totem and Taboo*, p. 202.

19. Robert Stein, "On Incest and Child Abuse," in *Spring 1987* (Dallas: Spring Publications, 1987), p. 64.

20. Jeffrey Masson, *The Assault on Truth*, p. 271. Masson, a former keeper of the Freud Archives, attacks Freud, as well as the psychoanalytic establishment, for attempting to keep the seduction theory in mothballs, stored away in the Archives, while the seduction of children runs rampant as a social and psychological disease. Perhaps his most scathing accusation is that it is the parents themselves, overwhelmingly fathers, who turn to their children for sexual pleasure. Masson's thesis is that Freud's original seduction theory was so controversial that had he not recanted it, it would have amounted to undoing the foundation of the psychoanalytic movement. Masson believes that the seduction theory needs to be "uncovered" and reevaluated in light of the increasing numbers of reports of the sexual abuse of children by their parents.

21. The statistics are from personal communication with Katie Bond from the American Humane Association; see also J. James, W. M. Womack, and F. Strauss, "Physician Reporting of Sexual Abuse of Children," (*Journal of the American Medical Association,* vol. 240, 1978, pp. 1145–1146). Another study by D. E. H. Russell, "The Incidence and Prevalence of Intrafamilial and Extrafamilial Sexual Abuse of Female Children," (*Child Abuse and Neglect,* vol. 7, 1983, pp. 133–146) of a random sample of 933 women in the San Francisco area indicated that thirty-eight percent had been sexually abused before the age of eighteen, and sixteen percent of those abuses were by a family member.

Also, Kee MacFarlane and Jill Waterman in *Sexual Abuse of Young Children* (New York: Guilford Press, 1986) indicate that there is considerable variation in estimates of the percentage of children abused by their fathers. David Finkelhor's survey, "The Sexual Abuse of Children: Current Research Reviewed" (*Psychiatric Annals: The Journal of Continuing Psychiatric Education,* vol. 17, no. 4, 1987) found that six to eight percent of the incestuous relationships involve the father or stepfather, while other family members, notably uncles and brothers, make up another sixteen to forty-two percent of the offenders. Another report by M. D. Schecter and L. Roberge, "Sexual

Exploitation" (in *Child Abuse and Neglect: The Family and the Community,* 1976) concluded that seventy-eight percent of reported incest involves fathers and daughters.

Since the literature on sexual abuse is only recently beginning to proliferate, and since it consists of various kinds of studies—some based on community surveys and others on retrospective reports—there is a wide variability in the statistics, making an assessment of the frequency of incidents difficult to determine accurately. This, coupled with methodological problems, confuses the accuracy of overall assessment, although most clinicians are coming to know firsthand the actual magnitude of the problem.

22. Neither Freud nor Jung had access to any statistics relating to child sexual abuse because there simply weren't any at that time. But even now, a "real" versus "imaginal" debate goes on. Since the publication of Masson's book as well as those by Alice Miller (*The Drama of the Gifted Child, Thou Shalt Not Be Aware,* and *For Your Own Good*), there seems to be a battle of sorts going on as to whether incest is important as an actual or an imagined event. Name-calling, insults, and projections are scattered throughout various discussions of the issue, indicating that some highly charged complexes are being touched upon. Some analysts warn that *countertransference* issues need to be examined carefully to assess the degree of unconscious identification with the "victims" of sexual abuse. (Paul Kluger, "Childhood Seduction," in *Spring 1987 (Dallas: Spring Publications, 1987).*

What strikes me as rather curious is what whenever incest is discussed as a "real" act, it generates either absolute emotional intensity or a flat overintellectualized response—whether being discussed by the victims themselves, the mothers, the perpetrators, the social workers, or the therapists. Most notable is the emotionality of some analysts who seem to be attempting to quell the recent outrage by those who are appalled by the alarming frequency with which child sexual abuse occurs.

Jung, many years ago, spoke of the "violent disapprobation of psychology's concern with symbolism"; perhaps we are facing an enantiodromia, a flipping into the opposite of disapproving the literal. If so, we may have inadvertently split again. Perhaps what this comes from is the "overimaginalizing" of the incest complex as only the symbolic pole of incest. The archetype of incest is bipolar; the literal, negative, and nasty endogenous pole is also crying out for its place. It seems to me that it is as relevant, as compelling, and certainly as important.

CHAPTER 5. *Sons and Their Fathers*

1. Joseph L. Henderson, "Ancient Myth and Modern Man," in *Man and His Symbols,* ed. C. G. Jung (New York: Doubleday, 1964), p. 128.
2. Erich Neumann, *Amor and Psyche: The Psychic Development of the Feminine.*
3. Murray Stein, "The Devouring Father," p. 65.
4. Ibid., p. 71.
5. Ibid., p. 73.
6. Henderson, "Ancient Myth and Modern Man."
7. One of the most remarkable manifestations of this can be seen in children's dreams. Feelings and attitudes of one parent about the other are often vividly portrayed in the child's dreams even when these feelings and attitudes have not been consciously revealed to the child.
8. Shere Hite, *The Hite Report on Male Sexuality.*
9. Frank A. Pedersen et. al., "Parent-Infant and Husband-Wife Interactions Observed at Five Months."
10. Frederick Feirstein, "Fathering," published in *The Psychoanalytic Review,* vol. 73, no. 4 (Winter 1986).

CHAPTER 6. *Man the Slayer*

1. Sigmund Freud, *Beyond the Pleasure Principle: The Standard Edition of the Complete Psychological Works of Sigmund Freud,* vol. 18 (London: Hogarth Press, 1920).
2. Elisabeth Young-Bruehl, *Anna Freud: A Biography.*
3. C. G. Jung, *Psychology and Religion: East and West,* para. 131, p. 76.
4. N. Feshbach and S. Feshback, "Children's Aggression."
5. A. Bandura, ed., *Psychological Modelling: Conflicting Theories.*
6. M. Strauss, R. J. Gelles, and S. K. Steinmetz, *Behind Closed Doors.*
7. G. T. Hotaling and D. B. Sugarman, "An Analysis of Risk Markets in Husband to Wife Violence: The Current State of Knowledge."
8. See Phyllis Tyson, "Male Gender Identity: Early Developmental Roots," in *Toward a New Psychology of Men: Psychoanalytic and Social Perspectives,* ed. R. Friedman and L. Lerner, a special issue of the *Psychoanalytic Review,* 73, no. 4 (Winter 1986).
9. Hervey Cleckley, *The Mask of Sanity.*
10. Erich Fromm, *The Art of Loving.*
11. C. G. Jung, *The Archetypes and the Collective Unconscious,* para. 485.

CHAPTER 7. *Men's Sense of Love*

1. Mary Ritchie Key, *Male/Female Language,* p. 26.
2. Erik Erikson, *Childhood and Society.*
3. John Bowlby, *A Secure Base.*

4. David M. Buss, "Love Acts: The Evolutionary Biology of Love."
5. Paul C. Holinger, *Violent Deaths in the United States;* and United States Bureau of the Census, *Statistical Abstract of the United States,* 1988.
6. Edwin Shneidman, *Definition of Suicide.*
7. Stuart Miller, *Men and Friendship,* pp. 140–141.
8. Psychoanalytic explanations range from viewing homosexuality as a completely normal sexual orientation to seeing it as a fairly severe form of psychopathology. There has also been a more recent trend to ascribe homosexuality to a biological or innate tendency. Some explanations cite the biological and evolutionary concepts of the inherent bisexual or ambisexual nature of the brain. A genetic contribution to homosexuality may remain a remote possibility, but the studies of identical male twins do not give unequivocal support to a purely genetic explanation. Developmental abnormalities and chromosomal aberrations certainly occur, but the incidence of these is relatively rare, and their contribution to homosexuality is not necessarily significant. Again, psychobiologists have attempted to construct an evolutionary basis of homosexuality using the rationale of the survival of adaptive traits. However, in view of the fact that homosexuals have so few children, the question of whether there is distinct "homosexual adaptation" makes these points of view seem dubious. See Edward Wilson, *On Human Nature* (Cambridge: Harvard University Press, 1978); and, by the same author, *Sociobiology: The New Synthesis* (Cambridge: Harvard University Press, 1975).

Other studies citing a neuroendocrine basis of homosexuality are often inconclusive or contradictory. At best, they state that there are some biological factors that may act in a way to predispose one to homosexuality. Even intentional hormonalization of certain species of animals does not guarantee a specific sexual orientation, and this is even more true the higher one goes on the evolutionary scale. As is true of other kinds of complex human behaviors, biological determinants are far less important than social learning. See John Money, *Gay, Straight, and In-Between: The Sexology of Erotic Orientation* (Oxford and New York: Oxford University Press, 1988).

Homosexuality is no less free of attempts at reductive explanations than are other complex human behaviors. Adequate explanations of human behaviors, and particularly those that are at variance with socially accepted behaviors, require a multivariate approach that accounts for the subtleties and complexities of the individual's life history. Human behavior is itself inherently complex, requiring complex explanations. Most behavioral research, however, is biased by the fact that the experimenters are interested, covertly or overtly, in establishing a particular point of view. Dichotomous thinking leads to the presumption that it must be either this or that which accounts for behavior, rather than both or neither. The increasing specialization of Western science has the effect of further decreasing communication between scientists until they are ready to argue for their respective points of view. Furthermore, in spite of a great deal of current touting of wholism, in practice many approaches to the study of human behavior and mental health are still beset with an archaic Cartesian duality of splitting the mind and the body.

9. Richard A. Isay, *Being Homosexual: Gay Men and Their Development.*

10. Kee Macfarlane and Jill Watermann, *Sexual Abuse of Young Children,* p. 9.

11. C. G. Jung, *Symbols of Transformation,* para. 396.

12. James Wyly, *The Phallic Quest: Priapus and Masculine Inflation,* p. 17.

13. Jung, *Symbols of Transformation,* para. 329.

14. John Beebe, in his introduction to Jung's *Aspects of the Masculine,* p. xiii.

15. Marie-Louise von Franz, *An Interpretation of Apuleious' Golden Ass,* p. 66.

Chapter 8. *Epilogue*

1. C. G. Jung, *Aion,* in *Collected Works,* trans. R. F. C. Hall, vol. 9, para. 116 (Princeton: Princeton U. Press, 1959).

2. C. G. Jung, *Psychology and Alchemy,* para. 330.

3. Edward F. Edinger, *Ego and Archetype.*

4. T. S. Eliot, *Four Quartets,* p. 59.

Bibliography

Alvarez, A. *The Savage God: A Study of Suicide.* New York: Bantam Books, 1972.

Anthony, Dick; Ecker, Bruce; and Wilber, Ken eds. *Spiritual Choices: The Problem of Recognizing Authentic Paths to Inner Transformations.* New York: Paragon House, 1987.

Arieti, Silvano. *Creativity: The Magic Synthesis.* New York: Basic Books, 1976.

Arraj, James. *Christian Mysticism in the Light of Jungian Psychology: St. John of the Cross and Dr. C. G. Jung.* Chiloquin, Oregon: Tools for Inner Growth, 1986.

Babcock, Winifred. *Jung, Hesse, Harold: The Contributions of C. G. Jung, Hermann Hesse, and Preston Harold to a Spiritual Psychology.* New York: Harold Institute, 1983.

Bachelard, Gaston. *Water and Dreams.* Dallas: The Pegasus Foundation, 1983.

Bachofen, J. J. *Myth, Religion, and Mother Right: Selected Writings of J. J. Bachofen.* Translated by Ralph Manheim. Bollingen Series 84. Princeton: Princeton University Press, 1967.

Bandura, Albert ed. *Psychological Modelling: Conflicting Theories.* New York: Aldine-Atherton, 1971.

Begg, Ean. *Myth and Today's Consciousness.* London: Conventure, 1984.

Bell, Donald H. *Being A Man: The Paradox of Masculinity.* San Diego: Harcourt Brace Jovanovich, 1984.

Benjamin, Jessica. *The Bonds of Love: Psychoanalysis, Feminism, and the Problem of Domination.* New York: Pantheon Books, 1988.

Bennet, E. A. *What Jung Really Said.* What They *Really* Said Series, edited by A. N. Gilkes. New York: Schocken Books, 1967.

Bettelheim, Bruno. *Symbolic Wounds: Puberty Rites and the Envious Male.* Rev. ed. New York: Collier Books, 1962.

Birkhauser-Oeri, Sibylle. *The Mother: Archetypal Image in Fairy Tales.* Edited and with a foreword by Marie-Louise von Franz. Translated by Michael Mitchell. Toronto: Inner City Books, 1988.

Bolen, Jean Shinoda. *Goddesses in Everywoman: A New Psychology of Women.* San Francisco: Harper & Row, 1984.

————. *Gods in Everyman: A New Psychology of Men's Lives and Loves.* San Francisco: Harper & Row, 1989.

————. *The Tao of Psychology: Synchronicity and the Self.* San Francisco: Harper & Row, 1979.

Bowlby, John. *A Secure Base: Parent-Child Attachment and Healthy Human Development.* New York: Basic Books, 1988.

Bronstein, Phyllis and Cowan, Carolyn Pape, eds. *Fatherhood Today: Men's Changing Role in the Family.* New York: John Wiley & Sons, 1988.

Browne, Angela. *When Battered Women Kill.* New York: The Free Press, 1987.

Brunner, Cornelia. *Anima as Fate.* Translated by Julius Heuscher. Edited by David Scott May. Dallas, Tex.: Spring Publications, 1986.

Bullock, Alan. *Hitler: A Study in Tyranny.* Abr. ed. New York: Harper & Row, 1971.

Buss, David M. "Love Acts: The Evolutionary Biology of Love." In *The Psychology of Love,* edited by R. Sternberg and M. L. Barnes. New Haven: Yale University Press, 1988.

Campbell, Joseph. *The Hero With A Thousand Faces.* Bollingen Series 17. Princeton: Princeton University Press, 1968.

————. *The Power of Myth.* New York: Doubleday, 1988.

————, ed. *The Mystic Vision: Papers from the Eranos Yearbooks.* Bollingen Series 30, vol. 6. Princeton: Princeton University Press, 1968.

Carotenuto, Aldo. *The Vertical Labyrinth: Individuation in Jungian Psychology.* Translated by John Shepley. Toronto: Inner City Books, 1985.

Cherfas, Jeremy, and Gribbin, John. *The Redundant Male: Is Sex Irrelevant in the Modern World?* New York: Pantheon Books, 1984.

Cicchetti, Dante, and Hesse, Petra, eds. *Emotional Development.* New Directions for Child Development Series, vol. 16 (June 1982). Edited by William Damon. San Francisco: Jossey-Bass, 1982.

Cleckley, Hervey. *The Mask of Sanity.* New York: New American Library, 1982.

Colman, Arthur and Colman, Libby. *The Father: Mythology and Changing Roles.* Wilmette, Ill.: Chiron, 1988.

Cook, Albert. *Language and Myth.* Bloomington: Indiana University Press, 1980.

Cowan, Connell and Kinder, Melvyn. *Women Men Love, Women Men Leave: Why Men Are Drawn to Women and What Makes Them Want to Stay.* New York: Clarkson N. Potter, 1987.

de Beauvoir, Simone. *The Second Sex.* Translated and edited by H. M. Parshley. New York: Vintage Books, 1974.

Diagnostic And Statistical Manual of Mental Disorders. 3rd ed. Washington, D.C.: APA, 1980.

Dieckmann, Ute; Bradway, Katherine; and Hill, Gareth. *Male and Female, Feminine and Masculine.* San Francisco: C. G. Jung Institute of San Francisco, 1974.

Dinnerstein, Dorothy. *The Mermaid and the Minotaur: Sexual Arrangements and Human Malaise.* New York: Harper & Row, 1976.

Dooling, D. M., ed. *A Way of Working: The Spiritual Dimension of Craft.* New York: Parabola, 1986.

Dourley, John P. *The Illness That We Are: A Jungian Critique of Christianity.* Toronto: Inner City Books, 1984.

Downing, Christine. *The Goddess: Mythological Images of the Feminine.* New York: Crossroad, 1981.

Dubos, Rene. *A God Within.* New York: Charles Scribner's Sons, 1972.

Dunne, Edward J.; McIntosh, John L.; and Dunne-Maxim, Karen, eds. *Suicide and Its Aftermath: Understanding and Counseling the Survivors.* New York: W. W. Norton, 1987.

Eaton, S. Boyd; Shostake, Marjorie; and Konner, Melvin. *The Paleolithic Prescription: A Program of Diet and Exercise and a Design for Living.* New York: Harper & Row, 1988.

Edinger, Edward F. *Anatomy of the Psyche: Alchemical Symbolism in Psychotherapy.* LaSalle, Ill.: Open Court, 1985.

————. *The Christian Archetype: A Jungian Commentary on the Life of Christ.* Toronto: Inner City Books, 1987.

————. *The Creation of Consciousness: Jung's Myth for Modern Man.* Toronto: Inner City Books, 1984.

————. *Ego and Archetype.* New York: G. P. Putnam's, 1972.

————. *Encounter with the Self: A Jungian Commentary on William Blake's Illustrations of the Book of Job.* Toronto: Inner City Books, 1986.

Eisler, Riane. *The Chalice and the Blade: Our History, Our Future.* San Francisco: Harper & Row, 1987.

Eliade, Mircea. *Rites and Symbols of Initiation.* New York: Harper & Row, 1958.

————. *Shamanism: Archaic Techniques of Ecstasy.* Translated by Willard R. Trask. Bollingen Series 76. Princeton: Princeton University Press, 1972.

Eliot, T. S. *Four Quartets*. London: Faber and Faber. 1944.

Erikson, Erik H. *Childhood and Society*. 2d ed. New York: W. W. Norton, 1963.

Farrell, Warren. *Why Men Are the Way They Are*. New York: McGraw-Hill, 1986.

Fausto-Sterling, Anne. *Myths of Gender: Biological Theories About Women and Men*. New York: Basic Books, 1985.

Feinstein, David and Krippner, Stanley. *Personal Mythology: The Psychology of Your Evolving Self*. Los Angeles: Jeremy P. Tarcher, 1988.

Feshbach, N. and Feshbach, S. "Children's Aggression." In *The Young Child: Reviews of Research,* vol. 2, edited by W. W. Hartrup. Washington, D.C.: National Association for the Education of Young Children, 1972.

Fisher, Helen E. *The Sex Contract: The Evolution of Human Behavior*. New York: Quill, 1983.

Fordham, Michael. *Explorations into the Self*. The Library of Analytical Psychology, vol. 7. Edited by Michael Fordham et al. Orlando, Fl.: Academic Press, 1985.

Forward, Susan and Torres, Joan. *Men Who Hate Women and the Women Who Love Them*. New York: Bantam Books, 1987.

Frank, Robert H. *Passions Within Reason: The Strategic Role of the Emotions*. New York and London: W. W. Norton, 1988.

Freud, Sigmund. *The Interpretation of Dreams*. Translated and edited by James Strachey. New York: John Wiley & Sons, Science Editions, 1961.

———. *Totem and Taboo: Resemblances Between the Psychic Lives of Savages and Neurotics*. Translation and introduction by A. A. Brill. New York: Vintage Books, 1918.

Friedan, Betty. *The Feminine Mystique*. New York: W. W. Norton, 1963.

Friedman, Robert M. and Lerner, Leila, eds. *Toward a New Psychology of Men: Psychoanalytic and Social Perspectives*. Special issue of the *Psychoanalytic Review* 73, no. 4 (winter 1986).

Friedman, Sonja. *Men Are Just Desserts*. New York: Warner Books, 1983.

Fromm, Erich. *The Anatomy of Human Destructiveness*. New York: Holt, Rinehart and Winston, 1973.

———. *The Art of Loving*. New York: Harper, 1956.

———. *For the Love of Life*. Translated by Robert Kimber and Rita Kimber. Edited by Hans Jurgen Schulz. New York: The Free Press, 1986.

———. *Sigmund Freud's Mission*. New York: Harper & Bros., 1959.

Furlong, Monica. *Merton: A Biography*. San Francisco: Harper & Row, 1980.

Garfinkel, Perry. *In A Man's World: Father, Son, Brother, Friend and Other Roles Men Play*. New York: New American Library, 1985.

Gay, Peter. *Freud: A Life for Our Time*. New York: W. W. Norton, 1988.

Gazzaniga, Michael S. *Mind Matters: How the Mind and Brain Interact to Create Our Conscious Lives.* Boston: Houghton Mifflin Co., 1988.

Gimbutas, Marija. *The Goddesses and Gods of Old Europe: Myths and Cult Images.* Berkeley and Los Angeles: University of California Press, 1982.

———. *The Language of the Goddess.* San Francisco: Harper & Row, 1987.

Goldberg, Herb. *The Hazards of Being Male: Surviving the Myth of Masculine Privilege.* New York: American Library, 1977.

———. *The Inner Male: Overcoming Roadblocks to Intimacy.* New York: New American Library, 1988.

———. *The New Male: From Macho to Sensitive but Still All Male.* New York: New American Library, 1980.

Goldbrunner, Josef. *Individuation: A Study of the Depth Psychology of Carl Gustav Jung.* Notre Dame: University of Notre Dame, 1964.

Groth, A. N. "The Incest Offender." In *Handbook of Clinical Intervention in Child Sexual Abuse,* edited by S. M. Sgroi. Lexington, Mass.: Lexington Books, 1982.

Grotstein, James S. *Splitting and Projective Identification.* Northvale, N.J.: Jason Aronson, 1986.

Grun, Bernard, *The Timetables of History.* Based on Werner Stein's Kulturfahrplan. New York: Simon and Schuster, 1979.

Guggenbuhl-Craig, Adolf. *Marriage—Dead or Alive.* Translated by Murray Stein. Zurich: Spring Publications, 1977.

Guntrip, Harry. *Schizoid Phenomena, Object Relations and the Self.* New York: International Universities Press, 1969.

Hall, Nor. *The Moon and the Virgin: Reflections on the Archetypal Feminine.* New York: Harper & Row, 1980.

Hannah, Barbara. *Jung: His Life and Work: A Biographical Memoir.* New York: G. P. Putnam's Sons, 1976.

Harner, Michael. *The Way of the Shaman: A Guide to Power and Healing.* San Francisco: Harper & Row, 1980.

Henderson, Joseph L. *Thresholds of Initiation.* Middletown, Conn.: Wesleyan University Press, 1967.

Hesse, Hermann. *Steppenwolf.* Translated by Basil Creighton. New York: Bantam Books, 1969.

Hillman, James. *Anima: An Anatomy of a Personified Notion.* Dallas, Tex.: Spring Publications, 1985.

———. *Emotion. A Comprehensive Phenomenology of Theories and their Meanings for Therapy.* London: Routledge and Kegan Paul, 1960.

———. *Loose Ends: Schism, Betrayal, Longing, Masturbation, Abandon-*

ment and other Primary Papers in Archetypal Psychology. Zurich: Spring Publications, 1975.

————. *Suicide and the Soul.* New York: Harper & Row, 1964.

Hillman, James; Murry, Henry A.; Moore, Tom; Baird, James; Cowan, Thomas; and Severson, Randolph. *Puer Papers.* Irving, Tex.: Spring Publications, 1979.

Hite, Shere. *The Hite Report on Male Sexuality.* New York: Ballantine Books, 1981.

Hobson, Robert F. *Forms of Feeling: The Heart of Psychotherapy.* London and New York: Tavistock Publications, 1985.

Hochheimer, Wolfgang. *The Psychotherapy of C. G. Jung.* Translated by Hildegard Nagel. New York: G. P. Putnam's Sons for the C. G. Jung Foundation for Analytical Psychology, 1969.

Hoffman, Edward. *The Way of Splendor: Jewish Mysticism and Modern Psychology.* Boulder and London: Shambhala Publications, 1981.

Holinger, Paul C. *Violent Deaths in the United States: An Epidemiologic Study of Suicide, Homicide, and Accidents.* New York: Guilford Press, 1987.

Hopcke, Robert H. *A Guided Tour of the Collected Works of C. G. Jung.* Boston and Shaftesbury: Shambhala Publications, 1989.

Hope, Murray. *The Psychology of Ritual.* Longmead: Element Books, 1988.

Hotaling, G. T. and Sugarman, D. B. "An Analysis of Risk Markers in Husband to Wife Violence: The current state of Knowledge." In *Violence and Victims* 1, no. 2 (1986): 101–24.

Isay, Richard A. *Being Homosexual: Gay Men and Their Development.* New York: Farrar, Straus, Giroux, 1989.

Jackson, John G. *Man, God, and Civilization.* Secaucus, N.J.: Citadel Press, 1972.

Jacobi, Jolande. *The Way of Individuation.* Translated by R. F. C. Hall. New York: New American Library, 1983.

Jacoby, Mario. *The Analytic Encounter: Transference and Human Relationship.* Toronto: Inner City Books, 1984.

————. *Longing for Paradise: Psychological Perspectives on an Archetype.* Translated by Myron B. Gubitz. Boston: Sigo Press, 1985.

James, John. *Why Evil? A Biblical Approach.* Baltimore: Penguin Books, 1960.

Johnson, Robert A. *Femininity Lost and Regained.* New York: Harper & Row, 1990.

————. *He: Understanding Masculine Psychology.* New York: Harper & Row, 1977.

————. *She: Understanding Feminine Psychology.* New York: Harper & Row, 1977.

————. *We: Understanding the Psychology of Romantic Love.* San Francisco: Harper & Row, 1983.

Jones, Ernest. *The Life and Work of Sigmund Freud.* Vol. 1, *The Formative Years and the Great Discoveries: 1856–1900.* New York: Basic Books, 1953.

Jung C. G. *Alchemical Studies.* Collected Works, vol. 13. Translated by R. F. C. Hull. Bollingen Series 20. Princeton: Princeton University Press, 1967.

————. *The Archetypes and the Collective Unconscious.* Collected Works, vol. 9, pt. 1, 2d ed. Translated by R. F. C. Hull. Bollingen Series 20. Princeton University Press, 1968.

————. *Aspects of the Feminine.* Translated by R. F. C. Hull. Bollingen Series 20. Princeton: Princeton University Press, 1982.

————. *Aspects of the Masculine.* Translated by R. F. C. Hull. Introduction by John Beebe. Bollingen Series 20. Princeton: Princeton University Press, 1989.

————. *Memories, Dreams, Reflections.* Recorded and edited by Aniela Jaffe. Translated by Richard and Clara Winston. New York: Pantheon Books, 1961.

————. *Psychological Types.* Collected Works, vol. 6. Translated by R. F. C. Hull. Bollingen Series. 20. Princeton: Princeton University Press, 1971.

————. *Psychology and Alchemy.* Collected Works, vol. 12. Translated by R. F. C. Hull. Bollingen Series. Princeton: Princeton University Press, 1968.

————. *Psychology And Religion: East And West.* Collected Works, vol. 11. 2d ed. Translated by R. F. C. Hull. Bollingen Series. Princeton: Princeton University Press, 1969.

————. *The Structure and Dynamics of the Psyche.* Collected Works, vol. 8. Translated by R. F. C. Hull. Bollingen Series. Princeton: Princeton University Press, 1968.

————. *Symbols of Transformation.* Collected Works, vol. 5. Translated by R. F. C. Hull. Bollingen Series. Princeton: Princeton University Press, 1967.

Kaplan, Helen Singer. *Disorders of Sexual Desire and Other New Concepts and Techniques in Sex Therapy.* New York: Brunner/Mazel, 1979.

Kast, Verena. *The Nature of Loving: Patterns of Human Relationship.* Translated by Boris Matthews. Wilmette, Ill.: Chiron, 1986.

Katz, Jack. *Seductions of Crime: Moral and Sensual Attractions in Doing Evil.* New York: Basic Books, 1988.

Kazantzakis, Nikos. *The Saviors of God: Spiritual Exercises.* Translated by Kimon Friar. New York: Simon and Schuster, 1960.

Kelsey, Morton. *Healing and Christianity.* New York: Harper & Row, 1973.

Kelsey, Morton and Kelsey, Barbara. *Sacrament of Sexuality: The Spirituality and Psychology of Sex*. Warwick, N.Y.: Amity House, 1986.

Kerenyi, Karl. *Goddesses of Sun and Moon*. Translated by Murray Stein. Irving, Tex.: Spring Publications, 1979.

―――. *Hermes: Guide of Souls*. Translated by Murray Stein. Zurich: Spring Publications, 1976.

Kerenyi, Carl; Widengren, Geo; Maag, Victor; von Franz, Marie-Louise; Schlappner, Martin; Frey-Rohn, Liliane; Lowith, Karl; and Schmid, Karl. *Evil*. Translated by Ralph Manheim and Hildegard Nagel. Edited by the Curatorium of the C. G. Jung Institute, Zurich. Evanston, Ill.: Northwestern University Press, 1967.

Key, Mary Ritchie. *Male/Female Language*. New Jersey: The Scarecrow Press, 1975.

Keyes, Margaret Frings. *Inward Journey: Art as Therapy*. LaSalle and London: Open Court, 1983.

Klama, John. *Aggression: The Myth of the Beast Within*. New York: John Wiley & Sons, 1988.

Kluger, Rivkah Scharf. *Satan in the Old Testament*. Translated by Hildegard Nagel. Evanston, Ill.: Northwestern University Press, 1967.

Knapp, Bettina L. *A Jungian Approach to Literature*. Carbondale: Southern Illinois University Press, 1984.

Koltuv, Barbara Black. *The Book of Lilith*. York Beach, Me.: Nicolas-Hays, 1986.

Kroeger, Otto and Thuesen, Janet M. *Typetalk*. New York: Delacorte Press, 1988.

Lamb, Michael E. *The Role of the Father in Child Development*. 2d ed. New York: John Wiley & Sons, 1981.

―――, ed. *The Father's Role: Applied Perspectives*. New York: John Wiley & Sons, 1986.

Lawrence, Nathaniel and O'Connor, Daniel (ed.). *Readings in Existential Phenomenology*. Engelwood Cliffs, N.J.: Prentice-Hall, 1967.

Layard, John. "Homo-eroticism in Primitive Society as a Function of the Self." *Journal of Analytical Psychology*, 4 (1959): 101–115.

Lee, John H. *The Flying Boy: Healing the Wounded Man*. Deerfield Beach, Fl.: Communications, 1987.

LeGuin, Ursula K. *A Wizard of Earthsea*. New York: Bantam Books, 1975.

Leonard, Linda Schierse. *Wounded Woman: Healing the Father-Daughter Relationship*. Boulder and London: Shambhala Publications, 1983.

Levinson, Daniel J. *The Seasons of a Man's Life*. New York: Ballantine Books, 1978.

Lewin, Roger. *Human Evolution: An Illustrated Introduction*. New York: W. H. Freeman and Co., 1984.

Macdonald, Gordon. *The Effective Father.* Wheaton, Ill.: Tyndale House, 1977.

Macfarlane, Kee and Watermann, Jill. *Sexual Abuse of Young Children.* New York: The Guilford Press, 1986.

McGill, Michael E. *The McGill Report on Male Intimacy.* New York: Harper & Row, 1986.

Mahdi, Louise Carcus; Foster, Steven; and Little, Meredith, eds. *Betwixt and Between: Patterns of Masculine and Feminine Initiation.* LaSalle, Ill.: Open Court, 1987.

Marone, Nicky. *How to Father a Successful Daughter.* New York: McGraw-Hill, 1988.

Masson, Jeffrey. *The Assault on Truth.* New York: Penguin Books, 1984.

Mather, John M. and Briggs, Dennie, eds. *An Open Life: Joseph Campbell in Conversation with Michael Toms.* Burdett, N.Y.: Larson Publications, 1988.

Meier, C. A. *Soul and Body: Essays on the Theories of C. G. Jung.* San Francisco: Lapis Press, 1986.

Merton, Thomas. *Zen and the Birds of Appetite.* New York: New Directions, 1968.

Michaels, Leonard. *The Men's Club.* New York: Avon Books, 1978.

Michelet, Jules. *Satanism and Witchcraft: A Study in Medieval Superstition.* Translated by A. R. Allinson. New York: Citadel Press, 1939.

Miller, Alice. *The Drama of the Gifted Child.* Translated by Ruth Ward. New York: Basic Books, 1981.

―――. *For Your Own Good: Hidden Cruelty in Child-Rearing and the Roots of Violence.* Translated by Hildegarde Hannum and Hunter Hannum. New York: Farrar, Straus, Giroux, 1983.

―――. *Thou Shalt Not Be Aware: Society's Betrayal of the Child.* Translated by Hildegarde Hannum and Hunter Hannum. New York: New American Library, 1984.

Miller, Arthur. *Death of a Salesman: Certain Private Conversations in Two Acts and a Requiem.* New York: Penguin Books, 1976.

Miller, Stuart. *Men and Friendship.* San Leandro, Calif.: Gateway Books, 1983.

Money, John. *Gay, Straight, and In-Between: The Sexology of Erotic Orientation.* Oxford and New York: Oxford University Press, 1988.

Monick, Eugene. *Phallos: Sacred Image of the Masculine.* Toronto: Inner City Books, 1987.

Moore, Robert L., ed. *Carl Jung and Christian Spirituality.* New York: Paulist Press, 1988.

Neumann, Erich. *Amor and Psyche: The Psychic Development of the*

Feminine. Translated by Ralph Manheim. Bollingen Series 54. Princeton: Princeton University Press, 1954.

———. *The Archetypal World of Henry Moore.* Bollingen Series 67. Princeton: Princeton University Press, 1959.

———. *Creative Man. Five Essays.* Bollingen Series 61, vol. 2. Princeton: Princeton University Press, 1979.

———. *The Great Mother: An Analysis of the Archetype.* Translated by Ralph Manheim. Bollingen Series 47. Princeton: Princeton University Press, 1972.

———. *The Origins and History of Consciousness.* Translated by R. F. C. Hull. Bollingen Series 42. Princeton: Princeton University Press, 1954.

O'Flaherty, Wendy Doniger. *The Origins of Evil in Hindu Mythology.* Berkeley: University of California Press, 1967.

Olsen, Carl, ed. *The Book of the Goddess Past and Present.* New York: Crossroad, 1983.

Ornstein Robert. *Multimind: A New Way of Looking at Human Behavior.* Boston: Houghton Mifflin Co., 1986.

———. *The Psychology of Consciousness.* 2d ed. New York: Harcourt Brace Jovanovich, 1977.

Ornstein, Robert and Ehrlich, Paul. *New World New Mind: Moving toward Conscious Evolution.* New York: Doubleday, 1989.

Osherson, Samuel. *Finding Our Fathers: How a Man's Life Is Shaped by His Relationship with His Father.* New York: Fawcett Columbine, 1986.

Parke, Ross D. *Fathers.* Cambridge, Mass.: Harvard University Press, 1981.

Peck, M. Scott. *The Road Less Traveled: A New Psychology of Love, Traditional Values and Spiritual Growth.* New York: Simon and Schuster, 1978.

Peck, Robert Newton. *A Day No Pigs Could Die.* New York: Dell, 1972.

Pedersen, Frank A. et al., "Parent-Infant and Husband-Wife Interactions Observed at Five Months." In *The Father Infant Relationship,* edited by Frank A. Pedersen. New York: Praeger, 1980.

Penney, Alexandra. *How to Make Love to a Man.* New York: Dell, 1982.

Pelletier, Kenneth R. *Toward a Science of Consciousness.* New York: Dell, 1978.

Pelletier, Kenneth R. and Garfield, Charles. *Consciousness: East and West.* San Francisco: Harper Colophon Books, 1976.

Perry, John Weir. *Lord of the Four Quarters: Myths of the Royal Father.* New York: Collier Books, 1970.

Pleck, Joseph H. and Sawyer, Jack, eds., *Men and Masculinity.* Englewood Cliffs, N.J.: Prentice-Hall, 1974.

Ponce, Charles. *Papers Toward a Radical Alchemy: Metaphysics.* Berkeley: North Atlantic Books, 1983.

Pruett, Kyle D. *The Nurturing Father: Journey Toward the Complete Man.* New York: Warner Books, 1987.

Puryear, Herbert B. *Sex and the Spiritual Path.* Virginia Beach, Va: A.R.E. Press, 1980.

Qualls-Corbett, Nancy. *The Sacred Prostitute: Eternal Aspects of the Feminine.* Toronto: Inner City Books, 1988.

Rank, Otto. *The Myth of the Birth of the Hero and Other Writings.* Edited by Philip Freund. New York: Vintage Books, 1964.

Redfearn, Joseph W. T. *My Self, My Many Selves.* Library of Analytical Psychology, vol. 6. Edited by Michael Fordham, Rosemary Gordon, Judith Hubback, and Kenneth Lambert. Orlando, Fl.: Academic Press, 1985.

Restak, Richard M. *The Mind.* New York: Bantam Books, 1958.

Roberts, Bernadette. *The Experience of No-Self: A Contemplative Journey.* Boston and London: Shambhala Publications, 1984.

———. *The Path to No-Self: Life at the Center.* Boston and London: Shambhala Publications, 1985.

Rowan, John. *The Horned God: Feminism and Men As Wounding and Healing.* London and New York: Routledge and Kegan Paul, 1987.

Rubin, Jerry and Leonard, Mimi. *The War Between the Sheets: What's Happening with Men in Bed and What Women and Men are Doing About It.* New York and Mahwah: Richard Marek Publishers, 1980.

Rubin, Lilian B. *Intimate Strangers: Men and Women Together.* New York: Harper Colophon Books, 1984.

Rubin, Theodore Isaac and Berliner, David C. *Understanding Your Man: A Woman's Guide.* New York: Ballantine Books, 1977.

Ruse, Michael. *Homosexuality: A Philosophical Inquiry.* Oxford and New York: Basil Blackwell, 1988.

Saggs, H. W. F. *Civilization Before Greece and Rome.* New Haven and London: Yale University Press, 1989.

Samuels, Andrew. *Jung and the Post-Jungians.* London: Routledge and Kegan Paul, 1985.

———, ed. *The Father: Contemporary Jungian Perspectives.* New York: New York University Press, 1986.

Sanford, John A. *The Strange Trial of Mr. Hyde: A New Look at the Nature of Human Evil.* San Francisco: Harper & Row, 1987.

Sanford, John A. and Lough, George. *What Men Are Like: The Psychology of Men for Men and the Women Who Live with Them.* New York and Mahwah: Paulist Press, 1988.

Sanford, Nevitt and Comstock, Craig. *Sanctions for Evil: Sources of Social Destructiveness.* San Francisco, Calif.: Jossey-Bass, 1971.

Schmookler, Andrew Bard. *Out of Weakness: Healing the Wounds That Drive Us to War*. New York: Bantam Books, 1988.

Schwartz-Salant, Nathan. *Narcissism and Character Transformation: The Psychology of Narcissistic Character Disorders*. Toronto: Inner City Books, 1982.

Seligmann, Kurt. *Magic, Supernaturalism and Religion*. Pantheon Books, 1971. (Published in 1948 as *The History of Magic*).

Sheldrake, Rupert. *A New Science of Life: The Hypothesis of Formative Causation*. Los Angeles: J. P. Tarcher, 1981.

———. *The Presence of the Past: Morphic Resonance and the Habits of Nature*. New York: Times Books, 1988.

Shengold, Leonard. *Halo in the Sky: Observations on Anality and Defense*. New York: Guilford Press, 1988.

Shneidman, Edwin. *Definition of Suicide*. New York: John Wiley & Sons, 1985.

Sjoo, Monica and Mor, Barbara. *The Great Cosmic Mother: Rediscovering the Religion of the Earth*. San Francisco: Harper & Row, 1987.

Skinner, B. F. *Beyond Freedom and Dignity*. New York: Knopf, 1971.

Smith, Homer W. *Man and His Gods*. Boston: Little, Brown and Co., 1952.

Spiro, Melford E. *Culture and Human Nature: The Theoretical Papers of Melford E. Spiro*. Edited by Benjamin Kilbourne and L. L. Langness. Chicago and London: University of Chicago Press, 1987.

Stein, Murray. *In Midlife*. Dallas, Tex.: Spring Publications, 1983.

———. "The Devouring Father." In *Fathers & Mothers: Five Papers on the Archetypal Background of Family Psychology*, by Augusto Vitale et al. Zurich: Spring Publications, 1973.

Stein, Robert. *Incest and Human Love*. Dallas, Tex.: Spring Publications, 1973.

Sternberg, Robert J. and Barnes, Michael L., eds. *The Psychology of Love*. New Haven and London: Yale University Press, 1988.

Stevens, Anthony. *The Roots of War: A Jungian Perspective*. New York: Paragon House, 1989.

Storr, Anthony. *Solitude: A Return to the Self*. New York: Free Press, 1988.

Stone, Merlin. *When God Was a Woman*. San Diego: Harcourt Brace Jovanovich, 1976.

Strauss, M., Gelles, R. J., and Steinmetz, S. K. *Behind Closed Doors*. Garden City, N.Y.: Doubleday Anchor Press, 1980.

Strongman, Ken T. *The Psychology of Emotion*. 3d ed. New York: John Wiley & Sons, 1987.

Te Paske, Bradley A. *Rape and Ritual: A Psychological Study*. Toronto: Inner City Books, 1982.

Tiger, Lionel. *Men in Groups*. New York: Random House, 1969.

Tripp, C. A. *The Homosexual Matrix*. New York: McGraw-Hill, 1975.

U.S. Department of Justice, Bureau of Justice Statistics. *Report to the Nation on Crime and Justice*. 2d ed. March 1988.

van der Post, Laurens. *Jung and the Story of Our Time*. New York: Pantheon Books, 1975.

von Franz, Marie-Louise. *C. G. Jung: His Myth in Our Time*. Translated by William H. Kennedy. Boston and Toronto: Little Brown, 1975.

————. *Projection and Recollection in Jungian Psychology*. Lasalle and London: Open Court, 1980.

————. *An Interpretation of Apuleius' Golden Ass*. Irving, Tex.: Spring Publications, 1980.

————. *Shadow and Evil in Fairytales*. Zurich: Spring Publications, 1974.

————. *The Way of the Dream*. Toronto: Windrose Films, 1988.

Wagenvoord, James and Bailey, Peyton. *Men: A Book for Women*. New York: Avon Books, 1978.

Watzlawick, Paul. *How Real is Real?*. New York: Vintage Books, 1977.

Wehr, Demaris S. *Jung and Feminism: Liberating Archetypes*. Boston: Beacon Press, 1987.

Welch, John. *Spiritual Pilgrims: Carl Jung and Teresa of Avila*. New York and Ramsey: Paulist Press, 1982.

Westman, Heinz. *The Springs of Creativity: The Bible of the Creative Process of the Psyche*. Wilmette, Ill.: Chiron, 1986.

Whitmont, Edward C. *Return of the Goddess*. New York: Crossroad, 1984.

————. *The Symbolic Quest: Basic Concepts of Analytical Psychology*. New York: Harper Colophon Books, 1973.

Wickes, Frances G. *The Inner World of Childhood*. Rev. ed. New York: New American Library, 1968.

Wilber, Ken. *Up From Eden: A Transpersonal View of Human Revolution*. Boston: Shambhala Publications, 1986.

Wilber, Ken; Engler, Jack; and Brown, Daniel P. *Transformations of Consciousness: Conventional and Contemplative Perspectives on Development*. Boston and London: Shambhala Publications, 1986.

Willeford, William. *Feeling, Imagination, and the Self: Transformations of the Mother-Infant Relationship*. Evanston, Ill.: Northwestern University Press, 1987.

Wilmer, Harry A. *Practical Jung: Nuts and Bolts of Jungian Psychotherapy*. Wilmette, Ill.: Chiron, 1987.

Wilson, Edward. *On Human Nature*. Cambridge: Harvard University Press, 1978.

————. *Sociobiology: The New Synthesis*. Cambridge: Harvard University Press, 1975.

Wilson, James Q. and Herrnstein, Richard J. *Crime and Human Nature:*

The Definitive Study of the Causes of Crime. New York: Simon and Schuster, 1986.

Wolman, Benjamin B. and Ullman, Montague (ed.). *Handbook of States of Consciousness.* New York: Van Nostrand Reinhold Co., 1986.

Woolger, Jennifer Barker and Woolger, Roger J. *The Goddess Within: A Guide to the Eternal Myths That Shape Women's Lives.* New York: Fawcett Columbine, 1989.

Wyly, James. *The Phallic Quest: Priapus and Masculine Inflation.* Toronto: Inner City Books, 1989.

Yablonsky, Lewis. *Fathers and Sons: Life Stages in One of the Most Challenging of All Family Relationships.* New York: Simon and Schuster, 1982.

Young-Bruehl, Elisabeth. *Anna Freud: A Biography.* New York: Summit Books, 1988.

Young-Eisendrath, Polly, and Hall, James A., eds. *The Book of the Self: Person, Pretext, and Process.* New York and London: New York University Press, 1987.

Credits

Thanks are extended to the following publishers, institutions, and authors for permission to reprint material copyrighted or controlled by them.

Princeton University Press for permission to quote from *The Collected Works of C. G. Jung,* trans. R. F. C. Hull, Bollingen Series XX. Vol. 5: *Symbols of Transformation,* copyright ©1956 by Princeton University Press; Vol. 6: *Psychological Types,* copyright ©1971 by Princeton University Press; Vol. 8: *The Structure and Dynamics of the Psyche,* copyright ©1960, 1969 by Princeton University Press; Vol. 9, 1: *The Archetypes and the Collective Unconscious,* copyright ©1959, 1969 by Princeton University Press; Vol. 11: *Psychology and Religion: East and West,* copyright ©1958, 1969 by Princeton University Press; Vol. 12: *Psychology and Alchemy,* copyright ©1953, 1968 by Princeton University Press.

HarperCollins Publishers, Inc. for permission to reprint excerpts from *Merton: A Biography* by Monica Furlong. Copyright ©1989 by Monica Furlong. Reprinted by permission of HarperCollins Publishers, Inc.

Viking Penguin for permission to reprint an excerpt from *The Complete Poems of D. H. Lawrence.* Copyright ©1964, 1971 by Angelo Ravagli and C. M. Weekley, Executors of the Estate of Frieda Lawrence Ravagli. Reprinted by permission of Viking Penguin, a division of Penguin Books USA, Inc.

Harcourt Brace Jovanovich, Inc. for permission to reprint an excerpt from "Little Gidding" in *Four Quartets,* copyright 1943 by T. S. Eliot and renewed 1971 by Esme Valerie Eliot, reprinted by permission of Harcourt Brace Jovanovich, Inc.

Special thanks to Frederick Feirstein for his permission to quote his

Index